Wealth and Taxation in Central Europe
The History and Sociology of Public Finance

German Historical Perspectives Series
General Editors:
Gerhard A. Ritter, Werner Pöls, Anthony J. Nicholls

Volume I
Population, Labour and Migration in 19th- and 20th-Century Germany
Edited by Klaus J. Bade

Volume III
Nation Building in Central Europe
Edited by Hagen Schulze

German Historical Perspectives/II

Wealth and Taxation in Central Europe
The History and Sociology of Public Finance

Edited by

PETER-CHRISTIAN WITT

BERG
Leamington Spa / Hamburg / New York
Distributed exclusively in the US and Canada by
St. Martin's Press, *New York*

First published in 1987 by
Berg Publishers Limited
24 Binswood Avenue, Leamington Spa, CV32 5SQ, UK
Schenefelder Landstr. 14K, 2000 Hamburg 55, West Germany
175 Fifth Avenue/Room 400, New York, NY 10010, USA

336.43
W342

British Library Cataloguing in Publication Data

Wealth and taxation in Central Europe: the
  history and sociology of public finance.—
  (German historical perspectives; (2)
  1. Finance, Public—Social aspects—
  Central Europe—History 2. Finance,
  Public—Political aspects—Central Europe
  —History
  I. Witt, Peter-Christian II. Series
  306'.3 HJ1000

  ISBN 0–85496–523–8

Library of Congress Cataloging-in-Publication Data

Wealth and taxation in Central Europe.

  (German historical perspectives; (2)
  Includes index.
  1. Finance, Public—Central Europe—History.
2. Taxation—Central Europe—History. I. Witt,
Peter-Christian. II. Series.
HJ1000.W4 1987   336.47   86–24490
ISBN 0–85496–523–8

The editors wish to thank the *Stifterverbund für die Deutsche Wissenschaft*
for their generous grant towards the production costs of this volume.

KP

Printed in Great Britain by Billings of Worcester

Contents

List of Tables

Editorial Preface

The purpose of this series of books is to present the results of research by German historians and social scientists to readers in English-speaking countries. Each of the volumes has a particular theme which will be handled from different points of view by specialists. The series is not limited to the problems of Germany but will also involve publications dealing with the history of other countries, with general problems of political, economic, social and intellectual history as well as international relations and studies in comparative history. The aim of the series is to help overcome the language barrier which experience has shown obstructs the rapid appreciation of German research in English-speaking countries.

The publication of the series is closely associated with the German Visiting Fellowship at St Antony's College, Oxford, which has existed since 1965, having been originally funded by the *Stiftung Volkswagenwerk*, later by the British Leverhulme Foundation and, since 1982, by the Ministry of Education and Science in the Federal Republic of Germany. Each volume will be based on a series of seminars held in Oxford, which will have been conceived and directed by the Visiting Fellow and organised in collaboration with St Antony's College.

The editors wish to thank the *Stifterverband für die Deutsche Wissenschaft* for meeting the expenses of the original lecture series and for generous assistance with the publication. They hope that this enterprise will help to overcome national introspection and to further international academic discourse and cooperation.

Gerhard A. Ritter   **Werner Pöls**   **Anthony J. Nicholls**

PETER-CHRISTIAN WITT

Introduction: History and Sociology of Public Finance – Problems and Topics

I

This paper,* as the first in this collection on wealth and taxation in Central Europe, is designed to raise a number of theoretical and methodological problems relating to the history and sociology of public finance. The purpose of the collection as a whole is twofold: on the one hand, it hopes to show that historians in Germany have again become seriously interested in questions of public finance;[1] at the same time, it aims to contribute to a more general renaissance of this genre of historical writing. However, I would like to avoid one possible misunderstanding at the outset: in speaking of the history of public finance and of its sociology I am *not* concerned to establish yet another specialised branch of historiography and to add 'the history of public finance' to existing approaches, such as social and economic history, constitutional history, administrative history or business history. A new discipline such as this would, like the older ones, then develop its

---

* The author would like to thank his colleague and friend Professor Volker R. Berghahn for preparing the translation.

1. In the late 1960s when the author prepared his doctorial dissertation (published as *Die Finanzpolitik des deutschen Reiches von 1903 bis 1913. Eine Studie zur Innenpolitik des Wilhelminischen Deutschland*, Lübeck and Hamburg, 1970), the interest of German historians in the history of public finances was limited to some specialists in early modern history. Today even mainstream historiography is ready to acknowledge the importance of this subject for any historical epoch, and quite a few excellent doctorial dissertations and *Habilitationsschriften* have been published in the last fifteen years.

1

own concepts, theories and methods and hence merely exacerbate the fragmentation and specialisation of historical writing, which has already gone too far. It is not my intention to inflict this on either history or sociology. What I have in mind may be first described by means of a simple observation. Modern industrial societies today raise and distribute up to 50 per cent, and in some cases an even higher proportion, of the national income via the state or via public institutions which, by law, are charged with quasi-official tasks. And yet — *although* these are the facts, *although* people constantly lament this situation and *although* every single citizen is directly confronted with the consequences of these realities — it cannot be said that much is known about public finance and its various aspects. As research became increasingly subjected to the general process of bureaucratisation which has affected the modern world, scholars, too, began to think in terms of areas of competence, and there appears to be only one discipline, namely finance and accountancy, which is considered competent to deal with problems of public finance. The trouble is that this discipline is a strange hybrid. To this day it has not been possible to define and demarcate it *vis-à-vis* other disciplines, such as constitutional law, economic policy analysis, economic theory, political science and sociology. Of course, attempts have been made to determine the subject matter of *Finanzwissenschaft* ever since it emerged as a subject in the universities, especially of Italy, France and Germany.[2] Recently, Fritz Karl Mann has put forward a proposal to deal with public finance within the framework of a tripartite *Finanzwissenschaft* consisting of finance theory, the political science of finance and the sociology of finance.[3] Unfortunately, this has not brought the problems any nearer a solution. After all, it is quite obvious that public finance, with its divergent elements, touches upon the interests of quite a number of disciplines. The public dimension is central to the preoccupations of the political scientist. The lawyer will see it as part of the existing legal order. Its economic aspects are covered by economic theory or by economic analysis. And as far as its social components are concerned, they form part of the most important areas of sociology. This explains

2. See F. Neumark, 'Types nationaux de Science des Finances', *Openbare Financien*, 1947, pp. 1–13 (repr. in enlarged and revised version, 'Nationale Typen der Finanzwissenschaft', in idem (ed.), *Wirtschafts- und Finanzprobleme des Interventionsstaates*, Tübingen, 1961, pp. 81–95); W. Gerloff, 'Wesen und Aufgabe der Finanzwissenschaft, ihre Stellung und Beziehung zu anderen Wissenschaften', in W. Gerloff and F.M. Meisel (eds.), *Handbuch der Finanzwissenschaft*, vol. 1, 2nd edn. Tübingen, 1952, pp. 1–65.
3. F.K. Mann, 'Die drei Finanzwissenschaften', *Finanzarchiv*, vol. 30 (1971), pp. 1–19; idem, *Der Sinn der Finanzwirtschaft*, Tübingen, 1978.

why all these disciplines have made public finance a major focus of research at some point in their history.[4] What has remained solely the territory of finance and accounting is the study of the formal organisation of public budgets and accounts, the development and implementation of the so-called budgetary principles and, finally, taxation.[5]

The inevitably truncated and simplified summary is designed to draw attention to the following problem: there is a specialised scholarly discipline whose subject matter is public finances; however, for reasons which I cannot go into here, this discipline has never made public finance *in toto* the object of its research, even if attempts have been made in this direction. One reason for this is that, as other disciplines cannot avoid dealing with public finances, they have tended to take their mandate seriously. On the other hand, the emergence of *Finanzwissenschaft*, which also included the study of public finances, has led those other disciplines to some extent to reduce their own work in this area to a minimum. If one looks at the present situation — and this applies not just to the German case on which most of my observations are based — one is struck by this: although public finances, if only because of their sheer volume, have never had a greater significance in history than they have today, they have never been treated with more neglect. Modern economic theory of the type which Rostow has rightly

4. I cannot mention even the major contributions of historians, political scientists, sociologists, economists or lawyers, because that would require many pages. I simply want to draw attention to the fact that, with few exceptions, most representatives of these sciences are no longer aware of their own scientific tradition. And this certainly has its price: much of the conceptual and empirical work done in the nineteenth and early twentieth centuries could be helpful for present-day research — and many so-called 'new approaches' or 'new results' look fairly 'old' when the scientific tradition of the subject is taken into account. This applies not only, for example, to economics, where anti-historic thinking seems to be fashionable, but also to history, likewise where, for example, social history could have gained by a careful evaluation of the writings of the so-called Historical School of economics. Fragmentation and specialisation have done further harm: very seldom researchers are able and willing to go beyond the limits of their own science; the mutual knowledge of the work done by other sciences has greatly diminished. And finally, there is one problem which at least the English-speaking part of the scientific community — few exceptions notwithstanding — is concerning: research from Germany, Italy, France, and so on, is largely neglected (especially in economics, sociology and political science but to a lesser degree this applies to history too), something which did not happen before the First World War.
5. See the numerous modern textbooks; but there are some remarkable exceptions: H. Haller, *Finanzpolitik. Grundlagen und Hauptprobleme*, 5th edn, Tübingen and Zurich, 1972; idem, *Die Steuern. Grundlagen eines rationalen Systems öffentlicher Abgaben*, Tübingen, 1981; F. Neumark, *Der Reichshaushaltsplan. Ein Beitrag zur Lehre vom öffentlichen Haushalt*, Jena, 1929; idem, *Grundsätze gerechter und ökonomisch rationaler Steuerpolitik*, Tübingen, 1970; for the development in the field of finance and accounting (*Finanzwissenschaft*) in general, see F.K. Mann, 'Abriß einer Geschichte der Finanzwissenschaft', in *Handbuch der Finanzwissenschaft*, vol. 1, 3rd edn, Tübingen, 1977, pp. 1–38; H. Kolms, 'Einige Bemerkungen zur Finanzgeschichte, *Christiana Albertina*, vol. 12 (1980), pp. 9–19.

called 'the barbaric counter-revolution'[6] has merely revived the ancient dogma that financial management by the public authorities is at its best only if it follows the rules of the free market and does not influence the functioning of a free-market economy. This classic obligation that public finances must be 'neutral' has proved completely useless for research, quite apart from the fact that it was out of touch with reality and must be seen as 'pure' ideology. Worse, the promising beginnings of the 1920s and 1930s which tried to develop a theory of public finance are liable to be cut off completely if the notion of neutrality is combined with one which is particularly popular with Conservative politicians. I am thinking of the idea that public finances are best handled like the private household budget of a parsimonious *pater familias*.

However, German sociologists have also found it difficult to warm to the theme of public finances. This is all the more remarkable as Max Weber, to whom sociologists like to refer, built his theories of macro-sociological organisations very much upon a penetrating empirical analysis of public finances and their historical development.[7] I might add that other founding fathers of sociology, like the celebrated Vilfredo Pareto, also started from an examination of public finances.[8] Similar points could be made with reference to other disciplines like political science or constitutional law, which should, in principle, also be concerned with public finance. However, it is not my purpose to pinpoint the deficiencies of other disciplines. My central point is, rather, to demonstrate that public finance does not command a great deal of attention today among disciplines which in the past rightly emphasised its importance. This state of affairs has far-reaching consequences for the historian dealing with this topic, and these consequences are of an empirical, theoretical as well as methodological nature.

II

As I have mentioned above, historians have in recent years again become more interested in the field of public finances. It is important to stress the relativity of this observation. If today's efforts

---

6. W.W. Rostow, *The Barbaric Counter-Revolution: Cause and Cure*, London and Basingstoke, 1984.
7. See esp. his *Wirtschaft und Gesellschaft*, 5th rev. edn, Tübingen, 1972.
8. V. Pareto, *Trattato di sociologia generale*, Florence, 1916 (French edn, *Traité de sociologie générale*, 2 vols., Lausanne and Paris, 1917, 1919, repr. Geneva, 1968; abr. German edn, *Allgemeine Soziologie*, trans. and ed. by C. Brinkmann, Tübingen, 1955).

are compared with those which were undertaken at the end of the
nineteenth and at the beginning of the twentieth centuries by the
so-called Historical School of economics,[9] it is easy to see that there is a
good deal of wishful thinking in my statement. This is particularly true
if one looks at how research, covering different epochs of financial
history, is divided up in terms of volume. Thus a good deal of work has
been done on the sixteenth and seventeenth centuries and on the period
of upheaval in the late eighteenth and early nineteenth centuries, the
Napoleonic Wars and its consequences.[10] Few satisfactory studies,
whether empirical or theoretical, exist for the period of rapid growth of
public finances, their politics and their management.[11] It might also be
mentioned that the major historical handbooks on this period do not
contain more than a few marginal references to public finances. Even
the *Handbuch der deutschen Wirtschafts- und Sozialgeschichte* devotes no more
than a few pages to the subject.[12] As to the *Handbuch der Finanzwissenschaft*, it will be found that the first impression (1926–9) contained an
excellent article of the history of public finances. The contribution to
the most recent third impression (1977), by contrast, is most
unsatisfactory.[13]

It is no coincidence that various historical periods have been covered
with varying intensity. It reflects the inherent needs and interests of
historical writing. Thus it is impossible to analyse the emergence of the
modern state without raising the question of public finances. The
modern state is synonymous with the modern fiscal state.[14] Nor can we

9. It is impossible to list the numerous books and articles in the field of history of
public finances which were published in these years, but one fine example is W. Gerloff's
*Die Finanz- und Zollpolitik des deutschen Reiches nebst ihren Beziehungen zu Landes- und Gemein-
definanzen von der Gründung des Norddeutschen Bundes bis zur Gegenwart*, Jena, 1913, which
should be mentioned because the work of its author — for many years co-editor of the
Finanzarchiv and also co-editor of the first two editions of the *Handbuch der Finanzwissenschaft* — and the work of his students have contributed so much to the survival of the
tradition of the Historical School of economics. For the broader context, the appropriate
sections of J.A. Schumpeter's *History of Economic Analysis*, London, 1955, are still especially valuable; cf. D. Krüger, *Nationalökonomen im Wilhelminischen Deutschland*, Göttingen,
1983.
10. See the articles by K. Krüger and H.-P. Ullmann in this collection; a very
important and promising approach is the article by H. Wunder, which discusses the
hitherto neglected aspect of peasant credit as part of public finance.
11. See my book *Die Finanzpolitik des deutschen Reiches* and some of the work done in the
research project on 'Inflation and Reconstruction in Germany and Europe, 1914–24'.
12. H. Aubin and W. Zorn (eds.), *Handbuch der deutschen Wirtschafts- und Sozialgeschichte*,
2 vols., Stuttgart, 1971 and 1976.
13. The first edition of the *Handbuch der Finanzwissenschaft*, 3 vols., Tübingen, 1926,
1927 and 1929 (co-editors Wilhelm Gerloff and Franz Meisel) is still the best one from
the historian's viewpoint, because it contains not only quite a few historical articles but
nearly all contributions elaborate the historical dimension of their specific subject.
14. Sometimes it proves to be necessary to repeat commonplaces, especially in such

understand the rise of the *Verfassungs-* and *Rechtsstaat* in Germany without the crisis of public finances which hit the German states as a result of the Napoleonic Wars.[15] Yet, to examine the history of public finances in Germany from the mid-nineteenth century (or from 1871 onwards at the latest) is tantamount to analysing the total activity of the state and to dealing with the overall development of Central European society. This enables us to investigate causal factors of change by turning to the history of public finances. For the most recent period of the fully developed 'fiscal state', on the other hand, public finances and the problems they reflect represent *symptoms* in the sense that they mirror all state activity and hence can be used to capture all state activity. If a pragmatic approach is to be taken, the following points might be made: a history of public finances which tries to investigate causal connections between absolutism, the rise of the *miles perpetuus*, standing armies and continual tax levies, may confine itself to a relatively small number of questions and a clearly delimited body of sources. A study of public finances since the second half of the nineteenth century, on the other hand, is likely to proliferate. The state, as we all know it, takes away and distributes money in many different ways; it directs funds and commodities and influences the lives of its citizens in a comprehensive fashion; in doing all these things, it not only uses its own public administration but also delegates tasks to quasi-official agencies. This means that anyone who undertakes a study of state finances finds himself confronted with a field that he can hardly ever hope to cover. The finance ministries of modern states have produced enormous amounts of papers and continue to do so.[16] In this respect they surpass all other ministries. The historian can therefore look at no more than a tiny proportion of this material, and it is not always clear how much information he is going to miss as a result of his own selectivity. To this pragmatic difficulty must be added a logical one. This is a point which explains at least indirectly why historians, even if they recognise the need for financial history, shrink before the task. If it is true that all state activity, and even the development of a society, is symptomatically reflected in public finances, and yet it is

---

cases where an *opinio communis* seems to be established but too little is done to elucidate the questions raised by such commonplaces.

15. See E.R. Huber, *Deutsche Verfassungsgeschichte seit 1789*, vol. 1, 2nd edn, Stuttgart, 1975; T. Nipperdey, *Deutsche Geschichte 1800–1866. Bürgerwelt und starker Staat*, Munich, 1983, pp. 272–402.

16. See P.-C. Witt, 'Beschreibung von Archivbeständen der Finanz- und Wirtschafts-ministerien', in T. Trumpp and R. Köhne (eds.), *Archivbestände zur Wirtschafts- und Sozialgeschichte der Weimarer Republic*, Boppard, 1979, pp. 286–311.

impossible to elucidate these connections sufficiently and the most one can do is to deal with specialised problems like budget policy or taxation, then it is also no longer possible to justify a narrowing of one's focus, unavoidable as it is from the point of view of the manageability of the massive sources. All one can do is to admit, in a mood of resignation, that one accepts a limitation upon the cognitive opportunities which are in principle opened up by the study of public finances.

However, it is relatively easy to demonstrate the kind of difficulties the scholar confronts when adopting this attitude. All studies tend to place a considerable theoretical and empirical emphasis on the distributive role of state budgets and so-called para-fiscal organisations. The approach usually taken by this kind of work is to start off with an examination of the overall growth of public expenditures. The next step is to look at the relative shifts relating to different items of expenditure. The conclusion drawn from this tends to be that since the middle of the nineteenth century the modern state changed from the liberal 'night-watchman's' state (*Nachtwaechterstaat*) to the interventionist welfare state.[17] It is also customary to regard the periods of the two world wars and their aftermath as periods of particularly rapid change in this direction.[18] The use of data in the way described here is certainly not 'incorrect'. But it should be added that problems are being weighted in a certain direction in the process. Interpretations of the older liberal 'night-watchman's' state and the modern interventionist state are, often even unconsciously, taken for granted here when they are not in fact based on a comprehensive analysis but on hypotheses which have been adopted without critical scrutiny. No more than a detailed parallel study of the *income* aspect of public budgets would reveal that. When one talks of the modern interventionist state, a tacit assumption is being made: that the state conducts, on a large scale, a policy of redistribution between the social classes and stands in the way of a further sharpening of inequalities of income and wealth. The trouble is that this assumption is untenable in this form.

If, on top of this, one adds a rigorous analysis of the system of tax assessment and tax levying, including an investigation of the system of subsidies granted via taxation, it is even less likely that a definition of the modern state, which is based exclusively on an analysis of the

17. A fine example for this type of reasoning is P. Flora et al., *State, Economy, and Society in Western Europe 1815-1975. A Data Handbook. Vol. I: The Growth of Mass Democracies and Welfare States*, Frankfurt, London and Chicago, 1983.
18. See for example, the articles in the volume published by the Deutsche Bundesbank, *Währung und Wirtschaft in Deutschland 1876-1975*, Frankfurt, 1976.

expenditure side of the public purse, can be upheld. Let me give you a
further very well-known example of what I mean by this. The introduction of a state insurance system against sickness and old age by
Bismarck is usually seen as the decisive turn towards the welfare state
in Germany. Even those historians who take a very critical view of
Bismarck's policy and argue that social insurance was an instrument in
his domestic struggle against the organised working class — so to
speak, the carrot that came with the stick of the anti-Socialist laws —
emphasise that *de facto*, though perhaps not by design, the functions of
the state underwent a decisive *qualitative* change. This view is perfectly
correct, and yet it is totally insufficient; this is because a totally different
picture emerges if one examines the system of public income which also
completely changed at this time. The main feature of this system was
an elaborate system of *subsidies* paid out to particular social classes. So,
on the one hand, there emerged a system of welfare payments through
which the state organised, via taxation and insurance contributions, an
interpersonal redistribution between people in employment and those
who, for reasons of poor health or old age, were unemployed. On the
other hand, that *same* state favoured certain strata which were considered the political and social pillars of the state. However, in this case
payments were not made in the shape of open subsidies. Rather,
subsidies were paid much more inconspicuously and, as far as the
recipients were concerned, more agreeably via the system of public
income. In this particular case it was high tariffs introduced from the late
1870s and a new design of taxes on beer, spirits and sugar. Contemporaries, incidentally, called these innovations, on the one hand, extension
of welfare policies and, on the other hand — and they did so without
tongue-in-cheek — 'protection of national labour' (*Schutz der nationalen
Arbeit*).[19]

There is not space to elaborate on these examples. The purpose of
my analysis should be clear: since the middle of the nineteenth century,
any sectoral examination of public finances raises the danger that, by
stating facts which are *per se* correct, one ends up with crude distortions
of reality. If this is so, the question arises of how and with what
objectives is it possible to write a history of finance at all, at least with
reference to the modern interventionist state. Is it possible to develop
methods and questions which might yield promising results for a
history of finance, bearing in mind that the contributions of other

19. See P.-C. Witt, '"Patriotische Gabe" und "Brotwucher". Finanzverfassung und
politisches System im deutschen Kaiserreich 1871–1914', in U. Schultz (ed.), *Mit dem
Zehnten fing es an. Eine Kulturgeschichte der Steuer*, Munich 1986, pp. 189–99, 284–7.

disciplines concerned with problems of public finances have not been exactly impressive?

III

In answering these questions one will have to return to the problem which constitutes the central concern of 'public finance' or of 'fiscal economics'. In this respect an important contribution can already be made by an investigation which concentrates on changing functional definitions of public finance as undertaken by the cameralists or by the classical economist. For such definitions, which are adapted to the practical needs of the epoch concerned, can provide keys to the perceptions of state and society of the time.[20] At the same time we can subject the continued existence of such definitions in our own time to ideology-critical scrutiny.[21] Another example could be obtained by reference to the dogmas of the classical political economists relating to public finances, which today have renewed significance. The classical political economists took recourse to older notions, as formulated, for instance, by Jean Bodin in his dictum 'Les finances sont les nerfs de la République'.[22] These were ideas which were taken up, for example, by William Petty or the German cameralists and which stated that public finances should be seen above all as a power-political instrument in the hands of the state to secure internal and external peace. The classical political economists then turned these ideas into dogmas that are around to this day in the shape of the state's obligation to observe neutrality or to minimise the impact of public finances on the free-market economy. If state activity was to be restricted to internal and external peace and this peace was, by the same token, seen as a purely idealist and immaterial good, then it was logical to demand that, to achieve its purpose, the state should take away from its citizens as little as possible. It was also logical to insist that, for the same reason, the state should treat its income and expenditure with parsi-

20. F.K. Mann, 'Reorientation through fiscal theory', *Kyklos*, vol. 3, no. 2 (1949), pp. 116–29.

21. For the methodological approach compare: R. Goldscheid, 'Staat, öffentliche Haushalte und Gesellschaft. Wesen und Aufgabe der Finanzwissenschaft vom Standpunkt der Soziologie', in *Handbuch der Finanzwissenschaft*, vol. 1, Tübingen, 1926, pp. 146–84; idem, *Staatssozialismus oder Staatskapitalismus. Ein finanzsoziologischer Beitrag zur Lösung des Staatsschuldenproblems*, Vienna and Leipzig, 1917; J.A. Schumpeter, 'Die Krise des Steuerstaates', *Zeitfragen aus dem Gebiet der Soziologie*, vol. 4 (1918), pp. 3–74 (repr. in idem, *Aufsätze zur Soziologie*, Tübingen, 1953, pp. 1–71).

22. J. Bodin, *Les Six Livres de la République*, 4th edn, Paris, 1579, p. 852 (L. 6, Ch. 2).

mony and economy. In these circumstances the comparison between
the public purse and the family budget of the parsimonious and caring
patriarch seemed compelling. The demand, derived from the notion of
'limiting state purposes' (*limitierenden Staatszwecken*), that the state
should not participate in economic life, appeared just as plausible as
another postulate, again derived from this notion. This was the postulate that since all citizens benefited relatively equally from the state's
purpose to preserve internal and external peace, they were all also
obliged to contribute relatively equally to this purpose. In other words,
taxes and other levies should not have any effect on the relative
economic position of the citizen.[23]

All these individual notions of the classical political economist added
up to a total picture which tended to view public finances and the
finance economy as a magnified replica of the private economy. This
was, and is, a very tempting idea. Its attractiveness lies above all in the
fact that such analogies can be understood by everybody. They can be
explained without much difficulty, especially in the context of systems
which require democratic legitimation for the exercises of government.
Finally, it was implicit in this notion of the finance economy being a
large replica of the private economy that the former, just as the latter,
was in one's own interest.

This explains why the notions of the classical political economists,
though they have undergone various changes, have survived into our
own time and have, in fact, very recently seen a revival in the United
States and Western Europe.[24] On the other hand, attempts were made
as early as the nineteenth century — first, as far as we know, in Italy
and Germany — to define the finance economy as an economic
organism in its own right and with its own specific rationality, and to
see it as a vehicle for the pursuit of non-fiscal objectives; that is, for
changing the existing property structures, class structures and, last but
not least, also economic structures.[25] It was only logical that a redefinition of the state's purpose should be combined in these circumstances
with a redefinition of the finance economy. Studies of public finances as
they actually existed, have initiated this process of redefinition. The
classical political economists had started off with postulates; finance
and accountancy (*Finanzwissenschaft*), as it emerged in the nineteenth
century, took an historical-genetic approach, as can be seen from the

23. See Mann, *Der Sinn der Finanzwirtschaft*, esp. pp. 3–41.
24. Rostow, *The Barbaric Counter-Revolution*, pp. 26–51.
25. Mann, *Der Sinn der Finanzwirtschaft*, pp. 129–41.

writings of Karl Rodbertus or Albert Schaeffle.[26] Building upon the
cameralist tradition, they had gained their rich empirical material
partly through their own research, partly through economics, which in
Germany experienced a process of historicisation and put source
material at their disposal. The new approach led Schaeffle and others
to argue, as he put it, that 'the shaping of finance was invariably
dependent on the basic historical structure of the organisation of the
national economy'. The classical political economists had developed
their dogmas concerning public finance by making analogies with the
private economy. Schaeffle and others, by contrast, put public finances
once again into their political and social context and, moving on from
this, they also determined their economic function. The scholarly risk
raised by this 'realistic' approach was twofold. To begin with, the
historical-genetic method resulted in a reduced emphasis on the theoretical aspects. This was a development which was even more marked
in economics in Germany than in finance and accounting. Secondly,
the historical-genetic approach fell into traps similar to those which
historiography in Germany was caught by in this period. By turning
the genuinely historical concept of *Verstehen* into their guiding principle,
affirmation of what had grown historically became the basic objective
of this kind of research. Gustav Schmoller's *Preußische Verfassungs-,
Verwaltungs- und Finanzgeschichte* (Prussian Constitutional, Administration and Finance History), which represents one of the most impressive
books of this period, still reflected these tendencies. On the other hand,
its title alone indicates how expressly Schmoller tried to integrate
public finances into their political and social context.[27]

A major further development in these approaches was then initiated
by Max Weber (and to some extent also by Vilfredo Pareto). Weber's
sociology of domination (*Herrschaftssoziologie*) largely emerged from his
studies of the social determination of public finance organisation.[28]
Big steps forward were taken by Rudolf Goldscheid and Joseph A.
Schumpeter. Unlike Schumpeter, Goldscheid was a representative of
that unorthodox Austrian variant of Marxism which in his particular
case found expression in an interest in finance and accountancy — an

26. J.K. Rodbertus, 'Zur Geschichte der römischen Tributsteuern seit Augustus',
Jahrbücher für Nationalökonomie und Statistik vol. 4 (1865), vol. 5 (1865), vol. 8 (1867); Albert
Schäffle, *Die Grundsätze der Steuerpolitik*, Tübingen, 1880; idem, *Bau und Leben des sozialen
Körpers*, 2 vols., 2nd edn, Tübingen, 1896.
27. G. Schmoller, *Preussische Verfassungs-, Verwaltungs- und Finanzgeschichte*, Berlin, 1921.
28. See Weber, *Wirtschaft und Gesellschaft*; F.K. Mann, 'Finanzsoziologie. Grundsätzliche Bemerkungen', *Kölner Vierteljahreshefte für Soziologie*, vol. 12 (1933/4), pp. 1–20; W.
Koch, 'Finanzsoziologie', in *Handwörterbuch der Wirtschaftswissenschaften*, vol. 2, Göttingen
and Tübingen, 1980, pp. 97–106.

interest quite alien to Marx himself. Writing under the impact of the
unresolved problems of wartime finance in the First World War,
Goldscheid aimed to bring about a fundamental reform of society by
way of a radical reform of finances. He propagated this idea in his book
Staatssozialismus oder Staatskapitalismus (State Socialism or State Capitalism), published in 1917. However, Goldscheid's aims are of lesser
interest for our purposes (even if they remain important for an understanding of his work) than is the route to his aims — that is his
hypotheses and methods. For an understanding of these hypotheses
and methods it is essential to note his combination of a Marxian class
analysis with the results of the historical school of German *Finanzwissenschaft*. Goldscheid called this combination *finance sociology*. He derived
from it the statement which was at the same time a hypothesis and a
programme for research: 'that the whole of the socio-economic order
concerned is nowhere else as clearly reflected as in public accounts'. He
added, 'the state cannot be constituted differently from its budget . . .
[and] every single private household is very closely related to the
state's budget'.[29] Put differently, 'It is the mutual functional interaction
between state finances and societal development which, through very
thorough analysis [permits us] to recognise the peculiar character of
the state in every historical epoch'.[30] Schumpeter did not share Goldscheid's belief that it was possible to transcend capitalism by means of
a thorough-going finance reform. Nor did he consider such a development desirable. He thus clearly dissociated himself from Goldscheid's
aims and methods. Nevertheless, in his article 'Die Krise der Steuerstaates' (The Crisis of the Taxation State), published in 1918, which was
designed as a critique of Goldscheid's approach, Schumpeter adopted
his finance-sociological perspective.[31] Above all, he demonstrated most
impressively just what this perspective can yield for the benefit of a
history of public finances. 'Finances', Schumpeter argued:

> are one of the best starting-points for the study of social movement, in
> particular, though not exclusively, of political movement. The full value of
> this perspective emerges above all at those turning-points — or rather
> turning epochs — when what exists begins to die off and to transform itself
> into something new; [those epochs] are invariably also periods of crisis of the
> old financial methods. [We mean this] in its original meaning — in the sense
> that state financial processes are an important element in the causal complex

29. R. Goldscheid, in *Handbuch der Finanzwissenschaft*, vol. 1, 1926, p. 147.
30. Idem, *Staatssozialismus oder Staatskapitalismus*, p. 3.
31. J.A. Schumpeter 'Die Krise', *Zeitfragen aus dem Gebeit der Sociologie*, vol. 4 (1918),
pp. 3–/4.

of any change; [we mean this also] in its symptomatic meaning — in the sense that all events leave their imprint upon the finance economy. . . . The intellectual origins of a nation, its level of culture, the shape of its social structure and the orientation of its policy — all this and many other things can be read up, stripped of empty phrases, in [the country's finance economy]. Whoever is capable of listening to its message will hear in it more clearly than elsewhere the thunder of world history.[32]

Goldscheid and Schumpeter had divergent ideas about the aims of finance sociology. But both of them understood it to be the 'social component' of the finance economy and the 'finance-economic component of social action'. Above all, they both considered it a particularly promising approach to the study of social and political conditions of the past. By arguing that both the symptoms and causes of change leave their imprint on the finance economy, they also pointed to the importance which the study of public finances can have for historical research. Finally, both of them used, at least implicitly, a dynamic rather than a static notion of public finances. It should also be mentioned, in view of what German historians tend to work on, that Schumpeter, and to a lesser degree Goldscheid, saw finance sociology and finance history as mutually complementary sciences which in some areas even displayed a direct congruence. This implied that if they were to advance knowledge, they also had to use the same questions and methods.

Fritz Karl Mann has so far been the only person to continue this tradition, which emerged from the financial crisis of the First World War. The power of this approach has been demonstrated in his work *Steuerpolitische Ideale*, one of the best works of recent German history of ideas, and in many of his articles on topics of finance sociology and history.[33] Mainstream historiography, on the other hand, has hardly taken any notice of this research, while recent writings on finance sociology are amazingly anti-historical in their orientation.

In these circumstances a history of public finance, which consciously applies the questions and methods of finance sociology, offers a promising starting-point for the analysis of political and social structures and power relationships and for the examination of the causes and symptoms of societal conditions and human action.

32. Ibid., pp. 5–6.
33. F.K. Mann, *Steuerpolitische Ideale. Vergleichende Studien zur Geschichte der ökonomischen und politischen Ideen und ihres Wirkens in der öffentlichen Meinung 1600 bis 1935*, Jena, 1937.

IV

By using the history of public finance in this way a number of methodological and practical problems raised by our approach have been resolved; for the manifest links between public finance and the totality of the political, social and economic developments of the modern welfare state notwithstanding, it is now possible to engage in an analysis which deals only with parts of the story. On the other hand, this limitation does not mean the successful removal of all the practical problems which appear in the path of the historian of public finance.

Gaston Jèze's study *Allgemeine Theorie des Budgets* (General Theory of the Budget) may serve as a guide here and remains topical to this day as a study of the broad budgetary principles in parliamentary-democratic states. He wrote that the budget was the 'bare bones' of the exercise of political domination 'stripped of all deceptive ideologies'. The budget was in his view of a 'social programme' with which it was possible to cement the status quo or to change — intentionally or, at times, accidentally — the existing distribution of power in society.[34] If, furthermore, we compare the size of state budgets with that of social insurance funds or other para-fiscal agencies, it is not too difficult to see that the former, both in terms of revenue and expenditure, must be the focus of all finance-historical research. Of course, this does not mean that studies dealing with its history of ideas or theory or with its constitutional or administrative development should be ignored.

By tradition the budget tends to be one of the best-kept *arcana imperii* in all countries. Thus it is a laborious enterprise merely to obtain a vague notion of its total size. This certainly applies to early modern states or individual German states well into the nineteenth century. Trying to learn something about individual sources of revenue or expenditure is an almost hopeless endeavour. Since the nineteenth century, itemised budgets which were formally approved by parliamentary assemblies and subject to retrospective accounting control, became more widespread. It might be thought, therefore, that a detailed and long-term analysis of budgets would be relatively easy and that data would be readily available for examining, for instance, changes in revenue and expenditure over a longer time-span with the aim of checking and studying changing governmental priorities. Equally, on the assumption that the budget is to be seen as a government programme *par excellence*, it should be possible to compare budget

34. G. Jèze, *Allgemeine Theorie des Budgets*, Tübingen, 1927, pp. VII–VIII.

projections with actual revenue and expenditure; the purpose of this comparison would be to arrive at firm conclusions about the implementation of the government programme and hence about the success or failure of a particular cabinet. In practice, however, there are many problems which have to be solved before any data can be used. An illustration of this is provided by a look at the German Empire after 1871.

(1) The first problem is related to the fact that from 1871 onwards Germany was a federal state in fiscal terms. This applies even to Hitler's 'synchronised' and otherwise highly centralised Third Reich. The country's public finances were organised in a three-tier system of Reich, federal states and local communities and communal associations. All three levels were interconnected in various ways through revenue and expenditure transfers, 'matricular contributions' and revenues which were distributed in accordance with a specific key. Moreover, since 1871 at least four major material disruptions have taken place in 1878, 1919/20, 1933/4 and 1945/51. Anyone hoping to study the total picture of the German financial development will face almost insuperable problems simply by virtue of the fact that revenues and expenditures at local level are available only for a few random sample years in the shape of rough, barely reliable estimates. If the finances of only one of the three levels are to be examined — such as those of the central government, it must always be borne in mind that the sum total of public revenues and expenditures must be corrected by all those amounts which are subject to transfer under the system of fiscal equalisation (*Finanzausgleich*). What is more, comparisons between different decades are further complicated by the fact that individual items became subject to changes related to shifting tasks stipulated by a new constitution. Obviously, the new Weimar Constitution of 1919 dealt differently with certain fiscal tasks than the Bismarckian Constitution of 1871.[35]

It is only from the 1950s onwards that official statistics take account of these problems with some degree of reliability.[36] For earlier periods

35. See P.-C. Witt, 'Reichsfinanzminister und Reichsfinanzverwaltung, *Vierteljahres-shefte für Zeitgeschichte* vol. 23 (1975), pp. 1–61; J.v. Scherpenberg, *Öffentliche Finanzwirtschaft in Westdeutschland 1944–1948*, Frankfurt, 1984; W. Ehrlicher, 'Der Finanzausgleich in der Bundesrepublik Deutschland, in *Handwörterbuch der Wirtschaftswissenschaften*, vol. 2, Göttingen and Tübingen, 1980, pp. 662–94.

36. Unfortunately, there is still no reliable account discussing the methodological problems of the older statistical publications of the Statistisches Reichsamt and the Statistical Offices of the *Länder*; but anyone using these statistics and able and willing to check them with the original material collected by the Reichsfinanzministerium/

the historian of finance is forced to compile and systematically prepare the raw data for long-term and international comparisons. Only thereafter can he begin to turn to what are his real analytical objectives. An illustration of this particular dilemma is provided by Mitchell's *European Historical Statistics* in other respects a most valuable work. Unfortunately, the book is useless for making international comparisons because it only lists 'Central Government Expenditure'.[37] However, while there were political systems whose expenditure was concentrated in the hands of central government, Germany up to 1933, for example, disbursed the majority of its public expenditure through bodies lower down the line. Mitchell does not cover this differentiation.

(2) Comparisons of public expenditure over longer periods face a further methodological problem which is of significance for the German experience between 1871 and the present. This is the question of how it might be possible to arrive at the *real* structure of public expenditure, which includes the level of inflation.[38] It might be possible to ignore this question if Germany had experienced moderate levels of inflation or deflation during this period. In fact, however, the country was hit by two enormous waves of inflation, which resulted from wars and high armaments expenditure. There occurred, on the other hand, a no less momentous deflation in the early 1930s. In these circumstances it is clearly unacceptable merely to work with figures on *nominal* expenditure or, even simpler than that, to skip the critical years from 1914 to 1923 and from 1935/6 to 1948/9 while including the years of deflation between 1930 and 1933/4. Certainly, such a simplification would make a mockery of Schumpeter's point that the financial historian's approach is particularly fruitful for the analysis of crisis periods. If crisis periods are therefore to be included, an extensive reconstruction job becomes unavoidable, which raises very difficult methodological problems. The gains to be made from such labours, however, may be gleened from my own reconstruction of the real expenditures of all public bodies and of the social insurance funds between 1930 and 1933.

Reichsschatzamt or the ministers of finance of the *Länder* will be aware of the problems mentioned. To some degree Benjamin Disraeli's dictum 'Lies, damned lies, statistics' does apply especially to financial statistics.

37. B.R. Mitchell, *European Historical Statistics, 1750–1970*, London and Basingstoke, pp. 697–733.

38. The methodological problems are manifold; deflating or inflating public expenditures with the wholesale price or the cost-of-living index seems to be inadequate; but the construction of price indices for the different items of public expenditure is very laborious and very often is not possible due to missing information; for the description of one possible approach, cf. my article, 'Finanzpolitik als Verfassungs- und Gesellschaftspolitik. Uberlegungen zur Finanzpolitik des Deutschen Reiches in den Jahren 1930–1932', *Geschichte und Gesellschaft*, vol. 8 (1982), pp. 386–414.

These studies have shown that the reduction in public expenditure, calculated in 1913 prices, was limited to exactly the same figure by which German reparations payments were reduced in the 1932/3 budget in comparison with payments in 1929/30. In other words, it is also in deflationary periods that the 'monetary illusion' plays an important part in guiding the actions of the politicians. Other results of this study cannot be mentioned here.[39]

(3) Long-term comparisons of public revenues also face problems which result from inflationary and deflationary pressures. But there are further difficulties which are related in part to changes in the political system and to shifting competences among the fiscal authorities at different levels. There are also questions which may be traced to unresolved dilemmas of *Finanzwissenschaft* and of economic theory. A lesser problem, though one requiring considerable labour for its solution, is that prior to 1918 there existed divergent tax systems in the various individual German states and their respective local authorities, none of which were fully comparable with the system adopted by the Reich government. There is the more difficult question arising from the fact that the individual states and local authorities had very considerable revenues from public utilities and similar enterprises. Given the monopoly position of these enterprises, the question is raised as to whether these revenues were of a taxlike character.

Moreover, there is the problem of how certain, specialised services are to be classified. Even if it were possible to sort out these questions, no more than a start would have been made for investigating more important problems. Thus, how does the state influence general economic activity with its expenditure? What are the implications of the introduction of an *Allphasenumsatzsteuer* over the alternative value-added tax during the debate concerning the introduction of a turnover tax in 1917? What is reflected in a decision of the 1880s to introduce, in conjunction with certain consumer taxes, a system of veiled subsidies — a system which has been retained to this day, notwithstanding the various changes in the political system which Germany experienced in this century? Finally, there is the most important question of all: what are the tax burdens on individuals or on specific groups and classes? These are, and have always been, explosive political questions, and to date neither economic theory nor fiscal theory has developed plausible answers; all that has been proven is that the classic division into direct and indirect taxes is useless for understanding problems of the

39. Witt, ibid.

incidence of tax. And yet it might be important to examine the explicit
or unspoken assumptions of various political groups about the tax
system. After all, their 'ideological' presuppositions do have a considerable bearing on the shaping of that system.[40]

(4) Finally, brief reference shall be made to another problem of the
history of public finance in Germany: there exist almost insuperable
obstacles when we come to analysing the processes of executive and
legislative decision-making during certain periods. This is certainly
true of the years from 1914 to 1918 and from 1933/4 to 1945 for which
we have no budgetary files from the Finance Ministry or other related
ministries. This is not because they became an accidental casualty of
Allied bombing during the Second World War; rather, they were
systematically destroyed. The significance of this action will be clear to
anyone who has dealt with *published* statistics, which are, of course, still
available. But it is also well known that the agencies which produced
them thought it virtuous to falsify and veil the naked statistical truth.[41]

We have deliberately highlighted the difficulties facing our approach
and illustrated them by reference to budgetary analysis. We have also
indicated a few solutions to these problems. This seemed wise in order
to demonstrate the limits which the history of public finance runs up
against. These limits are partly imposed by the sources, but also by the
lack of sufficient preliminary work on the part of the economic and
financial sciences. On the other hand, the discussion of these difficulties
also contains a programme of questions which the historian of public
finance should investigate in future and which may allow him or her to
hear, if not the thunder, at least the distant rumblings of world history.

40. Some of the problems mentioned here are discussed in my study 'Die Finanz- und
Wirtschaftspolitik des deutschen Reiches 1918–1924' (unpublished manuscript).
41. See Witt, 'Finanzpolitik', *Geschichte und Gesellschaft*, vol. 8 (1982), pp. 386–414.

HEIDE WUNDER

Finance in the 'Economy of Old Europe': The Example of Peasant Credit from the Late Middle Ages to the Thirty Years War

To Rainer Wohlfeil on his 60th birthday

I

(1) The historical treatment in the history and sociology of public finances is bound to be conditioned with hindsight by the concepts of the 'modern state' as a *res publica*.[1] It therefore finds itself dealing with strategies for raising money (taxes) and with expenditure policy for areas which are retrospectively defined as the 'public interest' — or, in the language of the fifteenth and sixteenth centuries, as the 'common weal'. These areas are concerned, first of all, with the armed forces and the creation and extension of bureaucratic government, administration and jurisdiction; then with the promotion of the

1. J. Engel, 'Von der spätmittelalterlichen respublica christiana zum Mächte-Europa der Neuzeit', in T. Schieder (ed.), *Handbuch der europäischen Geschichte*, vol. 3, Stuttgart, 1971, pp. 387–443; T. Mayer, 'Geschichte der Finanzwirtschaft vom Mittelalter bis zum Ende des 18. Jahrhunderts', in E. von Beckerath et al. (eds.), *Handbuch der Finanzwissenschaft*, vol. 1, Tübingen, 1952, pp. 236–72; H. Hassinger, 'Finanzwesen', in G. Aubin, and W. Zorn (eds.), *Handbuch der deutschen Wirtschafts- und Sozialgeschichte*, vol. 1, Stuttgart, 1971), pp. 293–9; D. Willoweit, 'Die Entwicklung und Verwaltung der spätmittelalterlichen Landesherrschaft', in K.G.A. Jeserich et al. (eds.), *Deutsche Verwaltungsgeschichte*, vol. 1, Stuttgart, 1983), pp. 128–9; P. Moraw, 'Die Anfänge des Reichssteuerwesens', in ibid., pp. 57–8; F. Lütge, 'Finanzgeschichte', in E. von Beckerath et al. (eds.), *Handwörterbuch der Sozialwissenschaften*, vol.3, Stuttgart, 1961, pp. 580–604; A. Erler, 'Finanzwesen', in A. Erler and E. Kaufmann (eds.), *Handwörterbuch zur deutschen Rechtsgeschichte*, vol. 1, Berlin, 1971, pp. 1130–3.

economy by developing the infrastructure of the country and by massively subsidising new branches of the economy in line with the mercantilist theory of money; and finally, with 'public welfare'. By and by the modern state succeeded in monopolising the exercise of 'legitimate power' and thus became the 'public authority' *per se*. On the basis of such claims to power, the state acquired new tasks automatically as society itself grew and changed.

A more comprehensive view of financial affairs has been developed by economists. It also includes the 'corporations of public law' in the history of modern public finances.[2] In addition to the direct 'line' of the princely state, corporative communal traditions are recognised as forming part of the genealogy of the modern state and its finances; indeed, communes were already public institutions at a time when princes remained imprisoned in 'private', patrimonial ways of thinking which were not remotely 'public'. While historians have recognised a political — 'public' — significance in the finances of kings and their territories, they have classified urban economy (using market, money, production and distribution as its points of reference) as no more than the private activity of individual citizens. At best, it is pointed out that urban merchants repeatedly put the royal finances in order between the fifteenth and eighteenth centuries be it in France or in Bavaria, and that urban taxes set an example for the taxation system of the modern state. The urban economy's contribution to the development of public finances has thus been assessed on the basis of its technical achievements and services (credit), while the achievements of the towns as communities have been underestimated.

The semantic history of the term 'finances'[3] helps to trace the process by which the state took over urban economic methods. In the fourteenth century, the German *finantien* meant sums of money loaned for a clearly defined period; as repayment frequently fell due in connection with obscure bill business, the term gained the negative meaning of 'usury'. Not before the seventeenth century was the now current definition adopted from the French, and then only for state revenues and expenditure. Nevertheless, the older German connotations remain

    2. K.T.v. Eheberg, 'Finanzen', in J. Conrad et al. (eds.), *Handwörterbuch der Staatswissenschaften*, vol. 4, Jena, 1927, pp. 1–98; idem, 'Gemeindefinanzen', in ibid., pp. 783–845; J. Landmann, 'Geschichte des öffentlichen Kredits', in E. Alexander-Katz et al. (eds.), *Handbuch der Finanzwissenschaft*, vol. 3, Tübingen, 1958, pp. 1–33.
    3. F. Kluge, *Etymologisches Wörterbuch der deutschen Sprache*, 17th edn, Berlin, 1957, pp. 197–8; *Deutsches Wörterbuch von Jacob Grimm und Wilhelm Grimm*, vol. 3, Leipzig, 1862, pp. 1639–40; J. Bouvier and H. Germain-Martin, *Finances et financiers de l'Ancien Régime*, 2nd edn, Paris, 1969.

indispensable because they refer to a central aspect of the matter — the fact that in public finances there was frequently a gap between revenues and expenditure, which had to be covered by credit if increases in revenues or savings were not possible. The history of public credit has thus been dealt with in great detail by researchers into public finances; it has also been acknowledged by historians, at least under the aspect of 'debts', as a cause of the development of a systematic state financial economy, of corporate rights to approve taxation and of corporative administration of debts.

The term 'credit', which is derived from the Latin *credere*, provides further information. The granting of credit is not merely a financial transaction but rests on an advance of trust from the creditor to the debtor. This is still the case today, because trustworthiness is a precondition for obtaining credit from 'public funds'. Therefore credit is not merely a technical banking term but is part of a system of societal norms in which 'loyalty and faith' (*Treu und Glauben*) also constitute conditions for economic activity. Credit shows, more clearly than revenues and expenditure, that qualitative as well as quantitative factors enter into the calculations of financial economy. Admittedly, since the late Middle Ages personal trust alone has not been sufficient to secure credit. The debtor had to offer one or more guarantors as well as landed property. Moreover, it became customary to 'publish' urban credit (which normally operated by purchasing bonds) by means of an entry in the municipal register in the presence of the town's officials.

The qualitative aspects of economic life in particular are lost from view in public finances if the process of change in economic life is only described as one of increasing rationality. The stereotypes which are always used to describe this change (natural economy — money economy; simple production of goods — capitalist production of goods; simple mode of exchange — market mode of exchange) suggest qualitative changes, but they simultaneously suggest that a development has occurred from 'primitive' to complex or 'superior' standards. In this instance, the conditions of the nineteenth and twentieth centuries are used to set the standard for the judgement of superior development. In this kind of analytical approach, the history and sociology of public finances are discernible only to a very limited extent, because it assumes the independence of the economic sphere as a historical constant instead of regarding it as the result of an extensive and comprehensive transformation. While the growing autonomy of the political sphere has been understood as 'modern state' by opposing it to the older concept of 'household' (*familia*), the 'economics of old Europe' (*alteuropäische Ökonomik*),[4] which up to now has been treated as part of the history of ideas, still requires further elaboration before the way in which it differs from 'political economy' can become fully apparent. First of all, it should be remembered that the history of public finances began in an agricultural society, but that agricultural society must not be equated with natural economy. While it is true that the volume of goods produced did not rise above a certain level in pre-industrial agricultural society, there was nevertheless a considerable economic dynamism. This level was determined, on the one hand, by such factors as soil, climate, systems of cultivation, technology, the ratio of people to available food, and fluctuations in harvest, and on the other hand, by systems of distribution and the strategies of every social group to protect or to improve its status. Researchers have assessed economic dynamism in late medieval and early modern agriculture only for signs of economic *modernisation*, characterising it as 'demesne state' (*Domänenstaat*), 'agrarian capitalism' or, at least, 'commercialisation of agriculture'. But the older economic systems can be only partly understood by such investigations, because they work with ideas which resulted from this transformation — state, national economy, capitalism — or from the analysis of isolated economic sectors. Without any doubt, the results of modern retrospective economic history are important for understanding the development of capitalism,[5] but the task of researching contemporary ideas and perceptions of economic activity and economic processes in their connection with real economic life remains imperative. Only thus are we able to understand and explain traditional patterns of economic behaviour. This aspect is often not considered at all, or is underestimated. The effects of such an assessment are most clearly revealed in the treatment of the peasants.

(2) Without the peasants, the lords could not have survived and an urban market would have been impossible, but in the history of public finances they are not present as active partners in the economic process. At most, peasant income has been of interest in order to determine the extent of their financial burdens and contributions, their feudal or market quotas. According to such calculations, it frequently appears little short of miraculous that the peasants managed to survive at all. However precise the details of econometric economic history may appear, they can clearly explain only one part of economic events. Just as traditional historians have failed to recognise the peasant as

---

4. O. Brunner, 'Das "ganze Haus" und die alteuropäische "Ökonomik"', in idem, *Neue Wege der Verfassungs- und Sozialgeschichte*, 2nd edn, Göttingen, 1968, pp. 103–27.
5. P. Kriedte, *Spätfeudalismus und Handelskapitalismus*, Göttingen, 1980.

homo politicus, so economic historians have not taken him seriously as an economic subject, as *homo oeconomicus*. He has been included neither in economic nor in political *public life* (state, market); instead, he has been regarded as part of the natural economy, in which agriculture and the subsistence economy are assumed to be one and the same thing. Accordingly, peasants have not been regarded as participating in economic life in the modern sense, but only as working their land in order to subsist.

Contradictory assessments of the peasants derive in part from the fact that scholarly investigations have revealed only some aspects of their situation and way of life, which at first sight appear incompatible with each other. The other reason is that economic and constitutional historians have taken scarcely any notice of important research into pre-industrial agricultural society. For example, fifty years ago Wilhelm Abel established that the peasant economy was fundamentally involved in the market economy from the height of the Middle Ages; thus the peasants — like their lords — profited from booms and suffered during crises, if not in the same way;[6] also, Karl Siegfried Bader, in his studies (1958–73) on the legal history of the village in the Middle Ages, has shown that it was not the individual peasant but rather the rural community as a corporate body which constituted a legal entity. As such, it undertook public functions, disposed of its own community budget and had its own community bookkeeping.[7] It is thus clear that knowledge itself is not lacking so much as the coordination of that knowledge, and perhaps also a recognised interest in investigating the peasants in the context of pre-industrial European society and the comprehensive transformations of the modern era.

The researches of Abel and Bader provide the basis for an integration of the peasants into a history of economic and political public life, and thus into a history and sociology of public finances. On the sociological aspect, I shall first of all refer to the peasantry as a class or social group (*Klasse* or *Stand*) and only secondly to sub-groups of this class and its forms of local organisation (village). A rural and village perspective will be used to discover what can be understood by the term 'public finances' in the agricultural society of the late Middle Ages and early modern period. My argument will not — as is usual — be based on the income and outgoings of the peasants, on prices and

6. W. Abel, *Agrarkrisen und Agrarkonjunkturen*, 1935; 2nd edn, Hamburg and Berlin, 1966.
7. K.S. Bader, *Dorfgenossenschaft und Dorfgemeinde*, Vienna, Cologne and Graz, 1974, pp. 427–60.

wages, but on the search for rural credit. In this process social relationships other than those which are familiar from economic history and agricultural constitutional history emerge. These, assessed alongside the research on the history of the rural economy which is already available, enable us to obtain a more accurate picture of the significance of credit in pre-industrial agricultural society.

Although peasant *debts* have been known to historians for some time, the peasants have not been included in the money market and the issue of agricultural *credit* has not been investigated. There is no general history of agricultural credit, only a large number of local and regional studies which often deal with the period before the Peasants' War of 1525 and with the consequences of the Thirty Years War. At first sight, indebtedness has a certain plausibility as a cause of social movements and as a consequence of war. However, the intense debate about the reasons for the participation of many prosperous peasants in the Peasants' War shows that indebtedness was not a vital factor in determining peasant positions.[8] It is true that a significant feature of rural indebtedness became apparent in the fifteenth century and in the period before the great Peasants' War — namely personal credits from Jews.[9] However, individual cases are contradictory and cannot be compared with other findings. We lack a model against which to interpret the peasant economy and its relations with other economic sectors. According to conventional categories, the history of rural credit begins only in the nineteenth century with the agrarian reforms.[10] Until then, the peasant economy was regarded as part of the manorial system and was thus classified as 'private' (i.e. as the 'private affair' of the lords of the manor), to which the state had no direct access, although in the absolutist states even 'private peasants' (*Privatbauern*) were already 'state citizens' (*Staatsbürger)* with corresponding obligations. In the eighteenth century there existed that strange notion that the lords of the manor were private individuals as regards the state, but public persons — that is, endowed with public authority — in their relations with the peasantry.

(3) The implications of this system can be observed with particular

8. G. Franz, 'Die Führer im Bauernkrieg', in idem (ed), *Bauernschaft und Bauernstand 1500–1970*, Limburg and Lahn, 1975, pp. 1–15.

9. C. Bauer, 'Probleme der mittelalterlichen Agrargeschichte im Elsass', *Alemannisches Jahrbuch*, vol. 1 (1953), pp. 238–50; G. Franz, *Der deutsche Bauernkrieg*, 10th edn, Darmstadt, 1975, pp. 58–60.

10. W.v. Altrock, 'Landwirtschaftliches Kreditwesen', in L. Elster (ed.), *Handwörterbuch der Staatswissenschaften* 4th edn, vol. 4, Jena, 1925, pp. 189–96.

clarity in the case of Prussia in the eighteenth century.[11] After the Seven Years' War a credit system had been established with state support to protect the Prussian landowning nobility against bankruptcy. However, the same was not done for the peasants, who had also suffered greatly during the military campaigns. A partial explanation for this phenomenon lies in the fact that in many Prussian provinces based on the manorial system the peasant farm counted for very little whereas the peasants' labour force was valued highly; in consequence, the number of hereditarily dependent peasants determined the value of manor. Often the peasants owned neither their houses nor their implements and livestock, and in many cases had only inferior (not hereditary) rights of possession to the land they cultivated. They therefore lacked the basic precondition for obtaining mortgage credit. But even peasants with superior rights of possession and home ownership were forbidden to obtain urban credit without the consent of the lord of the manor. Nevertheless, it was generally the case that the better their rights of possession, the more easily they could gain access to the money market in order to obtain personal credit. Under the conditions of the manorial system, rural credit was also possible and customary in another form, namely as credit for the local peasant community. In Silesia such communities obtained credit in the towns in order to buy-off feudal rights.[12] For the creditors this was a calculated risk, inasmuch as the value of the peasant holdings rose as the result of liberation from obligations and was therefore regarded as sufficient security. Even in the estate of Boitzenburg (Uckermark), which can be regarded as the extreme example of the manorial system, peasants with hereditary tenant rights were able to finance their legal proceedings with urban credit.[13]

The general creditworthiness of the peasants was not established until the agrarian reforms at the beginning of the nineteenth century; these gave the individual peasant ownership of the land, which he could mortgage. To begin with, however, all peasants lost part of the land which they had previously cultivated for their former lords because — due to the lack of credit possibilities — they had to pay the required redemption fee in land rather than money. Peasants with superior rights of possession lost 'only' one-third of their land in this

11. O. Hintze, *Die Hohenzollern und ihr Werk*, 9th edn, Berlin, 1916, pp. 380–7; K. Klatte, 'Die Anfänge des Agrarkapitalismus und der preussische Konservatismus', Diss., Hamburg, 1974, pp. 130–8.
12. J. Ziekursch, *Hundert Jahre schlesischer Agrargeschichte*, Breslau, 1915, pp. 220–6.
13. H. Harnisch, *Die Herrschaft Boitzenburg*, Weimar, 1968, pp. 126–7.

way, while peasants with inferior rights lost as much as half. These losses of land and the low agricultural prices after 1817 ruined many peasants, not least because they could not afford the new state taxes: they had to sell their land, mostly to the former lord of the manor. Other German states, where the 'emancipation of the peasantry' was achieved later, learned from the Prussian example and established special banks which credited the peasants with the sums necessary for the redemption payments on favourable terms (e.g. Saxony and Hessen-Cassel).[14] Such institutions were limited to this objective and were not intended for general agricultural credit. The peasants themselves remedied this lack by founding credit societies following traditions of older communal institutions.[15]

The example of Prussia dramatically reveals the problems of rural credit in the late absolutist period and the era of reforms. At the same time, it reveals that, from this perspective, the term 'public credit' does not only mean credit supplied by the state but also civic credit. If one accepts this overall view of the 'public sphere' (*Öffentlichkeit*) in state *and* society, then the history and sociology of public finances cannot deal solely with the origin of public life in the princely state. An assessment of the contribution of other institutions and corporations with a public character since the height of the Middle Ages is equally fundamental.

(4) In addition to the Reich and the territorial authorities, urban and peasant communities as well as religious and secular corporations (guilds, orders, brotherhoods, universities) also had a public character. Common to all these 'public bodies' was *immunity* — more or less exemption from outside interference and the ability to organise the 'freedom' thus acquired according to their own rules (*Zwing und Bann, Gebot und Verbot, Willkür*). They differed from each other in the way the respective associations were organised, whether as familia/household [16] or as *universitas*/community.[17] The difference between these two forms of organisation is usually described in simplistic terms as the contrast between lordship and community. However, such a contrast is only partially accurate, for dominion was exercised within the communities

14. C. Dipper, *Die Bauernbefreiung in Deutschland 1970–1850*, Stuttgart, 1980, pp. 123–5.
15. W.v. Hippel, *Die Bauernbefreiung im Königreich Württemberg*, vol. 1, Boppard, 1977, pp. 551–3; see also W.A. Boelcke, 'Zur Entwicklung des bäuerlichen Kreditwesens in Württemberg vom späten Mittelalter bis Anfang des 17. Jahrhunderts', *Jahrbücher für Nationalökonomie und Statistik* vol. 176 (1964), pp. 329–30.
16. H.K. Schulze, *Grundstrukturen der Verfassung im Mittelalter*, vol. 1 Stuttgart, 1985, pp. 95–151.
17. Bader, pp. 3–29; H. Wunder, *Die bäuerliche Gemeinde in Deutschland*, Göttingen, 1986.

and there were communal features within the manorial households. Elected community representatives governed the communities, and all those inhabitants without civic status were subject to their control. Similarly, in the great manorial households peasant jurors were entitled to discover the verdict in their courts of justice. It thus follows that the terms 'equal' and 'unequal', which are often used to describe the contrast of *familia*/household and *universitas*/community are only applicable to a limited extent, as both qualities were found in both types of organisation. However, we can speak of a 'monarchial apex', receiving its legitimation from tradition, in all forms of household rule; in contrast, community rule was the rule of a large group, which elected a ruling body with a limited brief for a limited period, and with the obligation to render account. For this reason Max Weber has described the town — as the prototype of community rule — as an 'illegitimate' form of rule.

The qualitative differences between these two forms of domination and their 'public spheres', emerge still more clearly when we compare their respective aims and the methods of finding the necessary means of achieving them. It is then revealed that in all forms of household rule, 'public' and 'private' spheres cannot be strictly separated. The lord's income appears in retrospect to be private, although public obligations such as legal protection of the tenants were bound up with it. A mixing of private and general interests can also be discerned in the structure of the income and expenditure of princes. In contrast, the bookkeeping of the urban communities was public from the very beginning, because it served to distribute commitments among the whole community of citizens. This process did not rule out the possibility of private arbitrariness on the part of individual magistrates or the entire council, which in many cases led to conflicts between the council and the community.[18] Nevertheless, the guiding principle of municipal bookkeeping was the *common weal*.[19] However obvious the orientation of municipal politics on the common weal appears at first sight, the ideological aspects should not be overlooked. The idea of the common weal had already emerged in the thirteenth century, during the debates on the 'King's Peace' (*Landfriede*), before being adopted by the imperial cities. No longer at stake here was the fair distribution of foreseeable municipal costs, but the raising of money for a specific policy which was not equally reasonable to all citizens. The common weal as a social

18. K. Fritze, 'Die Finanzpolitik Lübecks im Krieg gegen Dänemark 1426–1433', in *Hansische Studien*, Berlin, 1961, pp. 82–9.
19. U. Peters, *Literatur in der Stadt*, Tübingen, 1983, pp. 227–68.

aim thus only becomes necessary in a society in which group interests have already diverged widely; this was the case in the towns, where increasing social and economic distinctions led to great tensions. Later problems, relating to who ought to decide what should be done in the public interest, are already clearly apparent here.

Increased understanding of public spheres in the Middle Ages helps us to interpret some apparent inconsistencies in the assessment of the peasants' situation. These inconsistencies are explained by the fact that the peasants belonged both to the large household of the lord of the manor and to the peasants' own communities. The relationship of superiority and subordination between these two institutions was actually ambiguous; the peasants, therefore, moved in an area of conflict defined by their individual dependence on their lord and by their corporative independence and ability to act. There was, in addition, a third form of public sphere: within the communities and the manorial estates there existed the individual peasant household. Its head exerted authority over the members of the family and the household on a scale which established the peasant household as a particular sphere of 'law and order'. Although the peasant household can, with good reason, be included in a history of public authority, the fact remains that the different public spheres did not have equal *public rights* and *public power*. There emerges an order of rank in public spheres. As the princely state had already begun to subordinate or appropriate to itself these public spheres during the fifteenth century, awareness of these connections was lost at an early stage. As a major example we may report the princes' efforts in their relations with the Church. In the fifteenth century they even assumed authority over those monasteries in their territories which were incapable of reform. The secularisation of religious estates and religious tasks during the Reformation formed the first peak of their endeavours. The subordination of the communities and the heads of households, on the other hand, turned out to be a more lengthy process.[20]

II

The roots of public finances are consequently widely ramified. They should be sought in the multitude of public spheres in the Middle Ages and the early modern period, which had developed

20. Wunder, *Die bäuerliche Gemeinde in Deutschland*.

systems of finance which had partly common and partly specific traits. Since the twelfth century — from the time, therefore, when peasants began operating independently in the community and corporate peasant communities were created — the peasants were part of these systems too. Accordingly, an investigation of rural credit does not just contribute to the history of 'private' peasant economy; it also helps to reveal the history of 'public finances'. Because peasants moved simultaneously in various public spheres, we must look for peasant credit in the manorial system, in the community and in the peasant household itself. We must begin, however, with a short explanation of what was understood by credit in medieval society.

Georges Duby revealed graphically how a new credit system arose after the Germanic tribes had been christianised.[21] The converts were persuaded not to bury rich objects in order to provide a good life for their dead in the hereafter. Instead, they began to endow monasteries and cathedral churches with rich gifts and property, while the inmates responded with prayers for the poor souls of the donators. Monasteries, in particular, served the cult of the dead of their founding families; this also served to represent the founders' superior secular position. In this way the monasteries collected enormous wealth, which they did not leave unused. From the tenth century they provided credit for freemen, who found themselves in increasing economic difficulties at a time of incessant warfare. When the freemen were unable to discharge their debts, they were forced to place themselves in economic and legal dependence on their monastic creditors. However, this is not the whole story. This dependence offered the freemen a share in the privileged status of the manasteries and ensured them protection which they could no longer guarantee for themselves. Therefore, even freemen without the pressure of debts chose to become 'people of God's house' (*Gotteshausleute*), to escape the pressure of secular lords in exchange for security.[22] The early medieval crediting thus contributed to the growth in the number of dependent peasants (*Vergrundherrschaftung*).

In this period, the wealth of the monasteries should be regarded as part of public finances. However, it was a fund which was available only to 'public persons' — that is, persons with full legal capacities, the freemen. The proposition can be further substantiated. Until the investiture contest, most monasteries were regarded as the property of their founding families, who accordingly had the property of the

21. G. Duby, *Guerriers et paysans VII–XIIe siècle*, Premier essor de l'économie européenne, Gallimard, 1974, p. 66.
22. W. Rösener, *Bauern im Mittelalter*, Munich, 1985, pp. 27–9; Boelcke, p. 321.

monastery at their disposal. The great imperial monasteries therefore had to part with some of their lands in order to serve the interests of their royal patron and to achieve *feudalism* as a political system.[23] With the fief, the feudal lord provided for his vassal while the vassal committed himself to rendering certain services — especially loyalty — to his lord. This relationship can be defined as an exchange, in which material and spiritual goods were exchanged to express reciprocal bonds and obligations. From the lord's point of view this exchange could also be interpreted as credit: its pledge was the fief, which reverted in the event of the vassal's disloyalty or death.

The idea of unequal exchange, bound up with reciprocal obligations, permeated all economic, social and political (*herrschaftliche*) relations.[24] It also determined the trade of goods itself to a large extent.[25] This explains why exchange and credit cannot be neatly separated. Because material and spiritual goods are exchanged simultaneously in every exchange/transaction, no account can ever be made out down to last penny. One party always remained somewhat indebted to the other; as this debt may be described as credit, it is apparent that there is no clear distinction between exchange and credit. The interrelatedness partly explains the economic, social and political dynamism typical for the Middle Ages: no one wished to remain indebted to anyone else, and the 'debtor' would therefore attempt to reverse the relationship at the earliest opportunity. If one of the parties was no longer able to keep pace, then a one-sided dependence was created. Correspondingly, credits were used consciously — until the twentieth century in rural society — to establish and symbolise dependency.

Until the height of the Middle Ages, public credit — as shown above — served to establish feudal bonds and peasant dependence. The idea of reciprocity was nevertheless maintained by both sides. Public credit gained a new dimension with the emergence of urban and peasant communities. It applied to the independent family economies of peasants, craftsmen and merchants, to the narrow network of peasant and urban economy, and to the web of trading relationships both within regions and between the great economic areas of the Baltic, the Mediterranean and Western Europe.

---

23. K. Bosl, 'Staat, Gesellschaft, Wirtschaft im deutschen Mittelalter', in H. Grundmann (ed.), *Handbuch der deutschen Geschichte* (9th edn,) vol. 1, Stuttgart, 1970, pp. 736–42.
24. H. Codere, 'Exchange and display', in D.L. Sills (ed.), *International Encyclopaedia of Social Sciences*, vol. 5, New York, 1968, pp. 239–45.
25. E. Pitz, *Wirtschafts- und Sozialgeschichte Deutschlands im Mittelalter*, Wiesbaden, 1979, pp. 27–8.

The religious corporations continued to give credit, so far as their situation allowed. Yet the Church as a whole discovered new 'capital' in the form of the supererogation collected by Jesus and the saints, which stood at the disposal of all those who could purchase it.[26] This commercialisation of the distribution of the means of grace took account of the new urban development and allowed merchants and craftsmen, along with the privileged nobility, to obtain 'credit' for life after death. Such was the aim of the numerous donations, particularly from merchants, who thus bought the prayers of the poor in order to ransom themselves with funds from commercial profit, which violated the principle of reciprocity.[27] While Georges Duby has shown how buried — dead — wealth was transformed into capital during the early Middle Ages, late medieval economic attitudes show that the interest of the living in life after death continued to determine the circulation of money until well into the sixteenth century by leading them to make large donations to religious corporations (mortmain).

On the other hand, a demand for credit in its technical sense developed especially in inter-regional trade, but also in urban and regional business. The charging of interest violated both the older idea of reciprocity and the ethics of the Church. People evaded the ecclesiastical ban on interest by inventing the purchase of fixed interest securities on the basis of (i) house ownership, (ii) the Lombard credit as a short-term loan on merchandise and (iii) the bill business.[28] This objectification or depersonalisation of credit enabled a commercialisation of financial transaction to occur, although the human guarantor still played an important role.[29]

The general trend towards commercialisation can also be detected in feudal relationships. Feudal lords actually traded with their rights over land and people in order to obtain money. The mortgaging of sources of income which provided a fluctuating revenue against a fixed sum can be interpreted as credit. The purchase of offices, which has long been regarded as 'corruption', also belongs to this system of credit. Even the corporative administration of princely debts derives from the fact that

26. G.A. Benrath, 'Ablaß', in G. Krause and G. Müller (eds.), *Theologische Realenzyklopädie* vol. 1, Berlin and New York, 1977, pp. 347–64.
27. E. Maschke, 'Die Unterschichten der mittelalterlichen Städte Deutschlands', in E. Maschke and J. Sydow (eds.), *Gesellschaftliche Unterschichten in den südwestdeutschen Städten*, Stuttgart, 1967, pp. 1–74.
28. E. Loening and O. Loening, 'Rentenkauf und Rentenschuld', in J. Conrad et al. (eds.), *Handwörterbuch der Staatswissenschaften*, 4th edn, vol. 7, Jena, 1926, pp. 23–7; J. Favier, 'Die Entstehung der Bank', *Journal für Geschichte*, vol. 5 (1984), pp. 48–57.
29. E. Kaufmann, 'Bürgschaft', in A. Erler and E. Kaufmann (eds.), *Handwörterbuch zur deutschen Rechtsgeschichte* vol. 1, Berlin, 1971, pp. 565–9.

the sovereign forced the Estates to take over his debts. Consequently, he lived off their credit.[30]

A search for peasant credit in the history of public finances must take into account the older public spheres, on the one hand (manorial system, community, household), and the history of credit in the narrow sense, on the other. Medieval sources do not permit more precise insights into the economic situation and conduct of the peasantry until the second half of the fourteenth century. This determines the point at which our investigation can begin. The end of the period of research is determined by the chance fact that the only detailed investigations in which peasant credit plays a part deal with Württemberg before and during the Thirty Years War.[31] This war, however, constituted a generally recognised *caesura* in the history of public finances, [32] so that it can also be regarded as the end of an epoch for our own purposes.

Peasant credit in the manorial system

From the early Middle Ages lords made registers of their possessions and of the peasant families obliged to render dues to them. Debt registers, on the other hand, which systematically record peasant debts, became important only as a consequence of the 'crisis of the fourteenth century'. The German Order's administration in Prussia provides a good example for this proposition. After the end of the period of settlement in the second half of the fourteenth century, and especially after the defeats against Poland-Lithuania in the first half of the fifteenth century, the German Order had to take great care in its economic management. The Penny Debt Register of the Christburg Commandery, which for approximately forty years (1380–1420) recorded the arrears of hundreds of German and Prussian peasants, dates from this period.[33] The Order not only gave its peasants time to pay their contributions but also advanced them seed crops, livestock and foodstuffs. There were many causes of indebtedness, but chief among them were the unfavourable climate and the devastations caused by

30. I. Mieck (ed.), *Ämterhandel im Spätmittelalter und im 16. Jahrhundert*, Berlin, 1984.
31. W.A. Boelcke, pp. 329–30; idem, 'Bäuerlicher Wohlstand in Württemberg Ende des 16. Jahrhunderts', in ibid., pp. 241–80; W. von Hippel, 'Bevölkerung und Wirtschaft im Zeitalter des Dreissigjährigen Krieges. Das Beispiel Württemberg', *Zeitschrift für Historische Forschung*, vol. 5 (1978), pp. 413–46.
32. K. Krüger, 'Entstehung und Ausbau des hessischen Steuerstaates vom 16. bis zum 18. Jahrhundert — Akten der Finanzverwaltung als frühneuzeitlicher Gesellschaftsspiegel', *Hessisches Jahrbuch für Landesgeschichte*, vol. 32 (1982), pp. 103–25.
33. H. Wunder (ed.), *Das Pfennigschuldbuch der Komturei Christburg*, Cologne and Berlin, 1969.

war. A price list at the beginning of the manuscript tells us a great deal about the administration of the debts. It appears that overdue contributions of natural produce could be paid off in money, and that money to be paid could be converted into natural produce. It is not clear whether the peasants were prepared to draw on their savings in order to pay their dues. They probably preferred to get into debt with the Order.

Habitual peasant indebtedness reveals a typical form of peasant credit in the manorial system. The contributions which were deferred should be regarded as credit from the lord, who granted it — or was forced to grant it — in order to keep his farms occupied if there was a shortage of labour (as was the case in the fifteenth century). This form of credit indicates the ambivalence of the manorial system in the late Middle Ages. It was no longer based, as in the eleventh century, solely on the lord's household and his needs, but on the productivity of the individual peasant households. At the same time these attempted, with more or less success, to reduce their contributions to their lord.

Nevertheless, the lords remained in a position — even in the case of a severe crop failure — to credit their peasants with cereal and livestock, to wait for their due contributions for one or several years, or to do without them altogether. The majority of peasants, on the other hand, were badly hit by low prices and poor harvests. Obviously, many of them could not collect sufficient reserves in good years to enable them to cope with bad years. This fact was due less to the burden of regular contributions than to irregular payments such as consent to marriage, payments on a change of ownership, money paid on the death of the owner of the farm, and legal payments to buy freedom from punishments according to manorial or community law. These payments, which should also be regarded as part of the 'feudal quota', scarcely permitted the small and medium peasants to make savings; the sums removed from the household in this way had always to be restored through good management so that the farm could be continued. The lords would probably be inclined to defer payment of the annual contributions in order to obtain the more lucrative irregular payments in the long term.

There is one feature of the manorial system of credit which is astonishing at first glance. There were no interest charges — that is, no profit — which are inextricably linked with the modern understanding of credit. This was not due to the canonical ban, which defined the charging of interest as usury and thus as a mortal sin. It was rather the result of a different understanding of the term 'interest': in this case, the 'interests' of the lords in preserving their power. As the relationship between the lord of the manor and his peasants was regarded as reciprocal, the willingness of the lord to do without interests which were otherwise customary may be seen as a compensation for the fundamentally unequal exchange of lordly protection and peasant contributions. Still, it can be assumed that there were subtle strategies to recover peasant debts with a material profit for the lord. One possibility consisted of demanding that peasant debts be paid back in the form (money or produce) which benefited the lord. Another practice was to use different units of measurement for cereal which was being lent out and cereal being paid in; for example, market bushels for the former and the larger manorial bushels for the latter, or level bushels for cereal which was lent and heaped bushels for cereal being returned. In the most extreme cases the lord could force a heavily indebted peasant to sell up as a bad housekeeper, though such practices were condemned unanimously as abuses. In principle the lord –peasant relationship was not presented as a relationship based on exploitation but as a system which should guarantee to both the livelihood (*Nahrung*) befitting their rank.

This basic idea was undermined to the extent that the manorial system was overtaken by market relationship.[34] In the fifteenth century the wine-growers provided an extreme example of this tendency towards commercialisation.[35] To earn a living in wine-growing only a small amount of land was required, along with a large labour force and some capital to convert fields into vineyards. The capital was provided by lords and by burghers who wanted to participate in the profitable wine trade, while the smallholding families organised the labour and frequently obtained in return secure rights of possession on the land they worked. Because of the climate, however, German wine-growers faced more bad harvests than good ones. During the frequent bad harvests they could not afford to pay their contributions. In addition, they were forced further into debt because they did not grow their own grain but had to buy it. Their lords conducted themselves differently towards these debts than was the case in traditional agriculture. They did not wait until the wine-growers were in a position to pay their

34. See H. Wunder, 'Bäuerlicher Widerstand und frühmoderner Staat am Beispiel von Ordensstaat und Herzogtum Preußen', in W. Schulze (ed.), *Aufstände, Revolten, Prozesse*, Stuttgart, 1983, pp. 112–34.
35. See D. Scheler, 'Die fränkische Vorgeschichte des ersten Reichsgesetzes gegen Weinverfälschung', in *120, Bericht des Historischen Vereins Bamberg 1984*, pp. 489–504; Boelcke, p. 352.

arrears. Instead, they had the right to demand payment after the next harvest and before the market price for wine was fixed, which usually left the wine-growers at a disadvantage. Moreover, the wine-growers were not allowed to mortgage their land, so that their only opportunity to get money lay in obtaining credit from Jews in the towns. These are the reasons why many south-west German peasants complained against Jewish usury from the fifteenth century to the Peasants' War of 1525.[36] To sum up, the precarious position of the wine-growers was caused by the unfavourable climatic conditions prevailing in Germany, by the monoculture of wine resulting in total dependence on wine harvests and by the small size of their landholdings, which invalidated the otherwise applicable rule that good rights of possession encouraged the granting of mortgage credit on usual terms. Also, the general conditions for receiving urban merchant credit were unfavourable for the rural population. Agricultural prices remained low until the last third of the fifteenth century, so urban creditors found it more profitable to invest their money in other areas.[37]

Peasant credit and the community

For the late medieval and early modern period, peasant communities can be classified according to their economic structures (most important, cereal cultivation, livestock breeding, wine cultivation) and settlement patterns associated with them: (i) *local* village communities and (ii) communities of dispersed settlement, whose centres were the parish church or the seat of the court of justice.[38] They were based on the local neighbourhood in the village and its fields and on the institutionalised association of the neighbourhood as a peasant corporation. Both forms of association play their part in the system of peasant credit.

The most widespread and long-lasting form of peasant and rural credit was based on the harvest cycle. Jobs were done by the village craftsmen 'on tick' until the harvest. Only leading figures, such as the village priest, usually paid in cash. As the village blacksmith — the craftsman most in demand — was dependent on deliveries of iron from urban traders, this meant that peasant credit, based on the harvest cycle, had an effect extending beyond local craftsmen right into the

36. Bauer, *Alemanisches Jahrbuch*, vol. 1 (1953), pp. 238–50; Franz, pp. 58–60.
37. Boelcke, p. 337.
38. Wunder, *Die bäuerliche Gemeinde in Deutschland*.

towns.[39] It goes without saying that no interest was charged. These small instances of neighbourly help — equipment, food and consumer goods of all kinds — may appear to be insignificant economically, but they were immensely important socially. In this sense they were a significant cause of conflict, as is revealed by the many trials for witchcraft in which the refusal of neighbourly help offered a welcome cause for an accusation of magic.[40]

However, there was also credit in the current sense. The peasants needed smaller and larger sums of money:

— To buy out the children or siblings who did not inherit, in the case of inheritance or when the farm had been handed over at an earlier stage.
— To set up provision for parents or the surviving parent.
— To organise a wedding.
— To build a house.
— To buy land.
— To pay legal fines.

When they had no savings available the peasants had to obtain credit for these primary, *family-based* expenditures. The necessary sums could be borrowed from well-to-do peasants, priests and pastors, municipal officials, religious institutions, peasant communities and parishes.[41]

For *household expenditures* — such as were incurred when a farm was burned down — credit did not play an important role: all the neighbours helped with the building work, the wood came from the communal or manorial forests, and the lord of the manor allowed time to pay the contributions due, or reduced them.[42] On the other hand, as was the case in Pomerania after the Thirty Years War, when the utterly impoverished peasants simply had no capital at all and the lords of the manor rebuilt and equipped the farms out of their own resources, then the peasants were left with only inferior rights of possession; this

39. J. Richter, 'Zur Schriftkundigkeit mecklenburgischer Bauern im 17. Jahrhundert', *Jahrbuch für Wirtschaftsgeschichte*, 1981, III, p. 97.
40. J.A. Lilienthal, *Die Hexenprozesse der beiden Städte Braunsberg*, Königsberg, 1861, p. 141.
41. See Boelcke, pp. 326–8, 335–9; F.-W. Henning, 'Die Verschuldung westfälischer Bauernhöfe in der zweiten Hälfte des 18. Jahrhunderts', in H.-G Schlotter (ed.), *Landwirtschaft und ländliche Gesellschaft in Geschichte und Gegenwart*, Festschrift für Wilhelm Abel, Hanover, 1964, pp. 21–2.
42. K.-S. Kramer, *Bauern und Bürger im nachmittelalterlichen Unterfranken*, Württemburg, 1957, pp. 134–5; see Henning, p. 24.

eliminated the possibility of mortgage credit from the outset.[43]

The community budget was the precondition for community credit.[44] Into the community treasury flowed legal fines as well as revenues from the letting of agricultural and commercial utilities which belonged to the community. These revenues were used to finance the community beer, but also community expenses such as the allocation of public works as paid labour. These services did not exhaust the functions of the community treasury. In the study of types of community credit it is possible to distinguish three aspects. Firstly, credits from the municipal treasury: as the jury books of the Brandenburg Mark reveal, 'inheritance money' for orphans was invested in the community treasury and lent to trustworthy persons.[45] The community treasuries thus functioned simultaneously as 'saving banks'. The extent of credit granted from these funds cannot be calculated. Nevertheless, its importance for peasant demand can scarcely be exaggerated. This community credit was particularly important in the East German territories, where the peasants were often unable to gain access to the urban credit market because of their inferior rights of possession. Secondly, it is known that communal representatives obtained credit for community purposes. A further aspect appears in Württemberg, where communal credit was raised for those community members who were unable to do so themselves.[46] This means that in the local village community there were different criteria of trustworthiness than in the anonymous urban credit market. Thirdly, the efficiency of community credit can easily be recognised in the process by which lords of the manor and princes took advantage of the credit of their peasant communities in order to pass on to them the servicing of their debts. This can also be detected in Württemberg, where the duke forced communities and individual peasants who were known to be wealthy to borrow money for him.[47] This system of state-forced loans is maintained into the twentieth century.

The parishes had similar resources for credit at their disposal. Religious funds came into being by means of donations of varying sizes and were used profitably. Forced loans also existed here, as is revealed by Church inspections during the Reformation. Thus the Church

43. W. Kuhn, *Geschichte der deutschen Ostsiedlung in der Neuzeit*, vol. 2, Cologne and Graz, 1957, pp. 104–27.
44. Bader; H. Harnisch, 'Gemeindeeigentum und Gemeindefinanzen im Spätfeudalismus', *Jahrbuch für Regionalgeschichte*, vol. 8 (1981), pp. 126–74.
45. B. Hinz, *Die Schöppenbücher der Mark Brandenburg*, Berlin, 1964, pp. 126–7.
46. See Boelcke, pp. 328–9.
47. Ibid., pp. 329, 332–3.

inspectors in the Duchy of Prussia recorded that many parishes were compelled to grant credit to neighbouring nobles on favourable terms or entirely interest-free. In addition, the Church wardens had also made interest-free loans to parish members, peasants as well as small-holders (*Gärtner*).[48]

The idea of reciprocity, which was realised as unequal exchange in the relationship between the lords and their peasants, had other features in the community. In addition to everyday neighbourly help, the funds of the peasant community and the parish were also available to members of the village on the usual conditions and possibly also interest-free. Over and above that, community representatives followed the principle of neighbourly help in their conduct towards people who could not get credit themselves. This demonstrates that in the community the laws of the market did not operate as they did in the urban credit business.

Peasant credit in the household, in the family and among relatives

The peasant household appeared as a unit in its relationship to the lord of the manor and within the community. But when we are dealing with the role it played in the peasant credit system, we get a glimpse of its inner structure. Towards the end of the Middle Ages the number of legal documents regulating conflicts or possible conflicts over rights of possession within peasant families increased remarkably. They point to the fact that family relations were defined by prospective options of its members. The question of inheritance was crucial: who was to inherit: one child or all children? And how was this transfer, which was first of all a financial transaction, organised? Often the son or daughter who was to inherit had to buy the parental farm (*Erbkauf*). Sometimes the price was below the market price. It was used to buy out siblings and to provide for the parent(s) themselves. The inheriting child therefore usually was faced with the problem of how to raise the money for this deal. This was achieved partly by obtaining credit and partly by strategies to collect money within the family in order to avoid or at least to reduce dependence on credit from outside.

The amount of money needed to buy out those children who did not inherit depended on the right of inheritance — the right to the farm (*Anerbenrecht*) or division of the estate (*Realteilung*) — and on the

48. See 'Visitationsabschied des Kirchspiels Medenau 1569' (Geheimes Staatsarchiv Preußischer Kulturbesitz XX, HA, StA Königsberg, Ostpr. Fol. 1276).

number of children. Part of the money was brought to the marriage by the bride or bridegroom, which means that the choice of marriage partner was determined by their financial situation. Sometimes savings from paid work might be available to buy out departing siblings, in which case the amount which had to be borrowed was further reduced. Often the heir took over care of his smaller brothers and sisters along with the farm, so that their portion of the inheritance was not yet due.[49] In many cases adult siblings also remained on the farm and demanded their portion only when they married or left the parental farm for other reasons. In these last two cases the amount of credit required was reduced because the siblings were in effect granting an interest-free loan.

This strategy to reduce credit from outside was also used in numerous cases of remarriage. If widows or widowers wanted to remarry, division (*Schicht und Teilung*) was necessary in order to secure the children's inheritance, which appeared to be endangered by the children of the new marriage and also by possible mismanagement on the part of the new couple. However, the portion of the inheritance belonging to the children of the first marriage often remained within the farm and could be demanded only when they reached maturity. These portions could be interpreted as an interest-free loan to the new owners.

In the case of the transfer of a farm either *inter vivos* or by inheritance, two connected procedures may be observed. Firstly, there was a flow of money between peasant households of approximately the same economic standing, because the heir or heiress had to find a suitable spouse at the time of or even before the transfer of the farm. Yet this money would be removed from the new household by the purchase of inheritance (*Erbkauf*). Secondly, for their part, the siblings tried to use their portion of inheritance to make an advantageous marriage or to establish an independent livelihood. However, a marriage between social equals could usually be achieved in such circumstances only by the family members of a well-to-do peasant with a small number of children. More frequently, the children who were bought out faced a decline in their social status.[50] But it was precisely these disadvantaged brothers and sisters who were often forced to grant an interest-free loan to the heir to the farm.

The relationship of the heirs to the parent(s) they had 'bought out' could be one of superiority, too, but not necessarily so. In Upper

49. H. Rebel, *Peasant Classes: The Bureaucratization of Property and Family Relations under Early Habsburg Absolutism 1511–1636*, Princeton, NJ, 1983, pp. 194–2.
50. Ibid., pp. 194–8.

Austria, for example, in instances when they could not immediately pay the full amount due, the parents attempted, using their powerful position as creditors, to exert influence on the running of the farm and thus to compensate for their actual loss of power.[51] More common, though, seems to have been the heir's endeavour to reduce the parents' portion.

If the heir to the farm still needed money, he could turn to relatives who would lend him money interest-free. Among relatives, the interest consisted in an obligation to provide interest-free loans to each other as required. In this credit relationship between kinfolk, what was at stake was not short-term profit so much as long-term safeguard against risks which could not be calculated. Thus far, it is comparable with the neighbourly forms of lending and borrowing. The granting of interest-free loans within the family and the circle of close relatives was connected in part with the fact that family and relations constituted a social network; however, it was also tied to the current economic standing of the individual family members. A tendency towards compulsion, exerted by the stronger family members, is unmistakable. This feature is also apparent within the household, in the relationships between the heads of house and the servants, especially the maids. Not infrequently, the wage to which they were contractually entitled was held back under some pretext and thus treated like an interest-free loan.[52]

Discussion of typical forms of credit within the framework of the peasant household and in its relationships with other households has revealed that credit was not merely a matter of using money profitably but a means of symbolising reciprocal social obligations. This is particularly clear in the tendency to commit households to each other through reciprocal credits, so that repayment was understood as a termination of friendship. At the same time, this meant that peasant indebtedness certainly signified 'need', but not always real poverty.

With the complicated credit relationships within and between households and families now explained, we may return to the theory that the peasant household constituted the smallest public sphere (*Öffentlichkeit*) and should therefore be included in the history of public finances. Households and families controlled a large part of what is today the responsibility of public provision, namely social welfare and tasks of public order. Moreover, as a constituent element of the peasant com-

51. Ibid., pp. 212–16.
52. ibid., p. 217.

munity, the household also took over these tasks for the inhabitants of a community who were not provided for. In the household, provision and care were organised mainly in personal terms, while in the community they were organised in institutional terms. Moreover, the household also contained elements of *privacy*, in the peasant *family* which arranged its credit within the circle of *relatives*. Common to the public house-keeping of the peasant household and the community was the fact that they both granted and took advantage of interest-free credit. This was regarded not just as Christian but also as neighbourly and friendly. Here the older system is fundamentally different from the modern system of public finances. The latter is calculated totally in monetary terms and in an independent sphere of circulation capital, while the former is a combination of material 'investment' and social 'reward'.

Credit in the narrow modern sense also had its place in the peasant credit system as soon as an external relationship was established; that is, when credit had to be obtained on the credit market. The credit market was not composed solely of merchants and other citizens of the towns but also of rural inhabitants — clergymen, officials and well-to-do peasants. It is possible to distinguish between the 'modern' forms of credit, personal credit and mortgage credit. The disadvantages of personal credit have already been demonstrated in the example of the wine-growers. In contrast, mortgage credit had a 'public' character because the debtor's house and land — the material basis of a house-hold as the smallest public sphere — offered the security. In addition, credits on this basis in the late Middle Ages were documented by public officials in the town halls and later legally covered by means of interest notes. Also, the interest charges were publicly fixed.

'Bourgeois' granting of credit is well known; it is therefore useful to investigate rural creditors in more detail by studying at least one example: Georg Minner, who was the wealthiest peasant in Württemberg on his death in 1599.[53] He was in no way exceptional but can be seen as an example of a wide category of suppliers of money in sixteenth-century Württemberg.[54] However, I hesitate to describe Georg Minner simply as a peasant, for he confirms the fact that agricultural work by itself did not make people wealthy but could do so only in conjunction with trade.[55] Minner had made two advantageous

53. Boelcke.
54. See also A. Bärtschi, *Die Chronik des Jost von Brechershäusern*, Burgdorf, 1958, pp. 14–15.
55. G. Wunder, 'Bäuerliche Oberschichten im alten Wirtemberg', in G. Franz (ed.), *Bauernschaft und Bauernstand 1500–1970*, Limburg and Lahn, 1975, p. 143.

marriages and ran a market-orientated farm, but he was also involved in transport and with rural credit. As is revealed in his will, Minner generally followed the usual credit procedures (mortgage cover, guarantors). However, interest-free credits also appear in his registers. The fact that Georg Minner and others granted interest-free loans — mostly smaller sums — can be understood more easily in the context of the above reports on credit in peasant households. Minner lent these sums especially to family members or to people with whom he had a special relationship of personal trust. In contrast, he granted credit on the usual terms mainly to 'strangers', to people who lived in communities other than his home community of Kornwestheim. He provided them with the impersonal forms of the urban-bourgeois credit business, in which the customers had to fulfil a series of formal preconditions and in which the status of personal guarantors was the only remnant of the older concept of 'trustworthiness'. So long as the debtors paid the interest, he did not hesitate to allow them further credit. Even if they got behind, this did not prevent him from granting more credit; this, in the conditions of the sixteenth century, was apparently preferable to a legal prosecution.

Minner's records reflect the general trend towards increased indebtedness in Württemberg, despite its duke's ban on loans lasting over four years and despite the official controls on creditors.[56] The anxious duke and his councillors feared that excessive indebtedness on the part of the peasants might reduce their capacity to pay taxes. He therefore established a registration system which also recorded debts; these were deducted from the taxable wealth. It turns out that indebtedness had actually increased enormously in comparison with the fifteenth century, but the comparison also reveals that it comprised only 8 per cent of taxable wealth and was thus lower than in the fifteenth century up to the time of the Peasants' War.[57] The causes of increased borrowing were varied, as has already been demonstrated in the case of the wine-growers, who needed money when they faced bad conditions. The situation was different for the peasants in the cereal-growing regions. As a consequence of the increase in population during the sixteenth century, the demand for cereals, and thus also cereal prices, rose. At the same time, the incentive to buy land to secure the basis for a livelihood increased as well. Indebtedness can be traced back to these facts, which also caused a boom in house-building.

56. Boelcke, pp. 331–2.
57. Ibid., pp. 343–5.

Because of the high price of land it was no great risk to get into debt, since selling would have enabled repayment to be made without further ado. In such circumstances it was not surprising that burghers were also ready to grant credit to the peasants, which they had not done in the fifteenth century.[58]

The case of Württemberg thus reveals that peasants could use phases of high agricultural and land prices to strengthen their own position. This confirms Hermann Rebel's proposition that peasant indebtedness can also be an expression of peasant participation in economic dynamics.[59]

Monasteries and foundations continued to be particularly important as creditors in the system of peasant credit. They relied on investing their funds profitably in order to fulfil their duties. They were therefore willing to lend money to trustworthy peasants who were in a position to pay the local interest rates. This form of credit played an important role in south-west Germany, while north German monasteries pursued another policy: they preferred the nobility as debtors.[60] It seems that peasant guilds took the monasteries' part in the rural credit system, at least to some extent, because their funds were not that large.[61]

III

Finally, it remains for us to consider whether the 'history and sociology of public finances' can be further clarified by the history of peasant credit from the late Middle Ages to the Thirty Years War and whether the special features of the 'economics of old Europe' can be further elucidated.

(1) The long-drawn process by which a sphere of public power emerged, is more clearly revealed when we take late medieval patterns of domination as a point of departure. The public spheres of the fifteenth, sixteenth and seventeenth centuries cannot be understood by reference to the criteria of the abstract (political) public sphere of the modern state and bourgeois society. The diverse forms of the older social units *familia* and *universitas* possessed public character and partook in public

58. Ibid., p. 337.
59. Rebel, p. 66.
60. Boelcke, p. 326; R. Kleiminger, *Das Heiligengeisthospital von Wismar in sieben Jahrhunderten*, Weimar, 1962, pp. 100–3.
61. K. Köstlin, *Gilden in Schleswig-Holstein*, Göttingen, 1976; J. Richter, 'Spätfeudale Bauerngilden in Mecklenburg', *Jahrbuch für Wirtschaftsgeschichte*, 1983, no. 1, pp. 99–122.

functions. They were 'nationalised' (*verstaatlicht*) and 'socialised' (*vergesellschaftet*) only during a long process,[62] transforming 'common' interest into 'public' interest.

(2) The peasant household was the smallest public sphere and resembled the other types of household association, especially in its economy; this is revealed especially by its participation in the general process of commercialisation of production and by the structure of the peasant credit system. Nevertheless, the prospects for trade of the peasant household were restricted by its small size. It could profit from agrarian economic trends and even adjust to commercial demand (domestic industry) to a certain extent. However, it had little chance to increase its revenue through the exercise of public power as the larger household association — the state and manorial estates — were able to do. At most, this could be achieved by the big peasants, who had access to public community power through communal offices.

The peasant household never lost its public functions, but the legitimation for its power changed. The relative autonomy it had enjoyed in the late Middle Ages was redefined by the early modern state as a sphere of delegated tasks. Peasant credit thus belonged to the public finances so long as public credit did not become the passive credit of the state.

(3) Even more clearly than the urban economy, the economic life of the peasantry in medieval and early modern European society reveals that economic activities belonged to two systems which were in competition with one another but were also linked:

— The 'household' (*das ganze Haus*), whose main devices were directed towards securing a livelihood (*Nahrung*) for the household members, autonomy as regards intervention from outside, and friendship in relations between household members and neighbours.

— The market economy, which forced the peasants into the market and made them dependent on the market, but also made it possible for them to achieve independence from the lord of the manor, and — much later — from the village and field neighbours.

(4) The tensions between these two systems and their specific normative orientation have already been defined by Aristotle in his practical

---

62. This aspect has not been taken into consideration by J. Habermas, *Strukturwandel*

philosophy as the contrast between *oikonomía* and *unnecessary accumulation* (reprehensible striving for profit when this goes beyond the requirements of 'good life').[63] There were two basic reasons for the adoption of the Aristotelian argument of natural law by medieval scholasticism in order to support a Christian 'economic ethic', and particularly the canonical ban on interest: firstly, the 'natural' limitation of production in pre-industrial agricultural society, with the consequences of reciprocal system of unequal exchange; secondly, the eclipse of simple systems of exchange by complex market relationships, which led to social tensions through the polarisation of rich and poor. Aristotle was studied in an epoch of medieval history when problems emerged which were related to those of Aristotle in his time; his precepts did not deal with timeless 'archaic' relationships:

> The Aristotelian differentiation between *oikonomía* and unnecessary accumulation serves to clarify the economic foundations of the polity. A money economy based on excessive profit endangers the stability of a mixed constitution, the economic balance between oligarchy and democracy. For the basic preconditions of the polity, moderation and balance, are put in question by the accumulation of finance capital and money in the hands of a few.[64]

A comparable situation occurred in the Middle Ages with the emergence of towns, and demanded new norms in order to control social polarisation.

Although medieval scholasticism was able to utilise Aristotelian arguments of natural law, the fundamental differences between Aristotelian economics and 'the economics of old Europe' are very apparent. Aristotle was referring to the household of the Attic citizens who made up the polity, and thus also to that domestic rule over women, children and slaves which he regarded as 'natural'. It lay in the 'nature' of things that the master of the house was also the 'head' of the household and that — in accordance with the metaphor of the body — economic life was directed towards autarky, to an economic 'circulation' within the household.

der Öffentlichkeit. Untersuchungen zu einer Kategorie der bürgerlichen Gesellschaft, Darmstadt and Neuwied, 1962; for another new dimension of 'Öffentlichkeit', see also L. Hölscher, *Öffentlichkeit und Geheimnis. Eine begriffsgeschichtliche Untersuchung zur Entstehung der Öffentlichkeit in der frühen Neuzeit*, Stuttgart, 1979.

63. H. Rabe, 'Ökonomie', in J. Ritter (ed.), *Historisches Wörterbuch der Philosophie*, vol. 6, Darmstadt, 1984, pp. 1149–62; K. Lichtblau, 'Politische Ökonomie', in ibid., pp. 1163–73.

64. P. Koslowski, 'Haus und Geld. Zur aristotelischen Unterscheidung von Politik, Ökonomik und Chrematistik', *Philosophisches Jahrbuch*, vol. 86 (1979), p. 71.

In contrast, medieval life since the eleventh century had been based not on slave or unfree labour, but on independent peasant, craftsmen and merchant family economies which emancipated themselves from the older manorial system and formed themselves into urban and rural communities. It is true that most peasants remained bound within the *familia* of one or several lords, but with the new 'feudal' forms of production in family economies tied to the market, the modus of distributing the results of their labour changed in favour of the peasant families. It became all the more necessary to establish reciprocity in a new form. Otto Brunner has already assessed that the lord–peasant relationship was not based on force (as was the despotic rule over house-slaves) but on a legally regulated contractual relationship with reciprocal rights and duties. It should nevertheless be added that peasant status and rights could only be realised when the peasants themselves became 'public' persons and created communal corporations with legitimate power to act as did merchants and craftsmen in the towns at the same time.

This process did not just involve an adjustment of the distribution of production between lord and peasants. It also included the distribution of the merchants' profit, who did not 'work' themselves but 'dealt' with the results of the labour of others. They thus earned money in 'unnatural' ways — all the more so when their business itself was extremely unnatural, especially in the money trade.[65] The redistribution of this unnatural profit, akin to usury, likewise followed the principle of unequal exchange, but according to bourgeois-urban rather than rural methods. Thus merchants paid to free themselves from the eternal punishment with which usurers were threatened by exchanging donations for the prayers of monks, nuns and the poor, which were believed to be particularly pleasing to God. In this way wordly gain was exchanged for the gain of eternal life in a process which calmed but by no means eliminated the new dynamism in the economy. It can therefore be maintained that — unlike the pursuit of the 'good life' in Aristotelian economics — concern with life after death in late medieval Christian society did not decisively obstruct the growing independence of economic dynamics. Indeed, it even encouraged it, although medieval economic ethics, like those of Aristotle, were directed towards balance.

65. H.A. Oberman, *Werden und Wertung der Reformation*, 2nd edn, Tübingen, 1979, ch. 8, 'Oeconomia moderna', pp. 161–200; W. Trusen, 'Spätmittelalterliche Jurisprudenz und Wirtschaftsethik', Wiesbaden, 1961, *Vierteljahresschrift für Sozial- und Wirtschaftsgeschichte* Beiheft 43.

Any comparison of relations between the household and the community in the Aristotelian and medieval systems can only emphasise that, in the Middle Ages, the separation of 'private' and 'public' did not take place. The household was not the private concern of the master of the house, but one of many public spheres existing side by side. The number of people participating in the economy of 'old Europe' was incomparably greater than the number of those who made up the basis of the Aristotelian polity; this fact is explained by the new social forms of production, the division of labour between town and countryside, between men and women and the Christian evaluation of the working people. 'Community' appears as the new regulative political principle, directed towards the 'common weal'. Despite the fact that it has been ideologised, the idea of the 'common weal' alone signalises an altered social conception in comparison with the Aristotelian polity, which retained a pronounced aristocratic character in its connection with *oikos* and its aim of achieving the 'good life'. Its early modern reception underlines this feature: it was the nobility which recognised in Aristotelian economics the model of a noble life-style,[66] while in the nascent bourgeois society a gap developed between public and private virtues as well as between both these systems of virtues and economic virtues.

66. O. Brunner, 'Österreichische Adelsbibliotheken des 15. bis 18. Jahrhunderts als geistesgeschichtliche Quelle', in idem, *Neue Wege der Verfassungs- und Sozialgeschichte*, 2nd edn, Göttingen, 1968, pp. 281–93.

KERSTEN KRÜGER

Public Finance and Modernisation: The Change from Domain State to Tax State in Hesse in the Sixteenth and Seventeenth centuries – A Case Study

Was there a crisis in early modern Europe?* Historians have not yet found a final answer to this much discussed question. Helmut G. Koenigsberger[1] recently presented viewpoints of British and French historians in a German publication to stimulate the discussion in Germany about crises during the seventeenth century. Indeed, German historians have observed signs of early modern crises mainly in the sixteenth century. Reinhart Koselleck stated, very generally, 'Crisis becomes the structural signature of modern times',[2] while Rainer Wohlfeil characterised the age of Reformation as determined by a crisis that initiated a process of spiritual, social and political disturbance and reorganisation in Europe.[3] Rudolf Vierhaus demanded the consideration of social, economic and political causes of crisis.[4]

*The author would like to thank Charlotte Pattenden for the translation.

1. H.G. Koenigsberger, 'Die Krise des 17. Jahrhunderts', *Zeitschrift für Historische Forschung*, 1983, pp. 143–65.
2. R. Koselleck, 'Krise', *Geschichtliche Grundbegriffe. Historisches Lexikon zur politisch-sozialen Sprache in Deutschland*, vol. 3, Stuttgart, 1982, pp. 617–50.
3. R. Wohlfeil, 'Reformation in sozialgeschichtlicher Betrachtungsweise', in S. Hoyer (ed.), *Reform — Reformation — Revolution*, Leipzig, 1980, pp. 95–104.
4. R. Vierhaus, 'Zum Problem historischer Krisen', in K.G. Faber and C. Meier (eds.), *Historische Prozesse*, Munich, 1978, pp. 313–30.

All these causes can be found in the Germany of the sixteenth century. The demographic development from about 1530 onwards led to overpopulation, resulting in food scarcity and rising prices for agricultural products.[5] Those who were not employed in agriculture had to spend more and more money on food. The purchasing power for manufactured goods decreased. Real wages sank. The problems grew worse when the influx of silver from South America from about 1540 led to an inflationary development. Underemployment and social unrest were spreading. Foreign politics added to these internal challenges. The Turks had long constituted a danger to the Reich, but the struggle for defence turned to a new dimension with the battle of Mohács in 1526 and the first siege of Vienna in 1529. Mercenaries in great number were deployed against the Turkish mass armies. The high costs of their upkeep had to be raised by the whole Reich — territorial states and free cities — through special Turk taxes.[6] The burden of taxation increased with the worsening economic situation.

The Reformation led to religious conflicts that combined with the internal and external symptoms of crisis. The solution of these new problems demanded radical reorganisation. Thus began the formation of the early modern state — in Germany, the territorial state. The sudden increase of the state's public responsibility led to an expansion of state activities with the aim to ensure order, stability and effectiveness of the social and political system. This process can be interpreted as the first phase of modernisation.[7]

The formation of the early modern state had a high price, for the increase in military and foreign activities and, in home politics, the regulation of the state's new responsibilities burdened public finances to a hitherto unknown extent. Inevitably, therefore, the social and political crisis of the sixteenth century was accompanied by a crisis of state finances, as the military forces had to be financially supported and the expanding administration paid for. Traditional means proved insufficient; new financial sources had to be opened up — taxes. Looking at state finance, the change from the feudal state with 'predominant remuneration in kind and little developed infrastructure'[8] to the modern institutional state can be described as the transition from a domain state to a tax state.[9] In their ideal form, these two stages in

5. W. Abel, *Agrarkrisen und Agrarkonjunktur*, 3rd edn, Hamburg and Berlin, 1978.
6. W. Schulze, *Reich und Türkengefahr im späten 16. Jahrhundert. Studien zu den politischen und gesellschaftlichen Auswirkungen einer äußeren Bedrohung*, Munich, 1978.
7. H.-U. Wehler, *Modernisierungstheorie und Geschichte*, Göttingen, 1975.
8. O. Hintze, 'Wesen und Verbreitung des Feudalismus (1929)', *Gesammelte Abhandlungen*, 3rd edn, vol. 1, Göttingen, 1970, pp. 84–119.
9. See E.L. Petersen, 'From domain state to tax state: synthesis and interpretation',

state development can be systemised as follows on Table 3.1.[10]

In its form of government, the domain state is characterised by rulers governing personally and at their discretion. The central administration of the state was looked after by court officials with few staff — almost as a side-line. They held a relatively weak position in dealing with the local administration, which enjoyed far-reaching autonomy in matters of economy and management. Local offices were in the hands of individual families; ancestry was more important for the entry to office than education. The main task of any administration was to keep internal and external law and order; that is, to avoid violent conflicts as far as possible. In contrast with this, the pre-liberal tax state was governed by established institutions according to legally defined rules. The central administration was well staffed and split into departments with clearly defined authority; it kept control over the subordinate local administration at all times. The administration was in the hands of professional bureaucrats; office could only be taken after successfully completed training. In addition to the keeping of law and order, the state also regulated and actively shaped internal conditions of life.

Public financing in the domain state was predominantly based on payments in kind; any excess produced by the domain was collected and made available through the local administration. Taxes were seldom imposed and then once only to help in certain emergencies; their use was strictly limited to their original purpose. Loans were employed to bridge short-term financial difficulties; generally, such loans could only be obtained by guaranteeing a fixed interest to be paid in kind or by pledging parts of the domain as security. Both reduced the substance of the domain state. The tax state, on the other hand, was mainly financed through monetary taxes. Excess production by the domain took second place to the revenue from direct and indirect taxes that were now levied regularly and continuously; their use was no longer limited. Loans were established as part of the state's budget; they were only raised against fixed monetary interest and underwritten in the long term by the estates of the realm or by public guarantee funds.

The domain state, which was mainly agricultural, was a profitable producer in its own right and thus played an independent role in the economy. The main intentions of economic policy were to guarantee

The Scandinavian Economic History Review, vol. 23 (1975), pp. 116–48.
10. K. Krüger, 'Gerhard Oestreich und der Finanzstaat. Entstehung und Deutung eines Epochenbegriffs der frühneuzeitlichen Verfassungs- und Sozialgeschichte', *Hessisches Jahrbuch für Landesgeschichte*, vol. 33 (1983), pp. 333–46.

Table 3.1. The transition from domain state to tax state

	Domain state	Tax state
Financial Theory	Jean Bodin, Kaspar Klock, Melchior von Osse	Justus Lipsius, Bartholomäus Keckermann
Form of Government	Personal, few limits in decision making	Institutional, legally defined proceedings
Central administration	Small staff	Well staffed; specialised departments with clearly defined authority
Local administration	Almost autonomous	Regularly controlled by central government
Office holders	Families of rank	Professionally trained personel
State responsibilities	Keeping of law and order	In addition, active influence on and regulation of all ways of life
Way of financing	In kind	Money
Public finance	Surplus produced by domain	Taxes
Taxes	For infrequent aid, limited to specific purpose	Regular direct and indirect taxes
Loans	Short-term bridging loans against interest in kind or mortgaging of domain land	Long-term guarantees by the state or the estates of the realm against monetary interest
Role in economy	Independent, active and profitable producer	Taxation as means of participating of profits made by subjects
Economic policy	Market intervention to keep prices down; securing of food supply	Market supervision; subsidies for potentially profitable enterprises in trade and industry
Public enterprises	Agricultural and mining enterprises in conjunction with domain	Monopolies with guaranteed supply and fiscally fixed prices
Political participation	Little and infrequent activity of the estates of the realm	Initially on the increase; authorisation and administration of taxes, later often limited or taken away by the absolute state
Social consequences	Negligible; stabilisation of agricultural economy	Compulsion to increase productivity; social disciplining; redistribution of purchasing power
Statistics	Rare; surveys only to assist estimation of output	Frequent productivity surveys; tax registers of house- and landowners; registers of tradesmen and artisans

the food supply and to stabilise the traditional structure of employment. In a supply crisis it was the primary aim to keep food prices down; as the state could intervene in the food sector with its own products, this policy was generally successful. The domain state mainly controlled agricultural enterprises and, where appropriate, mines. Price policies were based on costs or on the economic aim of keeping prices down. The tax state, on the other hand, no longer played an active role in the economy but partook of the economic output of its subjects through taxes. By a mercantile policy it supported potentially profitable enterprises and thus promoted the economic dynamics of free enterprise. Increasingly slackening supervision took the place of market intervention. Predominantly non-agricultural public enterprises managed to acquire monopolies for retailing at fiscally fixed prices.

There was little political participation in the domain state. The estates of the realm met infrequently and there was no established organisational framework. The tax state, however, was dependent on the political collaboration of the subjects and therefore granted them — at least in the beginning — far-reaching rights of political participation. Through authorisation and administration of taxes, the estates acquired a high degree of organisation with clearly defined rights and established institutions. The absolute state, though, limited or put an end to the political influence of the estates.

The social impact of public financing through domains was comparatively small; on the whole it no more than stabilised the traditional agricultural economy and way of life. The tax state, however, led to social changes: an increase in the individual's economic output and financial efficiency was called for in order to meet the regular payment of taxes when due. This has to be seen as an important part of early modern social disciplining. Linked with the regular collection of taxes was a redistribution of both income and purchasing power, which led to changes in society — generally speaking, in the economic structure, and specifically, in the life-style of those subject to taxation, because they had to meet the increased financial demands.

The social and political changes outlined above can be followed clearly in the development of the territorial state of Hesse.[11] Landgrave Philipp (1504–67)[12] pursued an independent and active foreign policy

11. K. Krüger, 'Entstehung und Ausbau des hessischen Steuerstaates vom 16. bis zum 18. Jahrhundert', *Hessisches Jahrbuch für Landesgeschichte*, vol. 32 (1982) pp. 103–25.
12. W. Heinemeyer, 'Philipp the Magnanimous, Landgrave of Hesse', *Encyclopaedia Britannica*, 15th edn, 1974.

after 1520, which inevitably led to a crisis of public finance. This too took decades to overcome. The problems were solved by intensifying the cultivation of domain land and — in cooperation with the Landtag, the Hessian parliament — by opening up a new source of income in the form of direct and indirect taxation. The Reformation of 1526 brought some relief for the state finances, when large parts of Church lands were secularised. The domain increased in size; the great value of the profitable agricultural and forestry properties was realised and the land therefore was kept in state ownership. Selling or mortgaging of property was avoided as far as possible. Hesse differs in this respect from many other Protestant states that tried to solve their financial problems by disposing of parts of their domain. But by the selling their assets, they reduced the basic source of income and in the end only deepened their financial crisis.

Revenue from the domain consisted mainly of agricultural products, above all grain, with money making up only a small proportion of total income. Compared with the administration of money, it was more laborious and work-intensive to collect, store and use agricultural products. Keeping and settling of accounts was quite complicated and difficult to control. Revenue in kind, however, did have great advantages, too. The court and its officials' supply of basic foods and other essentials like firewood was ensured. In the agricultural boom of the sixteenth century the retail value of agricultural products rose in step with prices — excess produce could be sold at a profit. Furthermore, an income in kind enabled the state to pursue an active economic policy; food-supply crises in particular could be alleviated by market intervention. In this respect, the Hessian state was right to maintain a strong domain.

The management of the domain lay in the hands of the local administration. In 1530 this lowest level of state administration saw the beginning of fundamental reforms. Detailed instructions were issued to direct administration and accounting. The number of local officials rose with the increased duties. The landgrave ordered a completely new forest administration to be set up. Through close supervision and especially through strict auditing, the central organisation achieved a well-functioning administration and optimal fiscal utilisation of the districts. The intensification of state activities is shown here in the unity of general, financial and fiscal administration.

The central government developed a great interest in complete surveys of the income and expenditure of the domain state, in order to improve planning of the budget. The treasury, therefore, began to double as a central statistical office. Comprehensive state statistics were compiled there from local accounts. A climax of this work was undoubtedly the 'Ökonomische Staat' (Economic State) that Landgrave Wilhelm IV (1532–92) had compiled in 1570.[13] These statistics provide an insight into the finances of the domain state, but they also show — like a reflection in a mirror — how society was organised by the state. We are informed about the number of households in villages and towns, which local district they belonged to, local officials and clergymen and about the local finances both in money and in kind. An evaluation of these statistics — a task still to be accomplished, by the way — will provide the answers to further questions: the distribution of population in town and country; the burden of tributes and the appointments of clergy and government officials throughout the state.

Although Hesse ensured that it had a sound financial base by extending its domain, additional fiscal sources of income were still needed. One of the first extraordinary taxes levied was the 'Aid against the Turks' on behalf of the Reich in 1532. Only a year later, Landgrave Philipp demanded from the Hessian parliament the approval for a special tax aid for Hesse itself, namely to build fortifications and to provide dowries for the princesses. Philipp suggested an indirect tax on the consumption of beer and wine, but the town representatives at the parliament rejected this idea. Only twenty years later, after the financial crisis caused by the Schmalkalden War, when the parliament met in Homberg in 1553, did the towns agree to such taxes. With them the revenue of the prince was to be improved, debts discharged and fortifications paid for. The nobility agreed to the same taxes slightly later, in 1555. Originally, levying of this tax was limited to eight years, but it kept being renewed, for the last time in 1764 for the years to 1802. This tax on the consumption of beer and wine was therefore the first permanently raised tax in Hesse, an important foundation of the developing tax state.

Direct taxation based on the modern principle of productivity started with the Turk tax of 1532. This gradually replaced the older Hessian direct tax, the so-called land tax, that set fixed quotas to be paid by towns and rural districts. This tax did not take productivity into account and therefore burdened the country more than the towns. It is not astonishing, therefore, that the towns stuck to the old land tax. The central government, though, tried to bring about a fairer form of

13. *Der Ökonomische Staat Landgraf Wilhelms IV*, ed. L. Zimmerman (vols. 1–2) and K. Krüger (vol. 3), Marburg, 1933–77.

taxation on property and eventually succeeded. The old land tax became defunct. For the Turk tax of 1532 the Hessian parliament — following, by the way, the example of its Saxon counterpart — agreed to a combined direct tax on both property and income, supplemented by a poll tax. Converting these taxes into modern terms, the nobility had to pay 17 per cent income tax, Hessian clergymen 25 per cent, foreign clergymen 33 per cent and town- and countrymen 38 per cent. This was a high tax and very unevenly distributed!

The assessment of taxable property involved much administrative work; in the interests of fair taxation, however, this was not shirked. All movables and immovables — houses, farms, gardens, fields, meadows and woods — as well as tithes and interests in money or kind had to be calculated in monetary terms and added up. The resulting sum, later referred to as tax capital, provided the basis for assessing the rate of taxation. Tradesmen and artisans without real estate were to be assessed at a flat rate. Movables like household effects, foodstuffs for own consumption, savings (if not lent out for interest) and sometimes livestock, too, were to be tax free. These basic principles of Hessian property taxation underwent slight modification in 1544 and 1557, again in connection with Turk taxes for the Reich. The nobility kept their privileged status; clergymen and civil servants were only taxed on their private property, not on their salary. The principles of direct taxation as approved by the Hessian parliament in 1557 formed part of all future levies of property tax and were permanently confirmed in 1655[14] — they remained valid into the nineteenth century. We can therefore conclude that the tax state was finally established in Hesse by parliamentary decisions in 1553 (indirect taxation) and 1557 (direct taxation).

Special committees consisting each of one or two government officials plus representatives of towns or villages were commissioned to assess the rate of taxation for the direct taxes. They went from door to door and assessed the property of each person liable for taxation; their assessments were entered into a tax register. These tax registers have been passed down to us in great number; they form an important source of material about early modern social history. They still await their complete evaluation. Like a mirror of society, they reflect the structure of the population and its economic and fiscal productivity. The levy of direct taxes was soon faced with two major problems:

14. K.E. Demandt, 'Die hessischen Landstände im Zeitalter des Frühabsolutismus', *Hessisches Jahrbuch für Landesgeschichte*, vol. 15 (1965), pp. 38–108.

firstly, the extensive administration work in the course of tax assessment, and secondly, the no more than rough estimation of the taxable income from trade and industry. To ensure a fair distribution of the tax burden at all times, taxable property would have had to be assessed anew for each tax collection. The tax assessors, however, often shirked this effort and continued to enter the same tax quota after the first assessment. Any change of means led to unfair taxation. This was especially the case during the Thirty Years War, when war contributions[15] were raised in accordance with the old tax registers, without taking into account that the war had drastically changed all financial conditions. Taxation became arbitrary. There was no other way than thoroughly to renew and adjust the old tax registers.

The Hessian government first attempted a solution to this problem by directing, in 1631, that all properties had to be assessed jointly by government and local officials and that these assessments had to be entered into special books which were to be kept for control by the central government. These books are the first modern land registers in Hesse. The directive of 1631 was reissued in 1651 — both times the government did not quite reach the set goal. Only decades later, in 1680, did landgrave and parliament finally agree on standardised principles of taxation[16] that adjusted the 1557 acts to contemporary requirements, and these remained in force into the nineteenth century. In accordance with these principles, estate and income were converted into taxable property, the so-called tax capital. This tax capital served as the basis for calculating the direct-tax dues.

The administrative task of assessing the subjects' tax capital anew according to their economic productivity proved to be immense. In 1699 a special government department was therefore set up solely for this purpose: the so-called tax chamber (*Steuerstube*)[17] that had to coordinate and control all the work. This move soon met with success, but after only a generation it again became necessary to revise the tax-capital registers because of the country's economic development. From 1735 onwards, this task was carried out by two special central tax committees in cooperation with the local administration. They also solved the problem of taxing artisans and tradesmen fairly. So far only their real estate had been assessed exactly; their other income was only

15. See F. Redlich, 'Contribution in the Thirty Years War', *The Economic History Review*, vol. 2, no. 12 (1959–60), pp. 247–54.
16. *Sammlung fürstlich hessischer Landes-Ordnungen und Ausschreiben*, vol. 3, Kassel, 1777, pp. 143–7.
17. H. Philippi, *Landgraf Karl von Hessen-Kassel. Ein deutscher Fürst der Barockzeit*,

roughly estimated. Now, however, all income from trade and industry was individually and exactly assessed and converted into tax capital. From then on, the tax capital was the only measure of economic productivity and the only basis for direct taxation. The modern Hessian tax state had thus reached its full development. Henceforth, tax registers had to be checked and corrected annually.

The change from domain state to tax state can be demonstrated clearly with figures taken from the Hessian budget (Table 3.2). We look at the average rounded annual income and outgoings during three characteristic periods:[18] 1530–9, a decade of active Hessian foreign policy designed to spread the Reformation; 1560–8, a period of internal consolidation after the conflict between the denominations was settled by the Augsburg religious peace treaty; and 1694–1704, when the state had found new stability after the catastrophe of the Thirty Years War.

During the first period, from 1530 to 1539, Hesse had an annual total of 175,000 guilders at its disposal. One-third of this total or 58,000 guilders, in some way originated from the domain (domain administration and prince); 28,000 guilders, or 16 per cent, came from direct taxes. The most important sources of income, however, were subsidies and loans, giving 89,000 guilders, or 51 per cent of the total. This proves clearly that the ambitious Hessian policy of this period could not be financed from its own means; the domain state was too weak, the tax state still in the process of building up. Similarly, the structure of the 162,000 guilders' expenditure reveals the political priorities: ordinary expenses on behalf of the landgrave (mainly for administration) amounted to 79,000 guilders or 49 per cent, while 83,000 guilders, or 51 per cent, were extraordinary, on the whole military, expenses.

During the period of consolidation from 1560 to 1568, subsidies and loans disappeared completely as a means of financing. The total receipts sank to 163,000 guilders. The domain produced the highest receipts, with 101,000 guilders, or 62 per cent of the total. This can truly be taken as a success of the Hessian home policy to improve the domain administration and to increase its fiscal output. The receipts from direct and indirect taxation, however, had risen even faster to 62,000 guilders, or 38 per cent. This proves the establishment of the tax state. The way in which the total of 147,000 guilders was spent had noticeably changed as well. Ordinary expenses and expenses on behalf

Marburg, 1976, pp. 634–7.
  18. Philippi, pp. 677–80; K. Krüger, *Finanzstaat Hessen. Staatsbildung im Übergang vom Domänenstaat zum Steuerstaat*, Marburg, 1980, pp. 297, 469, 500.

Table 3.2. Annual state receipts and expenditure of Hesse (rounded averages in Guilders)

	1530–9 Guilders	%	1560–8 Guilders	%	1694–1704 Guilders	%
Receipts						
Exchequer	*43,000*		*63,000*		*285,000*	
Prince	*15,000*		*38,000*		*118,000*	
Domain receipts	58,000	33	101,000	62	403,000	52
Indirect taxes			*38,000*		*26,000*	
Direct taxes	*28,000*		*24,000*		*347,000*	
Tax receipts	28,000	16	62,000	38	373,000	48
Subsidies	44,000	25				
Loans	45,000	26				
Total receipts	175,000	100	163,000	100	776,000	100
Expenditure						
Ordinary Exp.	60,000	37	44,000	30	194,000	26
Prince	19,000	12	5,000	3	111,000	15
Extraordinary and military exp.	83,000	51	50,000	34	[373,000]	50
Amortizations and special exp.			48,000	33	71,000	9
Total expenditure	162,000	100	147,000	100	749,000	100
Balance	13,000		16,000		27,000	

of the landgrave had been reduced both absolutely and relatively to 49,000 guilders, or one-third, respectively. They had obviously cut down. The same applies to extraordinary and military expenses that went down to 50,000 guilders, or just over one-third of the total. But amortisation of debts cost 48,000 guilders, again almost one-third. That was the after-effect of an active foreign policy that had been financed by loans. The consolidation of public finances was only made possible by taxation.

At the end of the seventeenth century — from 1694 to 1704 — the annual total receipts had reached 776,000 guilders, almost five times as much as in the sixteenth century. That shows how much the monetary economy had expanded in the meantime. It was still the domain that, with 403,000 guilders, or 52 per cent, yielded the major part of the annual income, four times as much as during the 1560–8 period. Tax revenue, however, had increased sixfold to 373,000 guilders. This rise was due solely to direct taxation. Tax receipts had also increased in relative terms to 48 per cent of all income. Domain and tax state were almost in equilibrium. Total expenditure reached 749,000 guilders and was structurally similar to the first period, from 1530 to 1539. Some 305,000 guilders, or 41 per cent, were spent on ordinary expenses or on behalf of the prince. The military received an estimated 373,000 guilders, that is half the total expenditure. Some 71,000 guilders, or 9 per cent, were needed for amortisation of debts and for extraordinary expenses. Generally speaking, the few figures that have been presented here show that in an early process of modernisation Hesse expanded the monetary economy and changed from a domain state to a tax state.

Without any doubt the tax state led to changes in society as well, for the constant tax demands forced the subjects to manage their finances more effectively in order to be able to pay cash at the due dates. We still know little about this fundamental social and economic change, even though there is plenty of source material. It has to be evaluated through research into the sociological history of finances. A small sector of the Hessian social and economic structure, however, can be presented here. Three places are taken as examples: the village of Herleshausen; the small town of Waldkappel; and the medium-sized town of Homberg. In all these places the tax registers were renewed in 1744 and 1748 and all trades recorded in detail. These statistics help us to carry out a survey of occupational groups (Table 3.3).[19]

The village of Herleshausen had 663 inhabitants; 150 of these worked in a profession. The fifty-seven farmers made up the largest group, but in relative terms they represented only 38 per cent of the working population. Clothing trades appear as a strong group with forty people or 27 per cent. This shows that the village community no longer lived mainly on agriculture but was in the process of transition to a non-agricultural economy. Some 758 people lived in the small town of Waldkappel, 139 of whom followed some trade. There were only very few farmers. Clothing trades, however, dominated with seventy-two people, or 52 per cent. Victualling (twenty-four people, or 17 per cent) and building (nineteen people, or 14 per cent) played important parts, too. Homberg, finally, had 2,520 inhabitants, three times as many as Waldkappel. There were 472 craftsmen in Homberg, the largest group of which (183 people, or 39 per cent) again produced clothing. The victualling trade (seventy people, or 15 per cent) was in

19. A. Hinz and J. Trützschler, 'Stadtgeschichte und historische Finanzsoziologie. Die Sozialstruktur in Homberg nach der Katastervorbeschreibung von 1748', Zeitschrift des Vereins für Hessische Geschichte und Landeskunde, vol. 89 (1982–3), pp. 103–35, see pp. 120–7; Krüger, Hessisches Jahrbuch für Landesgeschichte, vol. 32 (1982), pp. 103–25, see pp. 121–5.

Table 3.3. Occupations in Hesse, 1744–8

	Herleshausen	Waldkappel	Homberg
Rural	57	4	11
Victualling	11	24	70
Clothing	40	72	183
Building	10	19	49
Distribution	4	7	36
Other trades	27	10	98
Miscellaneous	1	3	25

	Herleshausen		Waldkappel		Homberg	
	No.	%	No.	%	No.	%
Rural	57	38	4	3	11	2
Victualling	11	7	24	17	70	15
Clothing	40	27	72	52	183	39
Building	10	7	19	14	49	10
Distribution	4	3	7	5	36	8
Other trades	27	18	10	7	98	21
Miscellaneous	1		3	2	25	5
Total	150	100	139	100	472	100

relative terms as strong as in Waldkappel; the building trade (forty-nine people or 10 per cent) was slightly weaker. The large group of other tradesmen — mainly day-labourers — (ninety-eight people, or 21 per cent) shows a greater differentiation in occupational structure than that in Waldkappel.

Enumeration of occupation on its own does not, however, provide any information about economic productivity. This information can be gained by evaluating the tax capital. As mentioned earlier, all property (house and land) and all income from trade were converted into tax capital that was then used as a basis for taxation. The tax capital total for Herleshausen, Waldkappel and Homberg provide an interesting insight into their economic situation (Table 3.4).

If the tax capital total is divided by the number of inhabitants, we find an average tax capital per capita of 50 guilders in Herleshausen and Waldkappel, but only 40 guilders in Homberg. This is not astonishing if we consider that real estate constituted the major part of tax capital. Herleshausen was a village with farmsteads, Waldkappel a

Table 3.4. Tax capital in Hesse, 1744–8

	Herleshausen	Waldkappel	Homberg
Inhabitants	663	758	2,520
Tradesmen (farmers excluded)	93	135	461
Total tax-capital	33,183	39,220	100,583
– per inhabitant	50	52	40
Trade tax-capital	2,052	7,154	35,332
– per inhabitant	3	9	14
– per tradesman	22	53	77

small town with houses and gardens for most of its families; Homberg, however, was already too large for this, so that the number of house-owners and landowners was relatively smaller, which in turn led to a lower average tax capital per inhabitant.

If we look only at the trade tax-capital, a different picture emerges. On average, each inhabitant had a trade tax-capital of 3 guilders in Herleshausen, 9 guilders in Waldkappel and 14 guilders in Homberg. This shows a clear hierarchy in trade activities. The low figure for Herleshausen can easily be explained by the still agricultural structure of the village, but this does not apply to the two towns of Waldkappel and Homberg. For this, differences in trade productivity must be taken into account. They become obvious when the total trade tax-capital is divided by the number of non-agricultural tradesmen. Tradesmen in Herleshausen had an average trade tax-capital of 22 guilders, in Waldkappel 53 guilders and in Homberg 77 guilders. The result is an additional hierarchy of trade productivity and income from trade. To put it differently: compared to Homberg, tradesmen in Herleshausen were doing badly, and those in Waldkappel only moderately better.

This has been only a first rough analysis of social history by using the source material of the tax state as a reflection of society. The transition from domain state to tax state can be taken as part of the European process of modernisation. The details of this process still await research that, in turn, could also lead to a modernisation of historical research itself: financial history is wide open to new perception.

HANS-PETER ULLMANN

The Emergence of Modern Public Debts in Bavaria and Baden Between 1780 and 1820

I

In eighteen-century Europe one could clearly recognise dis-
similarities in the development of England, the Netherlands and
France on the one hand and of the German states on the other.* By the
early eighteenth century, England, the Netherlands and France had
already accomplished modern public debts by a 'Financial Revolution', while such a transition had not taken place in Central Europe.
Certainly, enlightened rulers had attempted to improve forms and
techniques of public debt in order to increase their room for manoeuvre
in financial and political affairs. However successful these measures
had been in individual cases, nevertheless, they did not initiate a
thorough and lasting modernisation of public debt. Such a development was hampered by the comparative backwardness of the economy,
by the underdeveloped banking system and by the fragmentation of
Germany into some 300 individual territories — but above all by the
rigid financial structure of the *ancien régime*.[1]

*This essay summarises my book *Staatsschulden und Reformpolitik. Die Entstehung moderner
öffentlicher Schulden in Bayern und Baden 1780–1820* (Veröffentlichungen des Max-Planck-
Instituts für Geschichte 82), Göttingen, 1986.

1. 'Financial Revolution': see G. Parker, 'The Emergence of Modern Finance in
Europe, 1500–1730', in C.M. Cipolla (ed.), *The Fontana Economic History of Europe*, vol. 2,
London, 1974, pp. 527–94; P.G.M. Dickson, *The Financial Revolution in England: A Study in
the Development of Public Credit 1688–1756*, London, 1967; J.C. Riley, *International Government*

As the Holy Roman Empire could not develop into a modern state with sound public finances, modern states and modern public finances emerged at territory level. This development, however, took place only within narrow confines. If one disregards Austria and Prussia, the framework within which changes were possible was — above all in the medium-sized and smaller territories — determined by the constitution of the Empire. The finances of the German territories thus had three peculiarities. Firstly, the prince did not have complete financial sovereignty. His financial power was externally restricted by the Old Empire and internally by the privileges of the Estates. Just how firmly the ruler's hands were tied by the constitutions of the Empire and the territories became most evident in the field of taxation. It is true that the prince had, to a large extent, unlimited power over his domain; as a rule, however, it was not he but the Estates who had the right to levy taxes. Secondly, the dualism of prince and Estates left its mark on all areas of public finances. They had a dual structure throughout, having thus two fiscal authorities, two exchequers and, of course, also two forms of debt. Thirdly, each innovation in public finance not only affected the balance of power between the prince and the Estates but also had to be enacted within the framework of the existing constitutions of the Empire and the territories. This well-nigh precluded larger-scale changes to the financial structure. Accordingly, the margin left for a modernisation of public debt remained narrow up to the end of the eighteenth century, and the relative backwardness of the German territories remained little changed.[2]

Only after the French Revolution and after the expansion of Napoleon's power was the rigid *ancien régime* set in motion by influence from abroad. This influence swept away for two decades the most important hindrances to reform – which had held back Germany – allowing the country to advance alongside the politically, socially and economically

---

Finance and the Amsterdam Capital Market 1740–1815, Cambridge, 1980; M. Marion, *Histoire financière de la France depuis 1715*, vol. 1, Paris, 1914. German states: J. Landmann, 'Geschichte des öffentlichen Kredites', in *Handbuch der Finanzwissenschaft*, vol. 3, Tübingen, 1958, pp. 1–35; J. Schasching, *Staatsbildung und Finanzentwicklung. Ein Beitrag zur Geschichte des österreichischen Staatskredites in der zweiten Hälfte des 18. Jahrhunderts*, Innsbruck, 1954; W. Däbritz, 'Die Staatsschulden Sachsens in der Zeit von 1763 bis 1837', Diss., Leipzig, 1906; H. Schmelzle, *Der Staatshaushalt des Herzogtums Bayern im 18. Jahrhundert mit Berücksichtigung der wirtschaftlichen, politischen und sozialen Verhältnisse des Landes*, Stuttgart, 1900.
    2. T. Mayer, 'Geschichte der Finanzwirtschaft und Finanzwissenschaft vom Spätmittelalter bis zum Ende des 18. Jahrhunderts', in *Handbuch der Finanzwissenschaft*, vol. 1, Tübingen, 1952, pp. 237–72; K. Th. Eheberg, 'Art. Finanzen II: Geschichte der Finanzen', in *Handwörterbuch der Staatswissenschaften*, vol. 4, Jena, 1927, pp. 9–98; E. Klein, *Geschichte der öffentlichen Finanzen in Deutschland (1500–1870)*, Wiesbaden, 1974.

more developed Western Europe. Thus the German states were exposed to intense pressure for modernisation. Owing to the severe financial problems caused at the turn of the century by wars, by the reshaping of the German territory and by reforms, public finances and, above all, public debts underwent an especially swift and pronounced period of change. Between 1780 and 1820 the development accelerated in a breathtaking fashion. As if in the speeded-up version of a film, we can witness how in these four decades the debt system of the *ancien régime* disintegrated and modern public debts emerged. In most German states this process took a similar course. I should like to elucidate its basic structures with reference to two states in southern Germany: Bavaria and Baden. My essay falls into two parts, or steps: the first is concerned with the main problem of the time in question, namely the *growth of public debt*; the second then investigates the methods in which the problem was solved, namely the *reform of the public debt system*.[3]

II

At the end of the eighteenth century the debts of the Electorate of Bavaria had amounted to around 20 million guilders. Twenty-five years later, in 1818, they peaked at 105 million guilders. This equalled an increase of 425 per cent. The debt per head had doubled from 15 to 30 guilders. Even more rapid than in Bavaria, the liabilities had risen in Baden from 65,000 guilders at the beginning of the 1790s to 31 million guilders in 1818, an increase of 48,000 per cent. The debt per head rose from half a guilder to 27 guilders; in other words, it had increased by more than fifty times. At the turn of the century, therefore, both states experienced so marked a growth in their public debt that, without exaggerating the situation, one can speak of a 'debt explosion'. In Bavaria and Baden alike, this 'explosion' had two causes: on the one hand, the high assumptions of debt and, on the other, the heavy credit-financing of public authorities.[4]

3. H. Berding und H.-P. Ullmann (eds.), *Deutschland zwischen Revolution und Restauration*, Königstein, 1981; F.L. v. Hornthal, *Ansichten über den wechselseitigen Einfluss der Umwälzung des Staats und des Staatskredits, unter Vergleichung gleichzeitiger ähnlicher Ereignisse in Deutschland und Frankreich, dann über einige Mittel, den so tief gesunkenen Staatskredit wieder zu heben*, Bamberg, 1816.
4. Bavaria (1793): *Kurzgefasste Geschichte des Bieraufschlages und vollständige Geschichte des königlich und landschaftlichen gemeinsamen Schuldenabledigungswerkes in Baiern* (Krenner, 18.4.1807), Bayerisches Hauptstaatsarchiv (= BHSTA) MF 19711. (1818): 'Summarische Uebersicht des gesammten Staats-Schulden-Standes des Königreichs Baiern', in

The extensive assumptions of debt were a direct consequence of the so-called 'territorial revolution' of the early nineteenth century, which radically restructured the political map of Central Europe. This led on the one hand to the creation of sound, rounded off, medium-sized states in southern Germany. On the other hand, these same events triggered off an unprecedented upheaval in public debt. The gist of the matter, after all, was that each area changed ownership together with all the encumbering liabilities. Territorial concentration thus led to an agglomeration of public debt. Bavaria had to take on liabilities to the tune of 93 million guilders. Baden had to accept new debts amounting to 15 million guilders.[5]

Alongside these high assumptions of debt, it was, as I have said, the financing of current expenditures by credit which was also responsible for the 'debt explosion'. This reflected the crisis of public finances in Bavaria and Baden, a crisis which left its mark on the entire period from the early 1790s right up to the consolidation of public finances in the aftermath of the Napoleonic Wars. These twenty-five years, which saw one financial crisis after the other, can be divided into four phases.[6]

The first phase stretched from the outbreak of the wars resulting from the French Revolution up to the dissolution of the Old Empire in 1806. The direct costs and indirect consequences of war led to a sudden strong increase in financial requirements. In addition, there were the financial consequences of the 'territorial revolution'. Finally, the reforms, which began in Bavaria as early as 1799 and in Baden in 1803, were also extremely costly. The increase in revenue could not keep pace with this rise in expenditure. The reason for this is to be found above all in the Old Empire's constitutional framework, which obstructed thorough-going tax reforms. In this way a gap opened up between the

---

Verhandlungen der zweyten Kammer der Ständeversammlung des Königreichs Baiern, vol. 2, Munich, 1819, p. 432. Baden (1793): *Übersicht des badischen Finanzzustandes von den 1790er und nachgefolgten Jahren bis in das Jahr 1805 mit Vergleichung der Perioden vor und nach dem ao. 1793 ausgebrochenen Kriege*, Generallandesarchiv Karlsruhe (= GLA) 237/1637. (1818): *Amortisationskasse. Rechnung pro 1818* (Scholl, 18.1.1824), GLA 62/20250. The debts of the *Distrikte* have to be added.

5. Fr. J. Haas, *Über das Repartitions-Princip der Staatsschulden bei Länderteilungen*, Bonn, 1831. Bavaria: see *Vortrag über den General-Finanz-Etat des Reiches für das Jahr 1818/19* (Schilcher, 4.1.1819), BHSTA StR 448. Baden: see *Zusammenstellung der Passiv- und Aktiv-Kapitalien, welche auf der Oberrheinischen/Mittelrheinischen Provinz haften: Zusammenstellung der Passiv- und Aktiv-Kapitalien der Niederrheinischen Provinz* (12.4.1809), GLA 237/1647; *Amortisationskasse. Rechnungen pro 1809 bis 1818* (Scholl, 13.10.1823 to 18.1.1824), GLA 62/20250.

6. The history of Bavaria's and Baden's public finances is scarcely explored for the entire epoch. There is only the unsatisfactory doctorial thesis by H. Klotz, 'Der bayerische Staatshaushalt von 1799–1818', Munich, 1952; research on Baden is lacking entirely.

mounting requirements of the emergent modern state and the continuing traditionalism of its financial foundations. This gap took the form of increasing budgetary deficits, which could be bridged only by credits. Between 1794 and 1804/5, the Electorate of Bavaria raised no fewer than thirty-one loans totalling 14 million guilders. And Baden, in order to patch over the most urgent budgetary needs, required thirteen loans with a total nominal volume of 8 million guilders. Neither of the two states, of course, could keep up such a tempo of new debt-incurment without impairing public credit and pushing up interest payment and repayment to alarming heights.[7]

The second phase, stretching from 1806 to 1809, was therefore marked by a consolidation of state finances. The Kingdom of Bavaria and the Grand Duchy of Baden made use of the considerable room for manoeuvre available after the fall of the Old Empire and the acquisition of complete sovereignty in internal affairs, and reformed substantial parts of the public economy. Since their reforms both took their bearings from the Franco-Westphalian model, they had — for all their differences in points of detail — clear common ground. And they were similar too in their effects. In the short term, the measures were successful. In both states they defused the financial crisis and reduced the amount of new credits. And in the long term, too, the reforms proved to be no less fruitful. In Bavaria and Baden alike they led to a lasting drive for modernisation, especially in the areas of financial administration, budgeting and the tax system, thus marking the decisive turning-point from the finance system of the territorial state and the *ancien régime* towards the public finances of the modern state. Only in the medium term did the reforms not meet with the success hoped for, because the wars against Austria, Russia and France put a premature end to several of the rationalisation efforts.[8]

In the third phase, between 1809 and 1815, the financial crisis accordingly continued, despite the financial reforms during the period of the Confederation of the Rhine. The picture is one of chronic budgeting deficits together with a permanent credit requirement rising in leaps and bounds in times of war — just as in the years before 1806.

7. Bavaria: see *Geschichtliche Darstellung des Gesamt-Staats-Schulden-Standes des Königreiches Bayern mit vorzüglicher Beziehung auf die vorliegende Tabellarische Übersicht desselben* (30.1.1810), BHSTA MF 19711. Baden: see *Amortisationskasse. Rechnung pro 1809* (Scholl, 13.10.1823), GLA 62/20250.

8. H.-P. Ullmann, 'Öffentliche Finanzen im Übergang vom Ancien Régime zur Moderne: die bayerische Finanzreform der Jahre 1807/08', *Archiv für Sozialgeschichte*, vol. 23 (1983), pp. 51–98; idem, 'Zur Finanzpolitik des Grossherzogtums Baden in der Rheinbundzeit: die Finanzreform von 1808', in E. Weis (ed.), *Reformen im rheinbündischen Deutschland*, Munich, 1984, pp. 99–120.

Now, neither Bavaria nor Baden was successful in raising loans abroad and the finance market at home would no longer take up their issues. The kingdom therefore had recourse to forced loans at home to finance its budgeting deficits. The compulsory loan of 1809 brought in 9 million guilders to the state coffers, and 18 million guilders came in through the lottery loan of 1812 and 1813. This, however, was not the end of it. Alongside these funded debts, the ministry of finance had to embark upon large numbers of short-term, so-called 'floating debts', largely against treasury bills. And in Baden in these years the state finances were scarcely in any better shape. Here too, the budget deficits could be covered only with help of compulsory loans and 'floating debts'.[9]

In the fourth phase, between 1815 and 1818/19, the incurring of new debt became markedly less frequent in both states. The end of the Napoleonic Wars reduced the heavy pressure on the state budgets. It remained, however, impossible, both in Bavaria and in Baden, to balance revenue and expenditure without raising new credits. For one thing, the burdens of the war years were still making themselves felt, and the grave economic crisis of 1816/17 did not leave state finances unaffected. And for another, the governments were unable themselves to carry through the measures necessary to rationalise public finances owing to the severe interdepartmental conflicts between the civil and military administrations. Therefore it was only under pressure from the parliaments after 1818/19 that the consolidation of state finance began to make tangible progress.[10]

The high assumptions of debt and the heavy credit-financing of public authorities, which had together resulted in the 'debt explosion' at the end of the eighteenth and outset of the nineteenth centuries confronted the financial administrations of Bavaria and Baden with legal, administrative, fiscal and economic problems. Both states at-

9. Bavaria: *Vortrag über die Resultate der Arbeiten des im Juli 1810 errichteten Finanz-Comité* (Schenk, 9.6.1811), BHSTA MF 56171/1; F. Segner, 'Die bayerische Staatsschuld, insbesondere seit Errichtung der Staatsschuldentilgungsanstalt (1. Oktober 1811)', in *Finanz-Archiv*, vol. 20, no. 2 (1903), pp. 222–98; *Tableau der Ausgestellten Tratten und Betrag der Zinsen und Provisionen vom Finanz-Jahre 1805/06 bis Ende Juni 1811*, BHSTA MF 19671. Baden: *Compte rendu* (Hofer, 13.7.1813), GLA 237/249; for the floating debt, see GLA 237/1732.

10. Bavaria: see *Protokolle des Geheimen Finanzkomitees vom 24.7.–21.9. 1816*, BHSTA MF 56171/3; *Vortrag an seine Majestät den König die Militär-Exigenz betreffend* (Montgelas, 18.11.1816), BHSTA N1 Montgelas 295; I. Rudhart, *Über den Zustand des Königreiches Bayern nach amtlichen Quellen*, 3 vols., Erlangen, 1827, esp. vol. 3, pp. 18ff. Baden: see *Gutachten der Finanzministerialkommission vom 21.8.1817*; *Protokoll des Staatsrates vom 8.11.1817*, GLA 237/7804; F.A. Regenauer, *Der Staatshaushalt des Grossherzogtums Baden in seinen Einrichtungen, seinen Ergebnissen und seinen seit der Wirksamkeit der landständischen Verfassung eingetretenen Umgestaltungen*, Karlsruhe, 1863, pp. 723ff.

tempted to obviate these difficulties by restructuring their system of debt.

III

The debt reforms undertaken by Bavaria and Baden at the beginning of the nineteenth century were made up of a number of partial reforms, each of which reacted to a concrete situation and pursued a different concept. The course and results of these reforms can be looked upon as a many-layered process of modernisation which, for reasons of analysis, will here be broken down into various partial processes and further examined with the help of several process terms. I am concerned with four strands of development: firstly with *legalisation* of public debt, secondly with its *unification*, thirdly with its *funding* and finally with its *commercialisation*.[11]

By the term *legalisation of public debt* is meant the dissolution of established legal relations and the embedding of public debt within new legal norms. Up to the end of the Old Empire the debts of the two territories remained tied to the legal forms which established themselves during the *ancien régime*. They were based on a dichotomy of all debt, a dichotomy which had its roots in the distinction between prince (*Landesherr*) and country (*Land*). The principle was that the ruler could incur debts only for his domain. The debts of the prince (*Kammerschulden*) so incurred were embedded in overlapping areas of law. In modern terms, we would say, these debts encompassed both public debts and private liabilities of the ruling house. Since the prince could not tax the country without first gaining the consent of its representatives, he was equally unable to contract any debts which would have placed an obligation on the person or goods of his subjects. The right to take on such liabilities lay only with the country itself. Alongside the debts of the prince, therefore, there were the separate debts of the country (*Landesschulden*), which had been incurred by the Estates themselves or had been passed on to them by the ruler for interest payment and amortisation. Neither the debts of the prince nor the debts of the country were public debts in the modern sense. On the contrary, for

11. The British, Austrian and, above all, the Franco-Westphalian models determined the trend of the reforms. See footnote 1 and J.F. Bosher, *French Finances 1770–1795: From Business to Bureaucracy*, Cambridge, 1970; F. Thimme, *Die inneren Zustände des Kurfürstentums Hannover unter der französisch-westfälischen Herrschaft*, 1806–1813, 2 vols., Hanover, 1895, esp. vol. 2, pp. 332ff, 507ff.

modern debt to emerge, two preconditions had to be fulfilled. Firstly, the debts of the prince had to be depatrimonialised; that is to say, the regent and dynasty could no longer claim the right to do with the state as they pleased. Secondly, the debts of the country had to be national-ised; that is to say, the Estates had to be removed, thus making the debts of the country the affair of the state.[12]

The dissolution of traditional legal relations quickened as the eight-eenth century gave way to the nineteenth. In Bavaria the Ansbach Family Compact of 1796 and the debt statute of 1804 ensured a strict separation of public and private debts. In Baden the development was delayed because the tradition of the patrimonial state was more strongly pronounced. Here it was only the two debt statutes of 1806 and 1808 that led to a depatrimonialisation of debt of the prince (*Kammerschulden*). The turning of debt of the country (*Landesschulden*) into state debt, however, developed in the two states in a largely parallel fashion. In the kingdom the Estates forfeited sovereignty and administrative rights in matters of debt in 1807, so that separate debts of the country were no longer necessary. From that point on, Bavaria had only state debts. Baden, which had not had any Estates since the late seventeenth century, had already made debts of the country an affair of the state in its newly acquired territory in 1806.[13]

While the old legal relations were dissolving, new legal forms ap-

---

12. For the demarcation between debts of the *Kammer* (i.e. the debts raised by the prince on his own account regardless of their purpose) and debts of the *Land* (i.e. debts raised by resolutions of the Estates), see J.J. Moser, *Von der Teutschen Reichs-Stände Landen, deren Landständen, Unterthanen, Landes-Freyheiten, Beschwerden, Schulden und Zusammenkünfften*, Frankfurt, 1769 (ND Osnabrück, 1967), pp. 1357ff; idem, *Persönliches Staats-Recht derer Teutschen Reichs-Stände*, 2 parts, Frankfurt, 1775 (Osnabrück, 1967), esp. part 1, pp. 117ff; A. Wagner, 'Art. Staatsschulden' in *Deutsches Staats-Wörterbuch*, vol. 10, Stuttgart, 1867, pp. 1–58. *Kammerschulden*: see W.F. Cassot de Florencourt, *Etwas über die Natur, die Veräusserung und Verschuldung der Cammergüter deutscher weltlicher Reichsstände*, Helmstedt, 1795; J.J. Moser, *Von dem Reichs-Ständischen Schuldenwesen. So vil es derer Weltlichen Churfürsten, auch Regierender Reichsfürsten und Grafen, Cameral-Schulden, und auch die Art, selbige abzustossen und zu bezahlen betrifft*, Frankfurt, 1774; *Landesschulden*: see H.A. Zachariä, *Deutsches Staats- und Bundesrecht*, 2 parts, Göttingen, 1867, esp. part 2, pp. 470ff.
13. Bavaria: see 'Pfalzbaierischer Haus-Vertrag von dem Jahre 1796 (12.10. 1796)', in Georg Karl Mayr (ed.), *Sammlung der Churpfalz-Baierischen allgemeinen und besonderen Landes-Verordnungen von Sr. Churfürstlichen Durchlaucht Maximilian Joseph IV*, 2 vols., Munich, 1800/2, esp. vol. 1, pp. 141–50; 'Schuldenpragmatik des Churhauses Pfalzbaiern vom 20.10.1804', in *Churpfalzbaierisches Regierungsblatt*, 6, 6.2.1805, pp. 201–12; 'Verordnung vom 8.6.1807', in *Königlich Bayerisches Regierungsblatt* (= KBR), 25, 13.6.1807, pp. 969–82; Baden: see 'Verordnung vom 1.10.1806', in *Vollständige Sammlung der Grossherzoglich Badischen Regierungsblätter von deren Entstehung 1803 bis Ende 1825*, 2 vols., Karlsruhe, 1826, esp. vol. 1, pp. 237–45; 'Grossherzoglich badische pragmatische Sanction über Staatsschulden und Staatsveräusserungen, über Privatschulden des Souveräns und der Mitglieder seiner Familie vom 18. 11. 1808', in ibid., pp. 555–9; *Gutachten über die Frage: Sollen alle Staatsschulden in eine Masse geworfen oder noch einzelne Landeskassen belassen werden* (Hofer, 17.12.1808), GLA 237/1656.

peared. They did so in two steps. At first the focus was on establishing legal regulations for the debt system. In Bavaria the Ansbach Family Compact and the debt statute made a threefold contribution to the emergence of modern debt law. They first mapped out with greater precision the legal domain of modern debt; then they established binding terms for the form state debts could take; and finally they laid down a multi-stage bureaucratic procedure to be followed when raising new credit. Regulations similar to those in Bavaria were established by the debt laws in Baden. They too gave the question of debt a firm footing in public law.

In neither state, admittedly, was such a legal regulation of debt sufficient to secure public credit in the long term. In both regions bureaucratic absolutism came up against a confidence barrier which it could not overcome with one-sided measures. In the second phase of the legalisation process, therefore, the constitutionalisation of debt became the major issue. In the light of the debt administration of the Estates in the *ancien régime*, the Bavarian financial bureaucracy was well aware of the close link between credit and representation. The constitution of 1808 accordingly made the first — albeit vain — attempt to secure constitutionally the collaboration of a representative organ in the management of debt. It was only in the course of th'e constitutional deliberations after 1814 that the opinion prevailed that the king and the bureaucracy could not maintain public credit alone. For this reason the constitution of 1818 assigned to the parliament the role of guarantor for public debt, conceded to it the right to approve loans and granted it further considerable means of influencing debt policy. In the grand duchy, as in the kingdom, the constitutionalisation of debt did not get beyond preliminaries during the years of the Confederation of the Rhine. The Baden constitution of 1808 did intend to grant certain competence in the field of debt to a representative organ of subjects, but the constitution never came into force. It was only the constitution of 1818, therefore, that put the question of debt on a constitutional footing.[14]

The second partial process is concerned with the *unification of public debt*. This meant the centralisation of the administration of debt as well as the consolidation of all debts into one single stock. At the end of the

14. Bavaria: see 'Konstitution für das Königreich Bayern vom 1.5.1808', in KBR, 22, 25.5.1808, pp. 985–1000, II/6 and 8; *Verfassungs-Urkunde des Königreiches Baiern*, (Munich) 1818, Titel VII, paras. 11ff; Baden: see F. v. Weech, *Geschichte der badischen Verfassung. Nach amtlichen Quellen*, Karlsruhe, 1868, pp. 151ff; *Die landständische Verfassungs-Urkunde für das Grossherzogtum Baden nebst den dazu gehörigen Actenstücken*, Karlsruhe, 1819, IV. Titel, paras. 57ff.

eighteenth century, the debts of Palatinate Bavaria were widely scat-
tered. As a rule, each of the individual Wittelsbach territories could
negotiate its own debts and administer them through a considerable
number of different pay-offices. In the management of debt, consequently, there was a motley spectrum of methods, a spectrum generally
characteristic of the *ancien régime* and its historical evolution. The
territorial shifts and the administrative reforms compelled changes to
be made: some because the newly gained lands threatened to make the
debt system even more confused than before, and others because a
reordering of states in the name of greater homogeneity could not
somehow leave the administration of debt untouched.[15]

The reorganisation of the debt system in Bavaria followed a course
more or less parallel to the reforms of the financial administration and
led, via various interim solutions, to the establishment in 1811 of the
Royal Bavarian Commission for the Amortisation of State Debt
(Königlich Bayerische Staatsschuldentilgungskommission). The latter
combined modern and traditional principles of organisation. On the
one hand, this commission was a central authority for the administration of debt and an authority which was for the first time responsible
for all the debts of the state of Bavaria. This was a fundamental step
forward from the decentralised debt administration of the *ancien régime*.
On the other hand, the commission remained tied to the fund principle
it had inherited. That is to say that neither the administration nor the
budget of this new institution was integrated into the general administration of public finance, and that the institution remained largely
independent, having its own separately accounted revenue, from which
it had to meet the outgoings for the repayment of debt. This recourse to
the outdated principles of fund economy was intended primarily to
ensure credit.[16]

Hand in hand with the centralisation of debt administration went
the consolidation of state debts. In 1811 all debts were joined together
to form one single stock. The advantages of this unification were fully
apparent. On the principle of 'one state, one debt', it swept away the
debt structure which had evolved in the course of time, thus levelling

15. *Geschichtliche Darstellung* (30.1.1810), BHSTA MF 19711.
16. Commission for the sinking fund: see 'Verordnung vom 20.8.1811', in KBR, 55,
11.9.1811, pp. 1063–71; F. Maier, *Geschichtliche Darstellung des Staatsschuldenwesens des
Königreiches Bayern mit Rücksicht auf dessen Kurrent-Finanz-Verwaltung*, Erlangen, 1839, pp.
9ff. Sinking fund principles: see T. Keller, 'Art. Fondswirtschaft', in *Handwörterbuch der
Sozialwissenschaften*, vol. 3, Stuttgart, 1961, pp. 799–803; Mayer, pp. 255ff. Sinking fund
of the Estates: *Kurzgefasste Geschichte* (Krenner, 18.4.1807), BHSTA MF 19711;
Schmelzle, pp. 222ff; Segner, pp. 232ff; K.O. Frhr. v. Aretin, *Bayerns Weg zum souveränen
Staat. Landstände und konstitutionelle Monarchie 1714–1818*, Munich, 1976, pp. 20ff.

out the highly disparate debt-burden of the various regions.[17]

In Baden the process of unification took a completely different course. It is true that the grand duchy did attempt to overcome the administrative chaos which the territorial changes had brought with them by introducing a reform of debt administration. Earlier than Bavaria, in 1808, Baden followed the Westphalian model and created an authority organised on the fund principle — the Amortisation Office of the Grand Duchy of Baden (Grossherzoglich Badische Amortisationskasse). In contrast to the Bavarian Commission for the Amortisation of State Debt, however, it was responsible not for all but, at best, for half the state debts of Baden, since three dozen minor debt offices continued to exist beside it. In the case of Baden, therefore, one can speak only of a partial centralisation of debt administration.[18]

This developmental lag was connected with the fact that Baden remained far more strongly tied to the debt system of the *ancien régime* than did Bavaria. This became even more apparent with the consolidation of debt. While Bavaria replaced the traditional debt structure by a homogeneous debt conglomerate, the grand duchy, for legal and historical reasons, retained the traditional dichotomy of all liabilities into debts of the prince and debts of the country. In concrete terms this meant that only a part of the debts, namely the debts of the prince, was unified and treated as a central state debt. The debts of the country, now termed 'provincial debts', remained on the other hand not only a separate debt conglomerate but also one without internal homogeneity. In contrast to Bavaria, therefore, Baden only partly consolidated its debts. The comparatively reticent unification policy of the grand duchy led to an impasse. For one thing, if there was no central debt administration then there was no hope of a fully coordinated debt policy, and for another, there now emerged discrepancies in debt-burdens within Baden, discrepancies which ran counter to the aims of the tax reform. The grand duchy therefore had ground to make up before its public debts were fully unified. This it did step by step, but the process which

---

17. 'Verordnung vom 9.9.1803', in *Churpfalzbaierisches Regierungsblatt*, 46, 16.11.1803, pp. 929–39; *Schuldenpragmatik* (20.10.1804), 6.2.1805, pp. 201–12; 'Verordnung vom 8.6.1807', KBR, 25, 13.6.1807, pp. 969–82; Verordnung vom 20.8.1811, KBR, 55, 11.9.1811, pp. 1063–71.

18. Amortisation: see 'Edikt vom 31.8.1808, Beilage Lit. E', *Sammlung*, vol. 1, p. 538; A. Siebert, *Über Entstehung und Entwicklung des öffentlichen Credits im Grossherzogtum Baden*, Leipzig, 1919, pp. 40ff.; idem 'Hundert Jahre Badischer Staatsschuldenverwaltung. Ein Beitrag zur Geschichte des Badischen Staatsschuldenwesens', in *Annalen des Deutschen Reiches für Gesetzgebung, Verwaltung und Volkswirtschaft*, 1909, pp. 743–72, esp. pp. 747f. Decentralised sinking fund: *Zusammenstellung* (12.4.1809), GLA 237/1647; *Gutachten* (Hofer, 17.12.1808), GLA 237/1656.

had been set into effect in Bavaria during the Confederation of the Rhine lasted in Baden until way into the 1830s.[19]

The third partial process is concerned with the *funding of public debt*. This meant the appropriation of certain revenue to pay the interest on and to pay off long-term debts. At the end of the *ancien régime* the debts of Palatinate Bavaria were funded on a great variety of revenue sources. Debts were met partly out of domain revenue, partly from indirect levies and partly from direct taxation. But that was not all: the individual debt conglomerates were also different in the quality of their funding. While one debt office could scarcely afford to pay the sum of interest due, another could both do that and undertake considerable amortisation. The high assumptions of debt and the heavy credit-financing at the turn of the century led also to a complication and deterioration in the funding of public debts. The amortisation of debts had to be halted in many cases, and even the payment of interest came again and again to a standstill. Both of these things did harm to public credit.[20]

The financial administration in Bavaria tried to meet these mounting difficulties with funding by setting up a central sinking fund from which the interest and amortisation payments on all the public debts in the kingdom were to be drawn. This step simplified the chaotic funding situation, but at the same time created unexpected financial problems. By concentrating the available means of funding, the administration had hoped to create a sufficiently large sinking fund. In fact, however, its measure served only to concentrate the funding difficulties at a single place, thus exacerbating the funding emergency still further. From the outset, therefore, the Commission for the Amortisation of State Debt had to struggle against well-nigh insoluble financing problems. In the budget 1811/12, for example, its current revenue of 5.5 million guilders was set against payment liabilities of almost 19 million guilders. In this situation there seemed to be only one set of alternatives: either the revenue of the Commission had to be increased or its outgoings had to be reduced. The former would have accumulated a large budget deficit; the latter would have ruined public credit. The

19. 'Edikt vom 31.8.1808', *Sammlung*, vol. 1, p. 538; *Gutachten* (Hofer, 17.12.1808), GLA 237/1656; *Notizen betr. das badische Schuldenwesen* (Nebenius, 1821), GLA Nl Nebenius; *Vortrag über das Schuldenwesen einzelner Landschaften im Grossherzogtum und über das Rechtsverhältnis nicht übernommener zu den übernommenen Schulden* (Sensburg, 1822), GLA 236/2427.
20. Consolidated debt: see Landmann, pp. 13ff; *Geschichtliche Darstellung* (30.1.1810), BHSTA MF 19711; *Kurzgefasste Geschichte* (Krenner, 18.4.1807), BHSTA, MF 19711. Quotation of Bavarian consols: see *Kurse der Staatspapiere 1797–1812*, Stadtarchiv Frankfurt Handel.

commission tried to obviate this set of alternatives and at first met with some success. In riskier and riskier, costlier and costlier credit operations it succeeded in fulfilling the obligations outstanding without at the same time burdening down the public budget with new expenditure. Such a funding policy, however, could not be maintained in the long term. In the summer of 1814, the Commission was faced with bankruptcy. Only after the Napoleonic Wars could it risk a change of course and adapt its payments to match the financial means at its disposal.[21]

In Baden the funding of debt caused fewer difficulties than in Bavaria. It is true that in the grand duchy also assumptions of debt- and credit-financing led to substantial differences in the form and quality of debt funding. As in Bavaria, so in Baden, a central sinking fund was set up in an attempt to overcome the problems that had arisen. In contrast to the kingdom, however, the grand duchy limited itself to assigning only a part of its debts — the debts of the prince, now termed 'state debts' — to this fund. This partial solution had one great advantage: it reduced the fiscal difficulties of debt funding. While the Amortisation Commission had to grapple with continual financial shortfalls, the Baden institution could not only manage regular interest payments on all its debts but could also meet its capital payments punctually. This advantage, admittedly, was matched by a severe disadvantage. The secure funding of state debt was achieved through a neglect of regional or provincial debt. Only at the end of the Confederation of the Rhine years did Baden take over these debt conglomerates little by little and thus ensured their reliable funding.[22]

The fourth partial process is concerned with the *commercialisation of public debt*. 'Commercialisation' refers to the restructuring of the debt system according to the principles of a market economy. This transition concerned first the *form of public debt*. Up to the end of the

---

21. Central sinking fund: see 'Verordnung vom 20.8.1811', KBR, 55, 11.9.1811, pp. 1063–71; *Vortrag* (Schenk, 9.6.1811), BHSTA MF 56171/1. Problems of consolidated debt: see *Generalrechnung der K.B. Staats-Schulden-Tilgungs-Kommission pro 1811/12 bis 1817/18* (Staatsschuldentilgungskommission, 23.2.1814 to 28.1.1822), BHSTA MF 22707. Bankruptcy: see *Berichte der Staatsschuldentilgungskommission vom 24.4 und 19.7.1814*, BHSTA MF 58218 bzw. 58312; *Vortrag an seine Majestät den König den dermaligen Stand der Staatsschuldentilgungsanstalt betr.* (Montgelas, 22.9.1814), BHSTA MF 22945. Parliamentary proceedings: see Maier, pp. 41ff; Rudhart, vol. 3, pp. 15ff; Segner, pp. 251ff.

22. Central sinking fund: 'Edikt', *Sammlung*, vol. 1, p. 538. Debt servicing: *Amortisationskasse* (Scholl, 13.10.1823 to 18.1.1824) (GLA 62/20250). Neglect of debts of the *Land* and provinces: see *Die Grossherzoglich Badischen Staatsschulden und die zu deren Tilgung zu treffenden Massregeln betreffend* (Holzmann, 5.1.1810), GLA 237/1653; *Plan betreffend Tilgung der kurz-, mittel- und langfristigen Schulden des Grossherzogtums Baden* (25.10.1811), GLA 237/1659; *Notizen* (Nebenius, 1821), GLA NI Nebenius; *Vortrag* (Sensburg, 1822), GLA 236/2427.

eighteenth century the rulers of Bavaria and Baden took up debts
predominantly in the form of personal loans. Debtor and creditor
entered into a personal agreement authenticated by a promissory note.
This was made out in the name of the credit grantor and reflected the
highly individual conditions of credit agreed on. Since these notes
could be traded only with difficulty, the creditors insisted on short
repayment periods and special securities. This traditional form of debt,
the personal loan, set narrow confines on the raising of new debt. This
form was not likely either to mobilise capital available at home or to
attract foreign capital. The growing need for credit at the turn of the
century compelled both Bavaria and Baden to accept more developed
forms of debt. Both states began to raise government-issued loans
against bearer bonds.[23]

In contrast to a personal loan, a government-issued loan was
brought about not by a personal contract but by a mass issue of bearer
bonds to a multitude of unknown persons. The creditors no longer
received promissory notes but securities of identical content, made out
to the bearer and tradable by mere handing over. Government-issued
loans against bearer bonds revolutionised the debt of both south
German states: they permitted not only long-term loans, since the
creditors received bonds which were easily transferable, but also made
special securities dispensable because the bonds embodied partial
claims on an overall body of debt. Above all, however, the government
loan concentrated the capital of many small investors and in this way
made possible credits of a size scarcely attained hitherto.[24]

23. Commercialisation: see M. Weber, *Wirtschaftsgeschichte. Abriss der universalen Sozial-
und Wirtschaftsgeschichte*, Berlin 1958, pp. 238ff; W. Sombart, 'Die Kommerzialisierung des
Wirtschaftslebens', in *Archiv für Sozialwissenschaft und Sozialpolitik*, vol. 30/31 (1910),
pp. 631–65, 23–66; Loans: see Landmann, pp. 11ff; O.v. Gierke, *Deutsches Privatrecht*, 3
vols., Munich, 1917, esp. vol. 3, pp. 575ff; K. Larenz, *Lehrbuch des Schuldrecht*, 2 vols.,
Munich, 1982/1981, esp. vol. 1, pp. 241ff; W.X.A. Frhr. von Kreittmayr, *Anmerkungen
über den Codicem Maximilianeum Bavaricum Civilem, worin derselbe sowohl mit dem gemeinen, als
ehemaligen bayerischen Landrechte genau collationirt, sohin der Unterschied zwischen alten und neueren
Rechte sammt Urquellen, woraus letzteres geschöpft worden überall angezeigt ist*, 5 parts, Munich
(1758), 1844, esp. part 4, pp. 84ff; Siebert, *Entstehung*, pp. 16ff.
24. History of ideas: J.E. Kuntze, *Die Lehre von den Inhaberpapieren oder Obligationen au
porteur, rechtsgeschichtlich, dogmatisch und mit Berücksichtigung der deutschen Partikularrechte*,
Leipzig, 1857, pp. 117ff. History: see L. Goldschmidt, *Handbuch des Handelsrechts*, 3 parts,
Stuttgart, 1891 (Aalen 1973), part 1, pp. 390ff; W. Sombart, *Die Juden und das Wirtschafts-
leben*, Munich, 1911, pp. 72ff; W. Zöllner, *Wertpapierrecht*, Munich, 1982, pp. 30ff; C.F.
Nebenius, *Der öffentliche Kredit. 1. (und einziger Teil): Über die Natur und Ursachen des
öffentlichen Kredites, Staatsanlehen, die Tilgung der öffentlichen Schulden, den Handel mit Staatspa-
pieren und die Wechselwirkung zwischen Kreditoperationen der Staaten und dem ökonomischen und
politischen Zustand der Länder*, Karlsruhe, 1829 (Aalen 1967), pp. 54ff; F. Ottel, 'Art.
Wertpapiere, II: Wirtschaftliche Funktionen; in *Handwörterbuch der Sozialwissenschaften*,
vol. 12, Stuttgart, 1965, pp. 5–8.

Bavaria and Baden first introduced the new form of debt for their foreign loans. With home debt the two states then went different ways. While the kingdom used large-scale compulsory loans to ensure the spread of bearer bonds at home as well, and indeed even began to transfer old bonds to the new scheme, the grand duchy was at pains to keep the bearer securities as far from the home market as possible. For this there was a good reason. The *obligations au porteur* as they were then called, gave the state a substantial advantage over other debtors and so impaired private credit.[25]

The new form of debt transformed, secondly, the *techniques of public debt*. In the age of the *ancien régime*, debtors and creditors normally had direct contact with one another. If need be, churches and monasteries assumed the function of financial institutions for their localities. Certainly, there were some spectacular credit transactions with court bankers or other bankers and merchants, but all in all the organisation of public debt through banks was, in Bavaria and Baden alike, in its infancy. At this stage neither state had any strong capital market to speak of.[26]

All this changed at the turn of the eighteenth century. Between the public debtors on the one hand and the private credit grantors on the other there was pushed a wedge of issuing houses, stock exchanges and specialised financial institutions, who took it upon themselves to market securities. The demand for credit, which grew in leaps and bounds in the two south German states, could not have been satisfied without the help of banks. Two-thirds of the new debt raised in Bavaria between 1794 and 1808 was transacted through financial institutions; in Baden they were involved in as much as 98 per cent of debt transactions. The banks could accomplish this position in the business because the new forms of public debt gave rise to a change in the banks' field of business. They were no longer themselves creditors of the state as they used to be, but now restricted themselves to negotiating the loans of Bavaria and Baden with the public. This shift in the banks'

25. Bavaria: see *Die dermalige Lage der Finanzen des Königreiches Bayern* (Utzschneider, 12.7.1810), MF 56170/1. Baden: see *Die der Amortisationskasse zu erteilende Instruktion über Abgabe der Amortisationskassenobligationen für andere Staatspapiere vom 28.2.1809*, GLA 237/7808.

26. Capital accumulation by clerical institutions: see D. Stutzer, 'Die wirtschaftlichen und sozialen Verhältnisse in den säkularisierten Klöstern Altbayerns 1803, in *Zeitschrift für bayerische Landesgeschichte*, vol. 40 (1977), pp. 121–62. Banks: see P. Sundheimer, 'Die jüdische Hochfinanz und der bayerische Staat im 18. Jahrhundert', in *Finanz-Archiv*, vol. 41 (1924), pp. 1–44, 259–308; Siebert, *Entstehung*, pp. 18ff. Capital markets: see E. Schremmer, *Die Wirtschaft Bayerns. Vom hohen Mittelalter bis zum Beginn der Industrialisierung*, Munich, 1970, pp. 219ff.

function lead to a rapid upswing of the issuing business at the turn of the century. This rise of the issuing houses facilitated Bavaria's and Baden's access to the capital markets.[27]

The two south German states could not satisfy their large credit needs at home but had to place their loans on capital markets elsewhere. All the Bavarian foreign loans and all those of Baden as well were issued at the Frankfurt capital market. With issues totalling 12.7 million guilders, Bavaria was the fourth largest lender there after Austria, Denmark and Prussia; Baden, with issues totalling 4.2 million guilders was in eighth place. The Frankfurt capital market, however, not only took up the new issues of the two states but it was also the most important place where the securities could then be traded. On the Frankfurt stock exchange Bavarian loans were regularly quoted from 1799 onwards and Baden loans from 1805 onwards — a sure sign that the turnover had already attained a considerable volume. While Baden remained entirely dependent on the Frankfurt market, the Augsburg market grew in importance for Bavaria from about 1809 on.

Admittedly, the kingdom could not place new issues here, but the home forced loans attained a high turnover on the Augsburg exchange.[28]

The new form and the changed techniques of public debt led thirdly to a new *creditor structure*. In Bavaria of the late eighteenth century, the Church and charitable institutions were among the most important creditors. Together they held fully two-thirds of all securities. In contrast, private creditors had only a 10 per cent share. In 1818/19 the creditor structure looked completely different. The Church and charitable institutions had forfeited their former position of eminence. They now held just one-third of all securities. Instead, it was now the private creditors who came to the fore. Together with the local communities they held 41 per cent of the securities registered by name and some

27. L. Metzler, *Studien zur Geschichte des Deutschen Effektenbankwesens vom ausgehenden Mittelalter bis zur Jetztzeit. Ein Beitrag zur Geschichte des Deutschen Bankwesens*, Leipzig, 1911; W. Lotz, *Die Technik des deutschen Emissionsgeschäftes. Anleihen, Konversionen und Gründungen*, Leipzig, 1890; F.W. Christians, 'Art. Emissionsgeschäft der Banken', in *Handwörterbuch der Finanzwirtschaft*, Stuttgart, 1976, pp. 297–311.
28. Issuing business: see A. Dietz, *Frankfurter Handelsgeschichte*, 4 vols., Frankfurt, 1910–1925 (Glashütten, 1970), esp. vol. 4/2, pp. 753ff. Frankfurt stock exchange: see O. Wormser, *Die Frankfurter Börse, ihre Besonderheiten und ihre Bedeutung. Ein Beitrag zur Frage der Börsenkonzentration*, Tübingen, 1919; H. Trumpler, 'Zur Geschichte der Frankfurter Börse', in *Bank-Archiv*, vol. 9 (1909), pp. 81–4, 100–1. Quotations: see *Geschichte der Handelskammer zu Frankfurt a. M. (1707–1908). Beiträge zur Frankfurter Handelsgeschichte*, ed. Handelskammer zu Frankfurt a. M., Frankfurt, 1908, pp. 24ff., 1101ff.; *Kurse* (1797–1812) Stadtarchiv Frankfurt Handel. Augsburg stock exchange: see L. Lieb, *Die Entwicklung der Augsburger Effektenbörse (1816–1896)*, Augsburg, 1930.

three-quarters of the bearer bonds.[29]

If, in conclusion, one surveys the transition in public debt in these two states in southern Germany, then both points of difference and areas of common ground emerge. A comparison shows that in the grand duchy the development took, in many respects, a different course than in the kingdom. Thus in Baden the break with the traditional debt system or the tendency to centralisation and consolidation of debts were less marked than in Bavaria, and the process of commercialisation also advanced more slowly. Above all, however, a comparison makes clear that these and other peculiarities are to be seen as specific variants of an accelerated process of modernisation, which had manifest common elements in the two states and, above all, tended in one and the same direction. In both regions the territorial debt system of the *ancien régime* finally dissolved, and the public debt system of the modern state took its place. Between 1780 and 1820, accordingly, Bavaria and Baden — and not only they but most of the other German states as well — experienced their 'Financial Revolution', almost a hundred years later than the countries of Western Europe. This reduced the developmental discrepancy which had existed in the Europe of the eighteenth century between England, the Netherlands and France on the one hand and the states of Central Europe on the other.

---

29. J. Hazzi, *Statistische Aufschlüsse über das Herzogtum Baiern, aus ächten Quellen geschöpft,* 4 vols., Nuremberg, 1801–1803, vol. 2, no. 2, pp. 148f.; *Geschichtliche Darstellung* (30.1.1810), BHSTA MF 19711; *Schuldenstand des Königreiches Baiern in Beziehung auf die Objecte worauf sie haften, nebst einer summarischen Nachweisung der Creditoren,* BHSTA MF 19730/2; *Verhandlungen,* vol. 11, pp. 109ff. Similar data for the creditors of Baden are not available.

HARM-HINRICH BRANDT

Public Finances of Neo-Absolutism in Austria in the 1850s: Integration and Modernisation

The emergence of the Austro-Hungarian monarchy is insep-
arable from the decisive role of the Habsburg dynasty. Within a
normative perspective of the formation of modern states, it can be said
that this monarchy never developed beyond the stage of monarchic
integration.[1] The notorious difficulty in giving a name to this amalga-
mation of territories simply represents the underlying structural dis-
unity of the Habsburg dominions.

Was that monarchy therefore a phenomenon *sui generis* amidst a
world of modern states? Otto Brunner repeatedly called it a 'monarchic
union of corporative states',[2] considering this a sufficient explanation of
its nature, even for the entire nineteenth century. With that description
he rightly underlined the overwhelming influence of the dynastic order
on the unity of the realm; on the other hand, this description seems
anachronously to imply the late medieval and early modern concepts of
Land and *Herrschaft*, disregarding any new process that may have been
involved in its development towards a modern state. An examination of
the eighteenth and nineteenth centuries reveals many such processes
integrating the Habsburg dominions, processes which follow contemporary European outlines but which often occurred some time later or
were concluded prematurely. One could therefore describe the Habs-

1. For the concept of stages of integration, which I follow here, see R. Smend,
Verfassung und Verfassungsrecht, Munich, 1928.
2. O. Brunner, 'Das Haus Österreich und die Donaumonarchie', *Südostforschungen*, vol.
14 (1955), pp. 122–44, esp. p. 126; frequently repeated by the same author.

burg monarchy as an unfinished state, thus accepting the general validity of the term 'state' in describing the pattern of development.

This view will be elaborated in order to clarify the nature of the whole era of so-called neo-absolute government between 1848 and 1860. Maria Theresa and Joseph II subjected their German and Bohemian Hereditary Lands (*Erblande*) to a process of absolute-bureaucratic modernisation which in its characteristics was similar to the administrative, power-political and economic integration we also find taking place in other European states. Under Joseph II's reign this modernisation leaped ahead of the rest of Europe in many respects and even assumed some characteristics of a revolution directed from above. In the field of social policy Joseph II aimed at abolishing the manorial and estate systems by decrees and by mobilising the peasant masses against their aristocratic and clerical opponents, which meant in fact a partial expropriation of the landlords. In the constitutional field he not only aimed at destroying the still powerful corporative states within the different *Lands* and at incorporating the patrimonial self-government into state administration, but, and above all, for the first time a ruler from his dynasty planned to impose the entire system of bureaucratic absolutism within the western half of his dominions on the Kingdom of Hungary. In doing this, however, he went far beyond the limits of his power. Due to the threat of a nation-wide revolt by his nobility, he and even more his brother Leopold were compelled to make far-reaching concessions to the privileged orders and to revoke the reform decrees. Leopold then finally re-established Theresian laws concerning the constitution, administration and social hierarchies.[3]

This experience deeply upset the court and the leading families, and, combined with the experiences of the French Revolution, they regarded the Josephinian reforms as the main threat to their society and interests. Thus enlightened despotism and revolution were taken to be born of the same mother and considered destructive to the integrity of the monarchy.[4] Consequently, the reforms of the Napoleonic era in Western and Central Europe, which had led to another substantial socio-

3. The problems of benevolent absolutism are discussed by K.O.v. Aretin in his introduction to K.O.v. Aretin (ed.), *Der Aufgeklärte Absolutismus*, Cologne, 1974, pp. 11–51. For Josef II, see P.v. Mitrofanov, *Josef II. Seine politische und kulturelle Tätigkeit*, 2 vols., German trans. Vienna and Leipzig, 1910; E. Bradler-Rottmann, *Die Reformen Kaiser Joseph II.*, Göttingen, 1973; K.-H. Osterloh, *Joseph von Sonnenfels und die österreichische Reformbewegung im Zeitalter des aufgeklärten Absolutismus*, Lübeck, 1970. For agrarian and tax reforms especially see R. Rozdolski, *Die grosse Steuer- und Agrarreform Josefs II. Ein Kapitel zur österreichischen Wirtschaftsgeschichte*, Warsaw, 1961; for Leopold's policy, see A. Wandruszka, *Leopold II.*, vol. 2, Vienna and Munich, 1961, pp. 249–383.
4. For an approach in terms of intellectual history, see E. Winter, *Romantismus, Restauration und Frühliberalismus im österreichischen Vormärz*, Vienna, 1968.

political push of modernisation, not only in the countries of the Confederation of the Rhine[5] but also in Prussia,[6] passed Austria by without any trace. Only since that time we may speak of a gap between Austria on the one side and most of the other states of the German Confederation on the other side, as far as economic, social and constitutional change are concerned. The transformation of this corporative society — with its subtle class hierarchies, with its ties based on property and pre-state power organisations — into a free society with common property rights, with a strict distinction between governmental and private spheres and with guarantees of the rule of law, remained unfinished and blocked until the 1848 Revolution. Above all, the manorial and estate systems were not changed. This meant for Austria that it became backward in exchange economics and productivity, which were both based on the division of labour and differentiation of production. Consequently, the pace of industrialisation slowed down markedly.[7]

The constitutional consequences led to the fact that in the western half of the empire the patrimonial courts remained untouched and, in addition to government authorities in the crown lands, the old corporative states maintained their strong political and administrative positions. Although the unifying tendencies of the imperial bureaucracy had a major influence on the formation of policy, the Estates of the

---

5. R. Wohlfeil, 'Napoleonische Modellstaaten', in W.v. Groote (ed.), *Napoleon I. und die Staatenwelt seiner Zeit*, Freiburg, 1969; H. Berding, *Napoleonische Herrschafts- und Gesellschaftspolitik im Königreich Westfalen 1807–1813*, Göttingen, 1973; E. Fehrenbach, *Traditionale Gesellschaft und revolutionäres Recht. Die Einführung des Code Napoléon in den Rheinbundstaaten*, Göttingen, 1974; H. Berding, 'Das Königreich Westfalen als Modellstaat', *Lippische Mitteilungen aus Geschichte und Landeskunde*, vol. 54 (1985), pp. 181–93. For Bavaria, see E. Weis, 'Die Begründung des modernen bayerischen Staates unter König Max I., 1799–1825', in M. Spindler (ed.), *Handbuch der bayerischen Geschichte*, vol. 4, Munich, 1974; for recently published articles, see E. Weis (ed.), *Reformen im rheinbündischen Deutschland*, Munich, 1984.
6. Recent collection of important contributions by B. Vogel (ed.), *Preussische Reformen 1807–1820*, Königstein, 1980; see the survey article of the editor.
7. For administration and constitution, see F. Walter, *Die Österreichische Zentralverwaltung*, ser. *II (1749–1848)*, 7 vols., Vienna 1934–56; V. Bibl, *Die Niederösterreichischen Stände im Vormärz*, Vienna, 1911; H. Schlitter, *Aus Österreichs Vormärz*, 4 vols., Vienna, 1920. For social structure and economic consequences, see K. Grünberg, *Die Bauernbefreiung und die Auflösung des gutsherrlich-bäuerlichen Verhältnisses in Böhmen, Mähren und Schlesien*, 2 vols., Leipzig, 1894; *Geschichte der österreichischen Land- und Forstwirtschaft und ihrer Industrien 1848–1898*, 7 vols., Vienna, 1899, especially Grünberg, 'Die Grundentlastung', vol. 1, pp. 1–80; J. Blum, *Noble Landowners and Agriculture in Austria 1815–1848*, Baltimore, 1948; R.L. Rudolph, 'The pattern of Austrian industrial growth from the 18th to the early 20th century', *Austrian History Yearbook*, vol. 11 (1975), pp. 3–43; N.T. Gross, 'Industrialization in Austria in the Nineteenth Century', Phil. Diss., Berkeley, 1966; W. Weber (ed.), *Österreichische Wirtschaftsstruktur — gestern, heute, morgen*, 2 vols., Berlin, 1961; J. Blum, 'Transportation and Industry in Austria 1815–1848', *Journal of Modern History*, vol. 15 (1943), p. 24–38; H. Matis, 'Technik und Industrialisierung im österreichischen Vormärz', *Technikgeschichte*, vol. 36 (1969), pp. 12–37.

Lands led more than a shadow existence and the crown lands were in many respects independent. They had laws of their own, different levels of taxation, different limitations of selling estates and different regulations concerning the right of settlement.[8] The consequences for the lands of the Hungarian Crown were that the king was not only bound to the approval of the Hungarian Reichstag in legislative matters, but beyond his traditional prerogatives there was no royal administration whatsoever. The manorial system and the semi-anarchic county administration (*Komitatsverwaltung*) remained the foundation of aristocratic power in Hungary. They continued their almost unfettered rule through county assemblies (*Komitatsversammlungen*), which exercised their right to give binding instructions to their Reichstag deputies, as well as their right to resist so-called unlawful decisions and decrees by central government.[9] After the failed attempt to introduce absolute government, the Hungarian nobles had the validity of this legislative complex confirmed in 1790 (later called the Hungarian National Law),[10] and the Vienna government took care not to take up that question again.

Until 1848 the Austro-Hungarian monarchy was divided into one part which was governed in a pre-absolute way and one part which was governed in an absolute way as far as constitutional law and administration were concerned, but in the latter, western, half of the monarchy one could also find a pre-absolute legacy which could at times dominate public life in one crown land or the other.

Now a word on the multi-nationality of the Empire, which, according to historical thought in the nineteenth and twentieth centuries, was the Empire's single greatest problem. We cannot, however, reduce all the difficulties of the Empire to an ethnic dimension. We can only understand the structural dilemma of the Habsburg monarchy in its full complexity by stressing three interrelated historical facts whose effects either reinforced or paralysed one another. Firstly, the Habsburg monarchy resembled a union of dominions with individual national or provincial legal traditions. Every *Land* had been constituted by its political aristocratic nation. Secondly, most *Lands*, and among

8. For a short survey including financial consequences, see H.-H. Brandt, *Der österreichische Neoabsolutismus: Staatsfinanzen und Politik 1848–1860*, 2 vols., Göttingen, 1978, vol. 1, pp. 12–25.

9. For Hungary, see ibid.; E. Andics, *Metternich und die Frage Ungarns*, Budapest, 1973; a good introduction into pre-March conditions is given by G. Barany, 'Ungarns Verwaltung 1848–1918, in A. Wandruszka (ed.), *Die Habsburgermonarchie 1848–1918*, vol. 2, Vienna, 1975, pp. 306–468, esp. pp. 312–28.

10. E.C. Hellbling, *Österreichische Verfassungs- und Verwaltungsgeschichte*, 2nd edn Vienna and New York, 1974, pp. 318–23; Wandruszka, *Leopold II.*, vol. 2, pp. 273–90.

them the largest and most important ones, were not homogenous ethnically but rather multi-national units. The plurality of *Lands* and the plurality of races never coincided. Thirdly, these nationalities normally had not the same position but were ranked in a system of social and political subordination. There were master races and servile races, or as they are called, 'historical and non-historical nations'. The latter had not established a leading class of their own and thus were left without political influence.[11]

One could envisage a Habsburg policy of working with the liberation movements of the small nations in order to break the powers of the particularistically orientated landed nobility through actively emancipating the peasants in all the nations, thus destroying the *Lands* for good. This would have been the conclusion of absolute-bureaucratic integration of the Empire on a social-revolutionary basis and in the second half of the nineteenth century might in the long run have been the basis for a federalisation along ethnic lines. The first steps towards such a policy can be found in Joseph II's reign. But after his death there was a freeze in this kind of development, and central government was happy with a policy of maintaining a balance of power, or even of seesaw politics, which supported the cultural wishes of the small nations from time to time but which was never willing to answer the unsolved constitutional question.[12]

Let us now leave behind this model of absolute-revolutionary integration and ask whether the opposite option, a conservative-corporative integration of the crown-lands might have been possible. This solution would have meant the union of the individual vested interests of the nobilities in the *Lands* within an assembly like the 'General Estates'. The corporate basis of such an assembly could later have been transformed into a modern representative body of a central parliament either in an evolutionary way as in Britain or in a revolutionary way as in France.

But it must be said that in Austria there had never been any attempt to establish central corporative units or central committees, either

---

11. R.A. Kann, *The Multinational Empire: Nationalism and National Reform in the Habsburg Monarchy 1848–1918*, 2 vols., New York, 1950; rev. edn (German), Graz and Cologne, 1964; R.A. Kann, 'Zur Problematik der Nationalitätenfrage in der Habsburgermonarchie 1848–1918. Eine Zusammenfassung', in A. Wandruszka (ed.), *Die Habsburgermonarchie 1848–1918*, vol. 3, Vienna, 1980, pp. 1304–38.
12. For the problems of domestic policy towards nationalities in the periods of restauration and pre-March, see J. Redlich, *Das österreichische Staats- und Reichsproblem*, 3 vols., Leipzig, 1920, 1926, vol. 1, pp. 59–88; see H.v. Srbik, *Metternich. Der Staatsmann und der Mensch*, 3 vols., Munich 1925, 1954, repr. 1957, vol. 1, pp. 423–524, and vol. 2, pp. 1–46; see Kann, particularly the chapters concerning the particular nationalities.

because the dynasty did not want to have them or because the dynasty was not able to establish these institutions. Normally, such ideas were initiated by the monarchs themselves when they needed funds or credit for their armies at times of war. During the wars with the Turks we find the first signs of a cooperation among corporative states in the German dominions and in Bohemia, but without the creation of a standing institution.[13] Until the Napoleonic Wars the Habsburg dynasty made intensive efforts to use corporative credit to fund their war transactions, but at the same time the dynasty was eager to isolate the different corporative states.[14] Only for the year 1816 have we any evidence of a centralist movement, when, again in connection with the strategy for dealing with the financial aftermath of the Napoleonic Wars, Metternich planned to combine corporative committees to form a central Council of the Empire.[15] The temporal and factual correlation between his and Hardenberg's policy in Prussia,[16] as well as the constitutional movements in the countries of the former Confederation of the Rhine,[17] is astonishing; for Austria its failure is also typical. Once we bring into focus the tight functional connection between financial or credit problems and tendencies to parliamentarisation, it is rather exciting to meet an application by the Austrian *Hofkammerpräsident* (president of the department of finance), in February 1848, to summon a united assembly of corporative states at Vienna in order to save the creditworthiness of the country (which had begun to vanish under the heralds of revolution) by a parliamentary declaration of liability. For a couple of days the pros and cons of this application were discussed in the light of the implicit political dangers, until the revolutionary actions put an end to this idea. Two reservations put forward by Metternich in the moment of emergency again show the specific Austrian dilemma: firstly, such a proposed body could be tempted to play the role of a constitutional assembly, and secondly and above all,

13. For a sketch of this problem, see Redlich, vol. 1, pp. 1–22.
14. F.v. Mensi, *Die Finanzen Österreichs von 1701–1740*, Vienna, 1890; A. Beer, *Die Staatsschulden und die Ordnung des Staatshaushaltes unter Maria Theresia*, Vienna, 1895, repr. 1972; Johann Schasching, *Staatsbildung und Finanzentwicklung. Ein Beitrag zur Geschichte des österreichischen Staatskredites in der 2. Hälfte des 18. Jahrhunderts*, Innsbruck, 1954.
15. E. Radvany, *Metternich's Projects for Reform in Austria*, The Hague, 1971.
16. For this aspect of Prussian reforms, see E. Klein, *Von der Reform zur Restauration. Finanzpolitik und Reformgesetzgebung des preußischen Staatskanzlers Karl August von Hardenberg*, Berlin, 1965. For the following decades, see H. Obenaus, *Anfänge des Parlamentarismus in Preußen*, Dusseldorf, 1984.
17. H. Obenaus, 'Finanzkrise und Verfassungsgesetzgebung. Zu den sozialen Bedingungen des frühen deutschen Konstitutionalismus, in G.A. Ritter (ed.), *Gesellschaft, Parlament und Regierung. Zur Geschichte des Parlamentarismus in Deutschland*, Dusseldorf, 1974, pp. 57–75.

it might perhaps be possible to force the corporative states in the western half of the monarchy to send delegates to such an assembly, but not the Hungarian Reichstag. The Empire would then have been split into two differently constituted parts; the existence of the monarchy would then be endangered.[18]

Immediately afterwards, the 1848 Revolution broke out, emphasising the extraordinary problems of constitutional movements in the Austrian Empire — now on the agenda was not only the power struggle within the state but firstly the struggle for the very existence of the Habsburg monarchy. The breaking away of the Italian provinces, the national revolt of the Czechs in Prague, movements for independence in Hungary, at first legally in the form of union only in the person of the monarchy [*Personalunion*], then, due to the outbreak of internal struggles in Hungary among the different nations, aimed at complete independence — all these events were signs of an imminent dissolution of the Empire. It was in vain that a constitutional Reichstag at Vienna, later moved to Kremsier, drafted a suitable outline of a constitution for the remaining German, Bohemian and Polish dominions. Court and army were not prepared to accept any restriction on monarchic prerogative whatsoever, and above all they were not willing to give up the unity of the monarchy.

Given the sharpening perception of danger and the final military victory over revolt and separatism, the court and armed forces were now ready to break with the old restoration system of simply maintaining balance and stability. They now started to experiment with the readoption of 'Josephinian' ideas of absolute-bureaucratic integration of the whole Empire, because they wanted to force a process of social modernisation and wanted to catch up with other countries in a very short time. At the same time their predominant aim was to re-establish the Austrian position as a great European power and its leading role in Germany and Italy. The new post-revolutionary regime had two faces. On the one hand, there was the Schwarzenberg ministry, a civilian government which judging by the names of its members expressed the desire for reform.[19] For a short period of time they believed it would be

18. For this remarkable episode, see Brandt, vol. 1, pp. 130–51, esp. 147–51.
19. For the Schwarzenberg 'coalition' ministry, see Walter, vol. 3, pp. 223–43; H. Rumpler, *Ministerrat und Ministerratsprotokolle 1848–1867. Behördengeschichtliche und aktenkundliche Analyse*, Vienna, 1970, pp. 30–2, with references. Out of the Liberal 1848 cabinets came Alexander Bach (Justice, then Interior), Philipp Krauss (Finance), Karl Krauss (Justice); Count Franz Stadion (Interior) was a kind of Austrian 'Whig'; Karl Ludwig Bruck (Trade), Triestine merchant and self-made man, had been member of the Paulskirche; the liberal-conservative Anton Schmerling (Justice for a short time) had been one of the most prominent figures in the Frankfurt parliament and government.

possible to draft a constitution for the whole monarchy involving some kind of representative body.[20] On the other hand, there was the court and military party, with their anti-revolutionary methods of suppression. In many parts of the monarchy, including all bigger cities, a state of siege was declared and maintained for years, thus substantial parts of the administration of justice and public safety were in the hands of the armed forces. Its central contribution to the salvation of the Empire brought the army its privileged role as a state within a state, a position consolidated by the military inclinations of the emperor.[21] At the same time government officials were busy drafting laws to fill in the framework of the imposed constitution: final settlement of relations between landowners and peasants after the legal emancipation of peasants (*Grundentlastung*); the reorganisation of state authorities, particularly on the lowest level; the imposition of the entire western administrative structure on Hungary; the organisation of municipalities as self-governing administrative bodies; the preparation of representative assemblies for *Lands* and districts; the reform of law and unification of law on the basis of freedom of settlement and disposable property; the promotion of free trade; the creation of a single economic unit within the monarchy; the reform of tariff laws and establishment of low protective duties; and the formation of chambers of commerce.[22] Behind these different laws we can see the thorough plan of mobilising all productive powers available. Government investment, especially in railway construction, rose by leaps and bounds. Nowhere else can we find more distinct marks of the new, powerful and centralised state than in these building activities.[23]

The whole reform movement, however, was stopped or abolished by the political reaction of 1851, certainly as far as constitutional matters were concerned,[24] and to a lesser degree as far as socio-economic matters were concerned. Thus followed the many strange socio-

20. For the imposed constitution of 4 March 1849, which never came into effect, see H. Schlitter, *Versäumte Gelegenheiten. Die oktroyierte Verfassung vom 4. März 1849. Ein Beitrag zu ihrer Geschichte*, Zurich, 1920; for the question of sincerity of governmental policy, see also Walter, vol. 3, pp. 431–4, and Rumpler, p. 32.

21. These aspects were emphasised by the earlier liberal historiography: W. Rogge, *Oesterreich von Világos bis zur Gegenwart*, 3 vols., Leipzig and Vienna, 1872–3, vol. 1; H. Friedjung, *Österreich von 1848 bis 1860*, 2 vols., Stuttgart and Berlin, 1918, vol. 1, chs. 6–8, 12–13; R. Charmatz, *Österreichs innere Geschichte von 1848 bis 1907*, 2 vols., Leipzig, 1909, vol. 1; V. Bibl, *Der Zerfall Österreichs*, 2 vols., Vienna, 1922–4, vol. 1.

22. See the survey (with references) in Brandt, vol. 1, chs. 3–4.

23. Brandt, vol. 1, ch. 4, sects. 2 and 4.

24. For the formal abolition of the 1849 Constitution by the 'Sylvester-Patent' (31.12.1851) and the reshaping government and administration, see Walter, vol. 3, pp. 486–579.

political contradictions which became a trade-mark of that neo-absolute government. On the whole they did not reconstruct pre-revolutionary (*vormärzlich*) absolutism but formed a pure bureaucratic centralism which did not care in the least for the traditional interests of the crown lands. This was a severe attack on the regional influence of the old powers, the nobility, and at the same time it left behind all liberal and constitutional thoughts and ignored the traditional Hungarian National and Constitutional Law. It was the Hungarian case that made many government officials realise how much had to be done in the fight against feudalism. This caused a renaissance of the Josephinian reform bureaucracy, which meant acts of absolute state formation using the means of the eighteenth century. At the same time this renaissance was a typical Austrian answer to the experiences of the last revolution. They had learnt their lesson, saying that the entire monarchy could not be integrated in a parliamentary way. Reform bureaucracy was the only institution with the power to carry through modernisation, since there was no possibility of the governed taking any part in that movement or controlling it, for such participation was held to be partly impracticable or too dangerous and partly bothersome or superfluous. In this situation the neo-absolute government was immediately placed under an obligation to succeed; failure could threaten the very existence of the system as a whole. There was the task of maintaining the newly unified empire by large security forces against internal opposition while at the same time satisfying the material expectations of the leading social classes through economic and social policy, since they were not allowed to take any role in politics. The success of such a policy depended largely on the Empire's ability to finance itself and on the ability to coordinate all its different actions.

This ambitious and expensive reform policy confronted a completely inadequate pre-revolutionary financial system[25] and thus immediately generated an exorbitant budget deficit. When trying to cope with the financial difficulties it was realised that there was a structural opposition between the two main groups of supporters of the new system, the army command and the bureaucracy.

If under those auspices public finances were to become the touchstone for this neo-absolute experiment of integrating the Habsburg dominions and of displaying power, then they would have to prove it simultaneously in a material and operational sense. Compelled to finance the new administration and at the same time to pay for

25. For pre-March finances, see Brandt, vol. 1, ch. 1, sect. 3.

infrastructural investments and an expanded army establishment, the
government should have been a functional unit capable of coping with
the problems of integrative budget planning and of correctly ordering
its priorities, free from any pressures of constitutional control. But here
the new system showed its crucial frailty. The conflict of interest
between military and civilian leaders fell together with the specific
shortcomings of the neo-absolute technique of governing. The 'Sylvester
Patent' (proclamation of New Year's Eve) of 1851[26] brought the
Ministerial Council to an end and reduced its former members to
politically irresponsible servants of their master. The emperor alone
should again be the only point of reference for the ministers. In the
background the Imperial Council (*Reichsrat*), as some kind of Crown
Council, was intended to play an important role as an advisory centre.[27]
In practice this form of autocratic reign led to a disintegration of
government activities that not even the Imperial Council could stop,
because the military branch made itself independent. In 1853 the
Ministry of War was dissolved and the administration of the army was
subordinated to the Army Supreme Command.[28] Thus supporting
even the civilian ministers' inclination to talk about the interests of
their departments directly with the emperor, this autocratic system of
government allowed military policy to be withdrawn from any responsible discussion within the leading administrative circles. Only the
emperor was entitled to set the necessary priorities on government
policy — a role he could hardly meet if only because of his youth.

The new system was at risk from the beginning due to these problems of leadership and coordination, and added to this, it was doubtful
whether it was able — inspite of the pre-revolutionary and inadequate
financial structure that needed immediate modernisation — to set in
train, quickly and permanently, the economic and financial powers of
the country needed by the rapidly introduced military- and bureaucra-
tic-power state. The military people around the monarch had high
expectations of the development of the empire.[29] Young Francis Joseph
was probably influenced by them to a great extent.

Anyhow, at the end of the Revolution the economic framework

26. See footnote 24. The text can be found in E. Bernatzik, *Die österreichischen Verfassungsgesetze mit Erläuterungen*, 2nd edn, Vienna, 1911, pp. 208–15.
27. For the *Reichsrat*, see Walter, vol. 3, pp. 434–79; Rumpler, pp. 32–40.
28. W. Wagner, *Geschichte des K.K. Kriegsministeriums*, vol. 1, (1848–66), Graz, 1966; A.
Schmidt-Brentano, *Die Armee in Österreich. Militär, Staat und Gesellschaft 1848–1867*, Boppard, 1975, ch. 1, sect. 1.
29. Optimistic views of Generalquartiermeister (chief of staff) Feldmarschall Hess
and Generaladjutant Grünne; see Brandt, vol. 1, pp. 281–3, and vol. 2, pp. 752–4.

seemed promising for the development of social, economic and financial policy. In the same way the first world-wide economic crisis of 1857, and in its wake economic depression, meant a severe challenge to all plans relating to economy and tax policy and led to a first disruption of the self-satisfied autonomy of reform bureaucrats. It prepared the decline of neo-absolute government. This economic development of the 1850s was therefore a significant factor in the political fate of the neo-absolute experiment.[30]

After 1857 the growing economic conflicts proved that government policy was unable to satisfy the materialistic demands of the most important social classes. This is true, above all, for agriculture. Government not only failed to back the emancipation of the peasants (*Grundentlastung*) by positive supporting measures but it also obstructed agricultural modernisation by fiscal exploitation of the compensation funds (*Grundentlastungfonds*)[31] and by prohibiting the foundation of banks specialising in mortgages. The opposition of the landlords, already opposed to the bureaucratic unitarian state on political grounds, was thus further fuelled by economic considerations.[32]

The whole investment and credit policy of government amounted to concentrating all funds in the railway network, to ensure the most rapid expansion possible; this was perfectly correct in terms of economic growth strategies but was impossible to justify politically. The original concept of a state-run railway building programme had to be given up because of severe budget deficits. The field was then open to private enterprise, but only foreign capital investors were able to apply for concessions, which were approved by government in large numbers. In

30. For the economic trends and business cycles in the 1850s, see Brandt, vol. 1, ch. 3, sect. 2; H. Matis, *Österreichs Wirtschaft 1848–1913. Konjunkturelle Dynamik und gesellschaftlicher Wandel im Zeitalter Franz Josephs I.*, Berlin, 1972, pp. 83–152.

31. By the Acts of 1848/9 the discharge of the peasants and the corresponding losses of feudal income had to be compensated to an amount of two-thirds of the capitalised value of the feudal rights. The entitled persons received 5 per cent bonds to the amount of their discharge capital, which had to be repayed by lot within forty years. In each crown land a compensation fund was erected for receiving payments of the peasants (50 per cent of the discharge capital within twenty years) and of the revenue offices (the other 50 per cent levied by surtaxes) and for paying interests and repaying the bonds disposed of by lot. In the western part of the realm (German and Bohemian crown lands) the total amount of discharge capital was about 210 million florins. Of this sum, 20 million florins had been payed off up to 1860 by lot and by free purchase, but at the same time 54 million florins which were available thanks to early payment of the peasants, had been transferred to the exchequer (for 5 per cent state bonds) for general state expenditure. See Brandt, vol. 1, pp. 299–301, and tables in vol. 2, p. 1066.

32. Governmental and capitalist interests and activities to penetrate the agrarian-dominated crown lands and the activities of the Bohemian and Hungarian landed nobility in establishing their own regional mortgage banks to maintain economic influence, blocked each other, so that nothing was effected during the decade of *Neoabsolutismus*. For this complex situation, see Brandt, vol. 1, pp. 301–15.

view of Austria's economic backwardness, the Western Europeans asked for and were granted several privileges, such as specially favourable import regulations for goods needed for their work.[33] This again was not a mistake in terms of national economy but gave rise to opposition by Austrian heavy industry, which was left empty-handed.[34] Similar difficulties were fostered by liberalising customs tariffs, which, in the economic crisis of 1857/8 drove the textile and iron industries into the camp of the government's enemies.[35]

The minister of finance also fared badly with his taxation policy. Due to poorly resourced tax authorities this amounted to placing the tax burden where it was most easily levied, on agriculture in the form of land taxes and on consumption of basic food stuffs. The early fiscal reforms were substantially influenced by the Revolution and combined the wish for more tax revenue with the socio-political desire for a more evenly shared tax burden. They tried to introduce some kind of income tax in accordance with the British example, which was regarded as the embodiment of a modern, elastic and socially fair system of direct taxation, but which did not fit in with the existing Austrian system of profit tax. Because of the traditional difficulties with inland revenue and various psychological barriers, the concept of income tax quickly degenerated into a surcharge on rates, building tax and trade tax.[36]

33. See Brandt, vol. 1, pp. 315–78, and tables vol. 2, pp. 1048–53. From 1839 to 1859, 565 million florins were spent on railway building in Austria, 260 million florins by the state, 305 million florins by private companies. State-run construction began in 1841, some of the private lines were purchased (about 30 mill. fl.), but from 1854 on private enterprise was newly admitted, and the complete state-line system was put up for sale (102.6 mill. fl.). Two main groups of railway companies developed competitively, backed by the house of Rothschild and by the French Credit Mobilier, and established by the investment of French, British and, to a lesser degree, German and Austrian private capital.
34. See Brandt, vol. 1, pp. 323, 352–3, 417–30, 436–8.
35. See Brandt, vol. 1, pp. 412–38. Bruck's tariff policy was guided by the superior aim to link up Austria with the German Zollverein. See A. Beer, *Die Österreichische Handelspolitik im 19. Jahrhundert*, Vienna, 1891, repr. 1972, chs. 5–7; H. Böhme, *Deutschlands Weg zur Grossmacht. Studien zum Verhältnis von Wirtschaft und Staat wahrend der Reichsgründungszeit 1848–1881*, Cologne and Berlin, 1966, ch. 1, sect. 1.
36. For the traditional Austrian system of direct taxation, the profit tax on land, buildings and trade, see Brandt, vol. 1, pp. 62–77. The 'income tax' of 1849, child of the 1848 Revolution, was introduced by Philipp Krauss (minister of finance, 1848–51), who had studied the British and some German examples; see Brandt, vol. 1, pp. 442–3, 444–65.

Results of direct taxation (mill. fl.)

	1851	1853	1855	1857	1859
Profit taxes	67.1	76.1	82.1	85.8	85.4
Income tax	3.7	6.4	7.8	9.9	10.8

Source: Brandt, vol. 2, p. 1072.

Commercial income remained under-taxed, as before 1848, since only fairly schematic tax-returns had to be submitted and since the tax authorities scarcely involved themselves in scrutinising balance sheets or double-bookkeeping. Also, annuity income or rents remained almost completely untaxed.[37] On the whole the difference in burden between country and city — a characteristic of direct taxation in pre-revolutionary days — actually widened after 1849. Here the most important factor is that the enormous surcharges levied by the compensation funds (*Grundentlastungsfonds*) and non-state-run regional administrative bodies (mainly municipalities) hit mainly the ratepayers. In addition to this, the peasants of the German and Bohemian countries were further burdened with direct compensation payments (*Entschädigungszahlungen*). The total level of burden on rural agriculture, which rose to 40 per cent or more of the land-register net profit (*Katastralreinertrag*),[38] did not, however, reach the same level as the real net profits due to lower land-register estimations (*Katasterschätzungen*), but the development of profit varied regionally and thus undermining the land-register as a stable basis for taxation enlarging the distortion even within agriculture. These distortions may have been overshadowed by high grain prices and good profits in the mid-1850s, but during the depression after 1857 the complaints against excessive tax burdens increased. They showed the government that another increase in rates was impossible without an overall reform of taxation.[39]

During the decade after the Revolution the Austrian authorities again put most emphasis on indirect taxes in their desire to open new wells of revenue. The abolition of manorial revenue on transfer of property offered the opportunity to expand the hitherto underdeveloped system of stamp taxes on documents and notary business. This newly developed taxation on buying and selling property again proved to be of the greatest fiscal importance in the sector of rural land and

37. Results of profit taxes (mill. fl.)

	1825	1835	1845	1850	1855	1857	1859
land tax	36.2	38.6	38.1	47.6	61.8	63.3	60.3
tax on buildings	3.5	3.7	4.5	6.5	10.8	11.8	14.8
tax on trade	2.3	2.4	2.8	3.0	9.5	10.0	10.3

Source: Brandt, vol. 2, p. 1072.

38. Brandt, vol. 1, pp. 291–3. Burdens in per cent of land-register net profit (western half of the realm): 21 per cent land tax, 3–5 per cent surtax for compensation of peasant's discharge, 7 per cent surtax for local government, 8–12 per cent direct payments of the peasants to compensation funds for peasants' discharge.

39. For the debates before 1857, see Brandt, vol. 1, pp. 542–52.

house property, because now all estates were subject to taxation. The new system, however, placed a burden on personal property, too, especially on stocks and shares, so that capital intended to finance the state or industry was now being taxed, even if only a little.[40]

In the sector of traditional excises the emphasis lay on production and products. Thus the excise on beer and spirits was transferred from town-gates to the producer,[41] an excise on beet sugar was introduced;[42] the excises on spirits and sugar were constantly increased during the following years.[43] In 1857 these fiscal demands went beyond the landlords' threshold of tolerance. The opposition to fiscal exploitation of agrarian secondary industries rose in the wake of recession and led to

40. For the pre-March system, see Brandt, vol. 1, pp. 84–6; for the legislation of 1850, see ibid., pp. 478–93, and tables in vol. 2, p. 1073.

Results of stamp taxes (mill. fl.)

	1847	1851	1858	1859
Total amount	7.3	17.2	32.1	31.3
Taxation of real property transfer	—	5.4	13.4	11.1

41. Originally, beer and spirits taxation was part of the general excise on consumption (wine, meat, grain, vegetables, etc.) which was confined to the bigger cities (gate taxation when imported) but which was the main object of revolutionary riots of the poor in 1847 and 1848. Since those events, it was the goal of administration to lower tariffs for vital goods or to modernise techniques of taxation psychologically by transferring tax collection from the gates to the sphere of production. But only a few goods were suitable to this change of taxation. See Brandt, vol. 1, pp. 77–81, 157, 465–8; Julius Marx, *Die wirtschaftlichen Ursachen der Revolution von 1848 in Österreich*, Graz and Cologne, 1965.
42. Before 1848 only the import of cane-sugar had been taxed by toll, whereas taxation of the growing beet-sugar production had been prevented by landlord lobby. After the Revolution, administration was successful in introducing beet-sugar taxation after heavy struggles in 1849/50. The basis of levy was (primitively) the weight of the beet when brought into the sugar factory. See Brandt, vol. 1, pp. 468–76.
43. Tariff per 100 kg sugar-beet (1 fl. = 60 Kreuzer): 1849, 5 Kr.; 1853, 8 Kr.; 1855, 12 Kr.; 1857, 18 Kr.
Spirits: Completely modernised tariff system, 1856, with considerable increase in rates, and the number of taxable items.

Results of excises (gross income, mill. fl.)

	1847	1850	1853	1856	1859
Spirits	1.8	3.2	6.9	9.4	11.6
Beer	5.6	7.5	8.1	7.6	13.4
Wine	2.5	2.5	4.9	4.8	5.3
Meat	2.9	2.6	5.0	5.4	5.3
Sugar	—	0.1	0.5	1.6	5.4
Other objects	7.8	7.0	4.4	4.9	3.7
Total Amount	20.6	22.9	29.8	33.6	44.5

Source: Brandt, vol. 1, pp. 473–8.

surveys. Protests by distillers and producers of sugar formed a substantial part of the widespread economic movement which tried to shake the position of tax authorities at the end of the decade.[44]

The imposition of the entire Austrian system of taxation on the lands of the Hungarian Crown was one of the most important actions of post-revolutionary reforms. It was hoped to increase inland revenue considerably, and thus bureaucracy was eager to pass all necessary regulations within a few years and tried to carry them out.[45] Hungarian burdens were thus brought into line with the burdens on the other parts of the Empire.[46] However, the enormous change in burden, affecting all branches of economic life, involved a considerable objective increase in tax;[47] subjectively, it was seen as a form of unjust treatment or punishment. A great deal of hardship was caused by the rigorous execution of the new level of taxation by the exchequer, which tried to carry it through within the shortest time possible, fighting any attempts at tax evasion.[48] In doing so, and by using Hungary for experiments with newly levied excises on wine and meat without regarding political dangers,[49] the bureaucracy undermined many of the

44. Brandt, vol. 1, pp. 572–89.
45. For the whole complex, see Brandt, vol. 1, pp. 493–534. 1849 introduction of the Austrian land-register, till 1853 transfer of a modified system of direct taxation; 1850 removal of the customs line between the western and the eastern part of the realm and introduction of the excise system and of the fiscal monopoly on tobacco.
46. Tax burden per capita (selected crown lands, per annum, in fl.)

	1841	1847	1851	1858	1859
Lower Austria and Vienna	17.45	19.65	22.37	26.60	27.15
Upper Austria	9.20	9.08	9.35	11.20	11.70
Carynthia	5.75	6.52	7.45	8.77	8.72
Bohemia	5.82	5.72	7.63	10.28	10.21
Lombardy	9.88	9.40	9.42	11.25	—
Hungary	1.43	1.68	4.28	6.28	6.18
Monarchy	4.57	4.97	6.57	8.55	8.33

Source: Brandt, vol. 2, p. 1080.

47. Growth rate of tax burden per capita and annum 1847–59 in all Austria 5.5 per cent, in the western half, 4.8 per cent, in the Hungarian half, 18.8 per cent. Estimated rate of economic growth within the same time per capita and annum 2–3 per cent. Brandt, vol. 1, p. 535; vol. 2, pp. 1035–41.
48. Arrears of land tax in Hungary (mill. fl.)

1847	1850	1851	1852	1853	1854	1855	1856	1857	1858	1859
6.0	19.7	15.2	10.3	10.4	8.7	7.6	5.4	4.7	5.1	6.0

Source: Brandt, vol. 1, pp. 77, 533.

49. Beyond the standard of the western half (only big cities) authorities first planned

positive results which could have been expected from the emancipation of the peasants in the eastern part.[50]

The growing resistance to neo-absolute tax policy was indicated finally by the debates on the reform projects proposed by the minister of finance, Bruck, in 1857 and later. A new system of direct taxation was to abolish income tax (*Einkommensteuer*) and thus restore the principle of profit tax. This principle, however, was to be flexibly adapted to the real development of profits; that is, it was to be index-linked. The most important change to the existing system of taxation was the inclusion of proceeds and capital returns in tax assessments and the introduction of profit tax on labour (*Arbeitsertragsteuer*) on as many people as possible and, above all, the dissolution of the stable crop yield land-register (*Bodenertragskataster*), which was to be replaced by a land-register of value (*Verkehrswertkataster*), subject to periodical revisions.[51] The possibility of carrying through such far-reaching changes in the system of rates (*Bodenbesteuerung*) was hardly promising, and the tax authorities also wanted to include administrative reorganisation in the reform programme. Bruck wanted to transfer almost all tax assessment and tax collection to regional and local bodies. This political aspect involved tax authorities in long and difficult arguments with the Ministry of the Interior. In addition, strong opposition arose among the landlords, who feared, not without good reason, that the Ministry of Finance mainly wanted to increase rates. Here again they regarded Bruck as an enemy of landed interest.[52]

Further fierce opposition arose with the proposal to extend the excise on wine and meat to total consumption, which had been tried earlier in Hungary. The arguments surrounding all these plans and the technical and political solutions to the problem of controlling administration, which Bruck offered within the context of his ideas on regional autonomy, offer insights into the socio-political anxieties of the neo-absolute regime, the narrow techniques of taxation at that time and their tight

---

to tax the entire consumption of the whole Hungarian population, then limited this to all places of 2,000 inhabitants and more, which still meant considerably larger taxation (Act of 1850). Several attempts to introduce total taxation in the next years failed under heavy conflicts between the different administrative authorities (Brandt, vol. 1, pp. 509–20).

50. See Brandt, vol. 1, pp. 531–4, with reference to contemporary reports.

51. For reform debates 1857–9, see Brandt, vol. 1, pp. 552–66. In contemporary Europe both systems of land taxation were known, but transition from the one to the other would have rendered forty years' work on the stable register almost worthless.

52. Opposition of the noble members of the *Reichsrat*, Brandt, vol. 1, pp. 563–6; noble opposition in 1860 on the eve of constitutional change: ibid., vol. 2, pp. 947–52. Introduction of local self-government, the debates about which filled the entire period of neo-absolutism within the ranks of bureaucracy, was one of the intricate problems of domestic policy, because here the future position of the landed nobility was in question.

connection with the problems of constitution and administration.[53] The failure of Bruck's plans for tax collection shows very clearly that attempts to increase inland revenue had reached a politically deter-mined limit by the end of the 1850s.

A crucial factor was the still basic nature of the taxation techniques, which greatly restricted the government's political tax reform options. Bruck doubtless favoured the interests of industry and banking. More important was the fact that movable capital and commercial business could hardly be taxed due to a common disapproval of inquisitorial checks of personal financial circumstances, whereas there was an easy access to rates. The relatively well-developed rates system was con-stantly open to further fiscal exploitation. But then political resistance on the part of those taxed stopped all further attempts. In the excise sector, shortcomings in tax collection were added to inadequacies resulting from a poorly developed system of trade. The few articles of mass consumption which were easily taxed without attracting too much attention, because of their locally concentrated industrial pro-duction, had already been registered. Given the internal political situation, it was simply impossible to collect the taxes imposed on consumer goods produced and consumed within the home — it would have involved the harassment of almost the entire population. Since any improvement in tax-collecting techniques seemed impossible, Bruck looked for a political solution: the psychological problems asso-ciated with levying taxes should be transferred from the state to the taxpayer, which should, through some kind of 'self-government', be responsible for a suitable distribution of charges, even at the price of an administrative step backwards. Not only did the local leading person-alities reject this solution, but the whole complex of self-government within the frame of bureaucratic principles of government was contra-dictory to the whole system and consequently extremely dangerous.

The hypothetical question of whether the Austrian national product (without regarding political and tax-levying questions) would have tolerated higher burdens — besides the basic impossibility of creating criteria for objective limits in a historical perspective — cannot be answered due to lack of statistical data; but one can make observations about this problem, which suggest a rather negative answer. The annual inland tax revenue rose between 1847 and 1858 by 80 per cent from 150 to 250 million florins. Of that increase a lot can be attributed

---

53. For the attempt to extend excises on wine and meat to total consumption, and the failure of legislation, 1857–62, see Brandt, vol. 1, pp. 566–72.

to the inclusion of revenue from Hungary. When we exclude Hungary arithmetically, we see that in the western half of the realm the average annual growth of inland revenue (about 5 per cent per capita) was substantially higher than the growth rate of production (about 2.5 per cent per capita).[54] This means that the fiscal share of the national product was increased. The burden grew in the western half of the monarchy, too.

Even if we had judged the possibilities of tax levying more optimistically under the hypothetical condition of better tax laws, we would still have to concede that there would have been no chance of increasing inland revenue to a level necessary to cope with the high annual budget deficits not even in the sector of state consumption (Table 5.1). The neo-absolute power state itself lived beyond its means, as the failure of its tax policy has shown. Neo-absolute government was not able to justify its existence in financial terms. The budget could not be balanced on the revenue column — only on the expenditure column (i.e. in terms of projected expenditure against actual expenditure).

Among the three branches of government expenditure — national debt, armed forces and civilian administration — the strict payment of interest rates on national debt remained untouched (Table 5.2), for everyone remembered the so-called national bankruptcy of 1811.[55] According to political criticism by the Conservative opposition, it was the building up of a hypertrophic bureaucracy and harsh absolutism that were mainly responsible for the ruin of imperial finances. After the defeat at Solferino, these Conservatives pushed ahead the dismantling of bureaucratic absolutism and their criticism strongly impressed the emperor (Table 5.3).[56] As the civil ministers saw it (and this is my

54. Tax burden: See footnotes 46 and 47.

Survey of gross tax revenue in selected years (mill. fl.)

| Year | Direct taxes | Indirect taxes | | | Tobacco | Stamps |
		Excises	Customs	Salt		
1820	49.0	12.0	9.7	22.4	6.1	4.4
1830	47.9	18.6	15.1	28.5	13.0	5.0
1840	46.9	23.1	21.1	31.6	17.0	6.8
1847	48.0	21.6	23.0	35.9	21.2	7.3
1848	25.8	15.3	11.6	14.6	16.7	4.3
1850	58.5	24.2	23.4	30.4	18.0	8.6
1853	82.5	30.6	23.4	34.3	37.5	25.8
1856	91.1	34.5	22.9	41.0	48.1	30.1
1858	95.5	43.1	22.3	41.3	51.5	32.1

Source: Brandt, vol. 2, pp. 1072, 1073, 1100.

55. Brandt, vol. 1, pp. 105–7, with reference to contemporary pamphleteering.
56. For the views of the neo-corporative party in 1860, see footnote 78.

Table 5.1. Survey over budget dates in the decade of revolution and neo-absolutism (mill. fl.)

	Receipts		Expenditure			Deficit					Floating debt[c]		
	Ord. net receipts (tax, national enterprise varia)	Extra-ordinary net receipts[a]	Civil admin.	Military	Debt service	Net	Without selling of rail-ways	Consoli-dated redeem	Profit-able invest-ment by central budget[b]	Gross deficit	Contrac-tion	Expansion	Receipts, loans
1847	155.0	0.4	60.3	61.0	36.0	1.9	—	5.5	33.1	40.6	—	37.8	16.1
1848	110.7	9.6	47.7	81.5	33.3	42.3	—	9.5	11.2	62.9	—	46.6	9.2
1849	100.4	33.9	50.4	148.5	34.6	99.3	—	10.4	10.4	120.0	—	143.2	—
1850	178.2	16.4	81.6	126.8	40.3	53.4	—	5.7	12.5	71.6	17.3	108.7	8.5
1851	205.6	16.8	96.9	130.5	40.9	46.1	—	5.9	19.3	71.3	—	—	99.2
1852	227.7	0.2	108.1	117.4	53.1	50.7	—	9.3	19.7	79.6	—	32.2	100.5
1853	235.3	0.3	114.3	119.0	52.6	50.2	—	8.6	24.3	83.1	51.0	—	69.5
1854	251.4	1.3	115.0	202.5	59.7	124.5	—	9.7	28.3	162.5	—	64.6	128.6
1855	258.5	26.8	121.4	212.1	68.3	116.4	143.2	20.9	32.6	169.9	—	13.3	153.5
1856	280.4	21.2	126.9	139.0	72.3	36.5	57.7	15.5	37.6	89.7	—	7.8	79.0
1857	283.4	42.2	137.2	126.9	75.4	13.9	56.0	11.5	31.3	56.6	167.2	—	228.8
1858	286.1	15.0	130.3	120.6	99.1	48.9	63.9	24.8	20.2	93.9	—	0.8	81.4
1859	288.1	12.9	120.1	239.7	86.5	145.4	157.7	12.0	8.2	165.6	—	157.4	66.9

[a] 1848/9: contributions levied by Austrian army. 1850/1: war indemnities from Sardinia. 1855–9: selling of state railways.

[b] Mainly purchase and construction of railways, interventions at the bourse (1847, 1858). The separate budgets of state property (estates, mines, etc.) are not included, only net delivery of profits is included in ordinary net receipts (first column).

[c] Paper money created by Nationalbank (issue of notes for credit without bankable cover) or directly by exchequer (assignates).

Source: Brandt, vol. 2, pp. 1072–103.

Table 5.2.   State of the Austrian debt (mill. fl.)

	Consolidated debt, capital reduced to 5 per cent interest level, minus property of sinking fund	Old paper-money debt till to 1816, capital reduced to 1 per cent interest level	Debt to be redeemed, nominal	Floating debt, nominal, minus cash	Interests, premium and other costs of debt[a]	Minus receipts of sinking fund
1815	8.8	285.6	17.9	—	—	—
1820	263.8	205.1	33.4	—	22.3	—
1830	363.4	122.1	129.1	20.1	35.5	—
1840	469.2	87.2	147.1	46.1	43.6	8.1
1847	606.7	61.5	129.3	57.9	46.3	10.4
1850	708.9	53.6	124.1	334.7	50.3	10.0
1853	918.5	44.0	168.5	324.0	66.3	13.7
1856	1429.3	36.7	194.5	437.0	82.3	10.0
1859	1674.0	27.8	164.5	372.3	95.7	9.2

[a] From 1837, the 1816 established sinking fund was out of function; its receipts of interests were remitted back for state expenditure.

Source: Brandt, vol. 2, pp. 1101, 1106, 1107; for problems of debt-restoring after the Napoleonic Wars, see ibid., vol. 1, pp. 103–29.

opinion, too), the central problem of neo-absolutist deficits lay in the exorbitant inflation of the military budget. Although the wars during the years of revolution were to blame at first, later, however, military staff was reduced only reluctantly and never reached its pre-revolutionary level, among other things because of the German conflict of autumn 1850 and the Crimean War.[57] Only the combination of foreign and domestic policy makes such a high number of troops understandable. In particular, the continuous watch on Lombardy, Venetia and Hungary made it seem sensible not to return to the former system of frequent grants of leave. Being in a state of constant mobility over years, troops also benefited from higher pay and better food.[58]

57. For military expenditure, see Table 5.1. Approximative presence of military persons (i.e. without soldiers on leave): 1840–5, 330,000; 1846–7, 350,000; 1848–9, finally 600,000; 1850, 600,000; 1851, 520,000; 1852, 440,000; 1853, 426,000; 1854–5 (Crimean War), 600,000; 1855 (October), 430,000; 1856, 417,000; 1857, 350,000; 1858, 346,000. Theoretically, state of war was assumed with 600,000; state of peace with 330,000 military persons (combatants and non-combatants). See Brandt, vol. 2, pp. 603–8.

58. After the end of mobility, new pay regulations secured the new level of income.

Table 5.3. Comparison of expenditure for civil administration of the provinces in 1847 and 1856

Grouping of Länder	Expenditure (000 fl.)		=growth 1847–56 in % of	=quota of total provincial expenditure (%)		=quota of provincial net receipts (%)		=expenditure per capita (fl.)
	1847	1856	1847	1847	1856	1847	1856	1856
1. Domestic administration and justice								
Lower Austria/ Vienna	1570	2103	34	33	26	7	6	1.31
German Alp.- Länder	3585	5256	47	36	29	15	16	1.29
Bohemian Lä.	1680	5760	243	29	40	5	11	0.83
Galicia	1673	3824	129	27	34	13	19	0.76
Hungarian Lä.	1141	11097	873	39	35	5	16	0.97
Lombardo-Venetia	5981	6524	9	36	38	13	13	1.17
2. Finance, administration and control								
Lower Austria/ Vienna	1057	1640	55	22	20	4	5	0.98
German Alp.- Länder	2538	5004	97	26	28	11	16	1.23
Bohemian Lä.	2544	4613	81	44	32	8	9	0.66
Galicia	2162	3139	45	34	28	17	16	0.63
Hungarian Lä.	726	8114	1018	25	25	3	12	0.59
Lombardo-Venetia	3195	3734	17	19	21	8	8	0.72
3. Public security (police, constabulary)								
Lower Austria/ Vienna	348	1190	242	7	15	1	3	0.72
German Alp.- Länder	169	1423	742	2	8	1	4	0.35
Bohemian Lä.	81	1038	1181	1	7	0	2	0.15
Galicia	86	724	742	1	6	1	4	0.14
Hungarian Lä.	—	3544	—	—	11	—	5	0.26
Lombardo-Venetia	1609	1964	22	10	11	4	6	0.38
4. Cult., education, local welfare (=only subsidy to local funds)								
Lower Austria/ Vienna	561	1141	103	12	14	2	3	0.68
German Alp.- Länder	988	1504	52	10	8	4	5	0.37
Bohemian Lä.	192	972	406	3	7	1	2	0.14
Galicia	1124	1505	34	18	13	9	8	0.30
Hungarian Lä.	200	1457	629	7	5	1	2	0.11
Lombardo-Venetia	2090	1335	−36	13	8	6	3	0.26

Table 5.3. *continued.*

Grouping of Länder	Expenditure (000 fl.)		=growth 1847–56 in % of	=quota of total provincial expenditure (%)		=quota of provincial net receipts (%)		=expenditure per capita (fl.)
	1847	1856	1847	1847	1856	1847	1856	1856

5. Non-profitable public investment (roads, water, public buildings)

Lower Austria/ Vienna	1212	1379	14	26	17	5	4	0.83
German Alp.- Länder	2650	3888	47	27	22	11	12	0.95
Bohemian Lä.	1295	2115	63	22	15	4	4	0.30
Galicia	1258	1945	55	20	17	10	10	0.38
Hungarian Lä.	—	5564	—	—	17	—	8	0.40
Lombardo-Venetia	3630	3952	9	22	23	10	9	0.76

Concerning domestic administration and justice in 1847, income and expenditure for patrimonial government should be mentioned but cannot be quantified. In any case, growth is smaller than shown in the table, except for the Italian dominions, with their developed state-administration. Attention should be paid to the growth in the cost of public security, which is due mainly to the militarily-organised constabulary.
Source: Brandt, vol. 2, p. 1095.

The continuous maintenance of a populous army was not only supported by political but also by internal military reasons. It was common knowledge that the pre-revolutionary armed forces had been rotten. The system of frequent grants of leave and the consequently growing number of unoccupied cadres had led to a deterioration in training. Compared to the draft system, the old inflexible system of conscription and cadres demanded permanently high numbers of soldiers if one wanted to improve the strike power. Field exercises, high agility in personal dispositions and continuous movements of troops and regroupings kept substantial parts of the army constantly on the move and caused substantial expenditure of marching toll, compensation and expenses of all kinds. All changes in staff were subject to increased costs since troops were stationed far away from their recruiting areas to cut off political ties with their homelands.[59]

The pay per capita was approximatively doubled in 1857 compared with 1847. Unlike this, the income of civil servants was not raised over the period. Being the main factor of stability of the neo-absolute regime, the army obtained a kind of insurance premium. For the whole complex, see Brandt, vol. 2, pp. 608–14; Schmidt-Brentano.
59. For these problems, see Schmidt-Brentano; sketched also in Brandt, vol. 2, pp.

If we are to judge these conditions, we must bear in mind that the administration of the whole military budget was carried out under complete isolation from any civilian participation or control. All attempts by the Ministry of Finance to participate through special committees in that detailed work of planning needs and supply in order to break up military autonomy, were put down by the commanders. The Conference of Ministers was unable to act as a directing or integrative institution. The sole institution responsible for balancing different interests remained the emperor himself, but that would have been asking too much of him, even if his impartiality could have been preserved in the face of his close relations with the military people around him.[60]

But, if we disregard structural shortcomings in leadership, excesses in organisation and possible maladministration of the Austrian army, the armed forces that were set up after the Crimean War on the basis of political and strategic ideas was financially unbearable.[61] The crucial dilemma within its structure lay in ,the fact that the display of military might demanded a costly army in peacetime, which, due to its financial consequences and their repercussions on the international prestige of the monarchy, made the basic strategy of security useless. A reduction of peacetime strength while maintaining the drive for greater military efficiency in preparation for the eventuality of war, would have meant a far-reaching reorganisation of the army — specifically, the dropping of stable cadres, the introduction of universal conscription with short-term service, the introduction of reserve officers and a regionalisation of the army following ethnic boundaries, thus abandoning the principle of dislocation. All these military reforms would have been doubtful for reasons of internal security. Military organisation and military finances remained bound by the problems of the Austrian multi-national empire in general and of the neo-absolute government in particular.[62]

As early as the end of 1858, it became clear to some members of government that these financial problems were a result of the specific shortcomings of neo-absolute rule which had now reached the point

---

610–25.

60. Wagner, vol. 1, Brandt, vol. 2, ch. 6.

61. The *Organisationsstatut* of 1857 scheduled for an offensive mobile army of 400,000 men (plus 100,000 volunteers in case of need) and a security force at home of 200,000 men in wartime; this meant 450,000 men in peacetime, which required a durable peace-budget of 110 mill. fl. (Brandt, vol. 2, pp. 620–3; the *Organisationsstatut* and its consequences are discussed by Schmidt-Brentano, pp. 129–37.

62. The structural problems are discussed by Brandt, vol. 2, pp. 622–4; Schmidt-Brentano, chs. 1 and 2.

where the slightest shake-up would have threatened the system's very survival.[63]

Parallel to the internal dangers, there was a weakening ability to maintain control in the Italian crisis, which had been set off by Napoleon III. Austria's poor performance in 1859 was mainly influenced by the state of its finances. Austrian actions just before the Italian War proves the extent to which the poor financial situation, worsened by the immediate drying up of credit, had crippled the monarchy's military and political options. Not only the discrepancy between a policy of ultimatum and effective military preparation for an offensive, but also being forced to execute such a policy of ultimatum itself, shows how little this extreme military policy was able to maintain its hegemonial position in Central Europe.[64] The early military retreat from Crimean War policies[65] spotlighted Austria's financial malaise, but during the Italian crisis its status as a great power and its financial soundness were questioned.

In terms of domestic policy, Austria's defeat in Italy meant a substantial loss of prestige for absolute government.[66] At the same time, opposition ideas and hopes won support, which posed an extremely dangerous political threat to the system, since the government's position was already shaken by economic attacks, by a chaotic currency situation and by forfeiting national credit. Thus finances were a crucial factor in the question of how many and what kinds of concessions were going to be offered.

If the neo-absolute method of government was to be watered down, all centrifugal forces would have to be released immediately, forces that

63. For the heavy internal struggles about budget problems and fears of imminent bankruptcy at the end of 1858, see Brandt, vol. 2, pp. 749–60.

64. The policy of ultimatum against Sardinia in March-April 1859 was motivated very strongly by the factor, that, in the given international constellation of powers Austria would not stand a period of full mobilisation without going to war for fear of financial collapse; and it was assumed, that exactly this was calculated by the French and Russian policy. At the same time, too little was done in time to provide the southern army with the reinforcement necessary to execute the ultimatum — similarly for financial reasons (Brandt, vol. 2, pp. 767–77; F. Engel-Janosi, 'L'"Ultimatum" austriaco del 1859' *Rassegna Storica Risorgimento*, vol. 24 [1937], pp. 1393–1425, 1563–1600, (including the texts of some council of war protocols).

65. For this complex, see Brandt, vol. 2, pp. 709–12 with critical reference to P.W. Schroeder, *Austria, Great Britain and the Crimean War: The Destruction of the European Concert*, Ithaca and New York, 1972; and W. Baumgart, *Der Friede von Paris. Studien zum Verhältnis von Kriegführung, Politik und Friedensbewahrung*, Munich and Vienna, 1972. See also B. Unckel, *Österreich und der Krimkrieg*, Lübeck, 1969.

66. Brandt, vol. 2, pp. 813–20, with reference to contemporary critics. First vague promises of changes in domestic policy in Francis Joseph's 'Laxenburg Manifesto', 15 July 1859; printed in G. Kolmer, *Parlament und Verfassung in Österreich*, 8 vols., Vienna, 1902–14, repr. 1972, vol. 1, pp. 21–2.

had been placed in custody ten years before in order to make way for a unitary state. Given the specific Austrian situation, any relaxation of the system would bring with it almost insoluble problems relating to the internal balance of power and its constitutional specification, and would call into question the unity of the Empire. In this connection, the compact national Hungarian opposition formed the strongest latent threat to central government. The liberal, predominantly German, central-constitutionalism played a somewhat provocative role rather than one which could be seen to be offering a solution to the problem of constitutional law. This aspect complicated still further the classic conflict between constitutional tendencies of power restriction and the maintenance of the monarchic prerogative, which had been earlier exacerbated by Francis Joseph's deep commitment to monarchic traditions. Over and above this dualism and problems of nationality and its centrifugal tendencies, there was the political movement of the royalist conservative high nobility, which rallied for a revision of their loss of power and function and which was committed to constitutional ideas of pre-absolute federalism within the historic crown-lands.

In 1859 signs of decay within neo-absolute government became apparent, but only the two groups which had easy access to court began exercising political pressure on constitutional development: the high nobility and the governmental reform bureaucracy. A change in system was not initiated by a broad people's movement but by the two dominating and, since the build-up of the modern state, competitive leading circles, whose political weights had shifted since 1849. They were forced by the obvious weakness of government to set the course for constitutional change in their direction. Both groups claimed, justly or unjustly, to be protagonists of broad political and economic interests.[67]

What was the high nobility aiming at? The answer is, the deprivation of power of the new bureaucracy and the abolition of the administrative unity of the Empire in favour of home rule for the *Länder* within the framework of neo-corporative states. In return, it would maintain the monarchic prerogative in central issues (army, foreign policy) and fight against modern constitutionalism. With this programme the Bohemian nobility continued their fight at a constitutional level for economic and political influence, a fight which had already begun in 1858 on economic and tax issues. This group later won additional political power when it allied itself with the Old Conservatives in the eastern half of the monarchy, who promoted themselves as holders of

67. Brandt, vol. 2, pp. 813–20, following the analysis of Redlich, vol. 1, pp. 460–87.

the key to the Hungarian problem, within a united Empire.[68]

On the other hand, the strength of the German-led reform bureaucracy lay in its connections with finances, trade and journalism of the Viennese centre, and with the German-dominated commercial employers in the *Länder* in and around the Alps and the German-speaking areas of Bohemia. It was therefore a coalition of those classes who had benefited most from the formation of a unitarian state and who now wanted to stabilise that unitarian state through a change from bureaucratic reformism to bourgeois constitutionalism. They wanted to safeguard the development of economic liberalism with its prospects for unfettered economic expansion.[69] The financial weakness of the Empire was both the motive for and means of attaining such constitutional changes. They wanted to save the unitary state from the defects of absolutism, as seen through the eyes of civilian administration and plutocracy, by introducing parliamentary control on military expenditure. This could have been brought about with the help of cooperation between the Ministry of Finance and the plutocracy by starting fictional troubles on credits.[70] The constitutionally minded bureaucracy were thus better equipped to destroy absolutism in the field of finances, but they did not have the answer to the specific Austrian constitutional problems.

Against these tendencies, beginning to take shape in the summer of 1859, the emperor intended to stand firm on the substance of an autocratically guided military and bureaucratic unitary state. He wanted to save that system by replacing its staff, by reforms in administration and by giving more influence to the Conference of Ministers. He also wanted to do away with the chronic budget deficits. The main point of reform was the formation of regional self-governing bodies, which were expected to ease the monarchy's financial burdens and at the same time create new ground for political action. It was also expected to encourage the Hungarians to cooperate with the new state.[71]

First of all, this 'reform programme' needed time. Government

68. Brandt, ibid., and Redlich, ibid. For conservative programmes and policies more details in W. Goldinger, 'Von Solferino bis zum Oktoberdiplom', *Mitteilungen des Österreichischen Staatsarchivs*, vol. 3 (1950), pp. 106–26.
69. Cf. Brandt, ibid., and Redlich, ibid. Description of the bureaucratic and economic bourgeoisie in G. Franz, *Liberalismus. Die deutschliberale Bewegung in der Habsburgischen Monarchie*, Munich, 1955.
70. This sort of combination played an important role in pushing Francis Joseph for constitutional concessions in January–March 1860 and from December 1860 to February 1861; see Brandt, vol. 2, pp. 874–84, 970–91.
71. For the new ministry Rechberg-Goluchowski and its governmental programme,

needed a lot of staying power in order to preserve the internal consistency of the programme and to maintain the autocracy during the cautious process of change. This kind of policy, however, was severely damaged in the autumn of 1859, when Bruck triggered off a credit-political crisis after he confessed to having secretly overdrawn government bonds.[72] This crisis — together with the inability to cope quickly with budget deficits — led to the abandonment of current neo-absolute policy and marked the beginning of constitutional experiment and concession.[73] Bruck himself made extensive use of this financial chaos in order to force the creation of a central representative body, which, although it was installed with only minimal political powers, nevertheless started the decisive internal landslide, because this body made topical the whole complex constitutional problem.[74]

---

see Brandt, vol. 2, pp. 821–32. For internal proceedings and views, a most interesting source is the private papers and memories of J.A. v. Hüber (in French), now partially edited in M. Cessi Drudi (ed.), *Joseph Alexander von Hübner, La Monarchia Austriaca dopo Villafranca. Résumé de l'an 1859* (=*Pubblicazioni degli Archivi die Stato*, vol. 35) Rome, 1959; and *idem* (ed.), 'Giudizi d'un Diplomatico sull'Impero Austriaco Dopo Villafranca', in *La Crisi dell'Impero Austriaco dopo Villafranca*, ed. by Istituto per la Storia del Risorgimento Italiano, Comitato di Trieste e Gorizia, Triest, 1961.

72. In 1854, during the Crimean War, a great subscription loan — the *Nationalanleihe* — of 500 million florins had been raised and payed in during the following years, mainly within state boundaries, so that a new open claim to the money market was not possible. Although one of the purposes, restoring of currency by the refunding of paper money to Nationalbank, was not even pursued, payments did not cover the current deficits. From 1857 to 1859 Minister Bruck, only verbally authorised by the emperor [!], secretly extended the amount of *Nationalanleihe* to 611 million florins; the additional issue of bonds was given to the sinking fund in exchange for elder bonds already redeemed by that fund, which were put into circulation again to hide the overdraft. This operation — thought to be typical of uncontrolled absolutist management of administration — was known only by few leading persons, who since 1858 forbade Bruck to publish the results of balancing the budget. In October 1859 Bruck at last made a publication arbitrarily, because advertisement of budget results had been continued since 1848 and could not be interrupted without causing a sensation, and probably — as I guess now — because he wanted to discredit absolutism and push for constitutional control, being sure that he personally would weather the crisis because of his indispensability. For the whole complex, see Brandt, vol. 2, ch. 6, sects. 5 and 6, and ch. 8, sect. 3.

73. As probably calculated by Bruck, the emperor held on to his minister so as not to be compromised himself, although influential court and government circles finally required Bruck's removal. Bruck then became head of reform movement, elaborated plans for financial control and in January 1860 required transition to semi-constitutionalism by transforming the existing Reichsrat into a partly representative body. See Brandt, vol. 2, ch. 8, sects. 3 and 4.

74. Imperial Patent of 5 March 1860, E. Bernatzik (ed.), *Die österreichischen Verfassungsgesetze*, 2nd edn, Vienna, 1911, pp. 217–221. The existing Reichsrat was to be reinforced periodically (at least once a year) by deputies of the provincial diets, selected by the emperor. The provincial diets had to be re-established on a neo-corporative base. This reinforced Reichsrat had to give advice on the annual budget and on all legislative matters proposed by government but had no right of decision and no initiative. A further concession of 17 July 1860 granted the Reichsrat the right to vote into being new taxes, new loans and increases in existing taxes (Bernatzik, p. 221.)

Since central government was very interested in the formation of a so-called *Verstärkter Reichsrat* (Reinforced Council of the Empire), concessions were hastily made to the Hungarians which led to the early abandonment of administrative control over the kingdom.[75] The threat of internal dangers from Hungary, the Italian complications which were again coming to a head, the problem of internal and foreign military safety and the financial troubles which pervaded all these other problems, constituted a background in the face of which the active political personalities supporting a centralised constitutionalism and the followers of an Old Conservative federalism now gathered. They forced the emperor to abandon the existing system of government.[76] In the first phase of this change, when the determined financial policy of the minister of finance threatened to lead to a constitutional system[77] and when the Hungarian problem was once more in the ascendancy, the emperor fell into line with the conservative nobility, whose programme connected the possibility of peace with Hungary with the maintenance of monarchic prerogative in the centre, which blocked constitutional development by neo-corporative regionalism and supported a money-saving cutback in bureaucracy. The so-called 'October Diploma' of 1860 was the result of such ideas.[78] In the second phase, after the failure of conservative policy on Hungary, highlighted by the Hungarian boycott of taxes, the German-dominated centralistic alliance of bureaucratic and constitutional powers successfully insisted that a solution to the everlasting finance and credit

75. Restoration of Hungarian self-government, which in consequence led to dissolution of the neo-absolutist administration on the regional and local level and later enabled Hungarians to refuse to pay taxes. See Brandt, vol. 2, pp. 900–3, 965–7, 975–93.

76. The background: complete failure of Bruck's attempt to place an Austrian loan in London, his loss of prestige, suspicion of him being involved into army-supply corruption, his dismissal and suicide, shocking the Austrian credit; Hungarian problems; military alarm in view of Italian unification; failure of an interministerial commission for budget saving to lower the level of expenses; failure of the ministry to present a balanced budget for 1861 to the assembled reinforced Reichsrat.

The Reichsrat was dominated by a majority group of conservative nobles and a minority group of centralist German liberals. In taking the financial disaster as a starting point of their criticism, both groups united in demanding a complete change of policy. They divided themselves at the end of the session in voting two different 'expertises' for the emperor which course should be followed in the future.

For the whole process from spring to autumn of the year 1860, see Brandt, vol. 2, ch. 8, sects. 5–7; Redlich, vol. 1, pp. 500–71. Debates and final resolutions printed in *Verhandlungen des österreichischen verstärkten Reichsrates 1860*, 2 vols., Vienna, 1860.

77. Bruck's follower and successor Ignaz v. Plener, pursued a policy of constitutionalising Austria with even more consequence and energy. In cooperation and even conspiring with the *Reichsrat*-minority and the press, he tried to extort concessions from the emperor by using the pressure of financial disaster. See Brandt, vol. 2, pp. 916–44.

78. For the events leading to the October Diploma (printed in Bernatzik, pp. 228–38), see Brandt, vol. 2, pp. 944–64. Broad discussion of content and political meaning in Redlich, vol. 1, pp. 572–671.

problems could only be found in centralised and constitutional institutions. Thus the catalytic power of the financial argument reached so far that, with the 'February Patent' of 1861, they found that centralistic solution to the constitutional problem which supported economic and bureaucratic interests combined with public finances.[79] The problem of the very existence of the Empire, however, remained entirely unsolved. The survival of the Empire was once more under threat.

The years to come were to prove that the new governing social groups and the integrative institution of a central parliament were not sufficient, under the special Austrian conditions, to tie together all the centrifugal ideas and tendencies. These findings specifically relate to Francis Joseph's axiomatic belief that it was impossible to rule Austria constitutionally.[80] A state whose machinery of integration was so inflexible was necessarily in constant danger of extinction.

79. The catalytic function of the financial question, in conjunction with the Hungarian difficulties, in the process leading from the October Diploma to the February Patent is elaborated in Brandt, vol. 2, ch. 8, sect. 8. For the February Patent, see Redlich, vol. 1, pp. 672–814.

80. For the emperor's reiterated statements, see F. Fellner, 'Kaiser Franz Joseph und das Parlament. Materialien zur Geschichte der Innenpolitik Österreichs in den Jahren 1867–1873', in *Mitteilungen des Österreichischen Staatsarchivs*, vol. 9 (1956), pp. 287–347.

JÜRGEN VON KRUEDENER

The Franckenstein Paradox in the Intergovernmental Fiscal Relations of Imperial Germany

Gerald Merkin, in memoriam

The fiscal history of Imperial Germany offers historians an opportunity to link the name Franckenstein with an illuminating counter-factual analysis, without invoking the famous novel written by Mary Shelley. In this case the subject is Georg Freiherr von und zu Franckenstein, an independent Bavarian patriot. He was a leading politician in the Centre Party, serving as leader of its parliamentary group (1875) and as vice-president of the Reichstag (1879).[1] Franckenstein's place in German financial history was assured when he added a clause to the important Customs Tariff Law of 1879, which brought the era of free trade to an end. This famous clause made the Reich financially dependent upon its member states. Even contemporaries soon recognised the linkage of the Reich's finances with those of the states as a major obstacle in the creation of a financial system befitting a modern nation-state, adapted to the rapid industrialisation of Germany and capable of supporting its claims to world-power status. Indeed, as the ambitions of the Reich grew, the effects of the 'Franckenstein clause' became ever more nightmarish. Far from being altered with time, this contemporary assessment has subsequently been generally accepted.

Previous historical judgements of the clause have been based on an

---

1. See K.O. Frhr. von Aretin, 'Franckenstein, Georg. . .', in *Neue Deutsche Biographie*, vol. 5, Berlin, 1971, pp. 329f.

evaluation of its financial efficiency. However, this was not the criterion used by Franckenstein himself. The clause was indeed intended to improve the condition of the public finances, or at any rate those of the states for Franckenstein. But two other motives were more important. His primary concern was not financial and economic efficiency, but a desire to strengthen — or at least to maintain — the position of the Reichstag in its relationship with the Reich government, and that of the states in their relationship with the Reich. Ultimately, therefore, Franckenstein was pursuing constitutional objectives. He hoped to use the clause, which modified intergovernmental fiscal relations, as a tool to secure his constitutional and federal, or particularistic, aims. Any historian wanting to provide an accurate assessment of the Francken-stein clause must therefore decide whether this original intention was fulfilled. I hope to show that the clause did not merely fail to achieve its constitutional and particularistic objectives but that its effects were actually diametrically opposed to those which its creator had intended. This paradox gives even more weight to previous historical criticism of the Franckenstein clause.

The paradox will be analysed in four stages. It will be based upon a survey of the system of public finances in Imperial Germany in 1871 (Sect. I). Against this background there will be an assessment of the customs tariff reform of 1879 and the development of the Franckenstein clause (Sect. II). Thirdly, the financial effects of the clause will be investigated (Sect. III). Finally, the counterfactual method will be applied to delineate the probable course of events if the Franckenstein clause had *not* been enacted, in order to expose the nature of the paradox (Sect. IV).

I

Germany in 1871 was a federation consisting of the Reich and its twenty-five member states (or twenty-six, including Alsace-Lorraine). These states and their municipalities varied greatly in size, population, economic strength, tradition and constitutions.[2] Political activity was carried out at three levels. The first of these was at the

---

2. On the Reich Constitution of 1871, see E.R. Huber, *Deutsche Verfassungsgeschichte seit 1789*, vol. 3, 2nd edn, Stuttgart, 1970, pp. 766ff. See the recent contributions on constitutional history by W.J. Mommsen, K.E. Pollmann and W.P. Fuchs in O. Pflanze (ed.), *Innenpolitische Probleme des Bismarck-Reiches* (Schriften des Historischen Kollegs, Kolloquien 2), Munich and Vienna 1983, pp. 195–256.

centre, through the Kaiser, the Reich chancellor and Reich authorities, the Federal Council (Bundesrat) representing the states, and the Reichstag; the chancellor, Federal Council and the Reichstag were forced to cooperate in order to pass legislation. Secondly, at the level of the states, political power was exercised by the princes, the state governments and the state parliaments. Thirdly, authority was wielded at local, municipal level. This threefold division of sovereign authority is characteristic of a basic federal structure. In principle the structure was maintained in the Weimar Republic and in the Federal Republic of Germany, but with three major differences:

(1) Imperial Germany did not have a fully developed parliamentary system but a so-called 'constitutional system'. It was constantly subject to the latent or overt demands of the parliamentary representatives for greater political power and participation. This fact had a significant effect on the development of financial policy.

(2) Whereas the Weimar Republic had a stronger central authority and the Federal Republic was given a moderately federal constitution, the unitary and federal elements in Imperial Germany were arranged much more in favour of a federal system. This situation emerged as a result of the historical development of the Reich as a federation of previously sovereign states. It found constitutional expression in a number of ways; for example, in the fact that, although the Reich had the power to make financial legislation, it had no financial administration of its own and was consequently entirely dependent on the states for the levy of taxes and duties.

(3) Unlike its successor states, Imperial Gemany was deeply affected by the tendency of Prussia to exert its own hegemony. Constitutionally and *de facto*, the Reich was a federal state dominated by Prussia. This relationship was formally recognised by two crucial personal unions: the Prussian king was also the German Kaiser, and the Prussian prime minister was also Reich chancellor. It was also revealed by the fact that many Reich tasks, such as control of the budget, were actually dealt with by the Prussian authorities. In material terms — in its size, population and economic and military power — Prussian hegemony was almost overwhelming.

In all modern states the links between the political structure and the fiscal system are very close. Thus the extent of parliamentary control over the budget reveals a great deal about the constitutional nature of any state. Similarly, the intergovernmental fiscal relations, (i.e. the arrangements for the distribution of revenues, expenditure and authority in financial affairs) reveal an enormous amount about the federal character of a state and the division of power between the central authority and the member states. In constitutional terms, the Reichstag in Imperial Germany had, unlike many state parliaments, unrestricted budgetary rights; that is, the right to appropriate revenues and expenditures. The Reichstag was elected by general, direct and secret ballot, and represented the strongest democratic element in the constitution.

When we examine the second factor, concerning intergovernmental fiscal relations, a detailed analysis of the 1871 constitution[3] reveals that the financial position of the Reich in its relationship with the states was intended to be rather stronger than historians have sometimes believed. According to Article 70 of the Reich Constitution, the Reich was responsible for all joint expenditures; initially, these comprised the costs of the army, navy and foreign affairs. To this end it received all joint revenues, namely: (1) customs duties; (2) joint excise duties on salt, sugar, tobacco and spirits; and (3) joint revenues from the post and telegraph services.

The states were thus relieved of the responsibility of expenditures for military matters and foreign affairs. In return, however, they had to cede control of their sources of revenue from customs duties and indirect taxes, with some exceptions for the three south German states, to whom certain exclusive rights were granted. Thus far, the financial system appeared to be comprehensible and reasonable, favouring neither central government nor the federal powers of the states.

In order to ensure that the Reich had an independent financial position to enable it to cope with its increasing tasks, the Constitution also subjected the issue of surpluses and deficits in the Reich budget to the same principle that regulated the division of expenditure and income. If joint revenues were higher than joint expenditures, the surplus was not to be distributed among the states but included in the federal budget of a following year as *joint* (or federal) revenue. On the other hand, should expenditures exceed revenues, the ensuing deficit should be covered by contributions from the member states 'so long as federal taxes have not been introduced' (the so-called *clausula Miquel* in Article 70 of the Reich Constitution). These contributions, following an example set in the German Confederation of 1815, were referred to as

3. The clauses of the Reich Constitution which deal with financial law are gathered in Section XII (Art. 69–73); see the text in G. Franz, *Staatsverfassungen. Eine Sammlung wichtiger Verfassungen der Vergangenheit und Gegenwart in Urtext und Übersetzung*, 3rd edn, Darmstadt, 1975, pp. 189f.

'matricular contributions'. The states' obligation to provide matricular contributions when required ensured that there could be no deficit in the Reich budget.

Two points emerge from these constitutional provisions. Firstly, the Reich was constitutionally entitled to introduce federal taxes to cover its ordinary requirements (i.e. to raise *direct* taxes) like the states; extraordinary requirements, according to Article 73 of the Reich Constitution, could be covered by the issue of bonds. Secondly, the matricular contributions were intended as a temporary arrangement, a stop-gap measure to balance the budget until the introduction of direct federal taxes. The whole character of these antiquated contributions, which were calculated like a poll tax on a *per capita* basis and inevitably introduced an element of unpredictability into the financial affairs of the states, made it impossible for them to be seen as anything else. The clear intention of the Reich Constitution was thus to provide for a complete separation of the financial systems of the Reich and the states.[4] In 1879 the introduction of the Franckenstein clause destroyed this plan; it was also connected with the emergence of the dogma that the Reich must be denied access to direct taxation.

II

The Reich and the states made a sound financial start as the result of the payment of war reparations by France.[5] It soon became apparent, however, that both were finding it increasingly difficult to balance revenues and expenditure in the face of the Great Depression (1873–96) and the inexorable increase in the social demands upon them. The states' room for manoeuvre was limited both by the municipalities, which bore the main socio-political burdens of coping with the economic crisis, and by the Reich itself, as it was compelled to demand increasing matricular contributions. Bismarck originally attempted to provide new sources of revenue for the Reich in the form of various projects for transfer taxes and excise duties. The opposition of the Reichstag, which demanded 'a more extensive, unified measure of tax

4. This was the opinion of P. Laband, 'Eine staatsrechtliche Erörterung zum Entwurf des neuen Zolltarifgesetzes', *Deutsche Juristen-Zeitung*, vol. 7 (1902), p. 2.

5. Fundamental to the development of the financial history of Imperial Germany still is W. Gerloff, *Die Finanz- und Zollpolitik des Deutschen Reiches nebst ihren Beziehungen zu Landes- und Gemeindefinanzen von der Gründung des Norddeutschen Bundes bis zur Gegenwart*, Jena, 1913.

reform', ensured the failure of these schemes.[6] The chancellor therefore
tried to achieve his objective by combining the reform of trade policy —
which was leading him away from free trade towards protective tariffs
— with domestic fiscal reform. We cannot know whether protectionist
aims or finance policy objectives were more important to him in this
undertaking. However, the prospect of considerably increased revenue
from customs duties, and from the modified tax on tobacco, certainly
played a significant part in determining his approach. Bismarck hoped
that this scheme would make the matricular contributions unnecessary, relieve the states and municipalities from the burden of direct
taxes and, most of all, ensure that the Reich was financially self-
supporting.[7]

The last objective, combined with the violent political struggles
which the tariff-reform programme had aroused in any case, brought
fundamental constitutional and federal issues into the debate. The
Reichstag, recalling the era when Prussia was without a budget,[8] was
profoundly mistrustful of a chancellor who was so closely tied to
Prussia. For their part, the states — especially in south Germany —
feared that their sovereign rights would be further eroded. Bismarck
hoped to forge a parliamentary majority to settle these issues by
breaking with the National Liberals and turning instead to the Conservatives and the Centre Party. Such a move involved a radical change of
course in domestic politics, making it possible that Bismarck's real
motive in the debates on customs-tariff reform was that of 'securing his
own power and the power of the government which he led'.[9] However,
the Centre Party, which had been humiliated by the *Kulturkampf*, was
won over only at the price of a compromise which gave rise to the
Franckenstein clause. This stated: 'Those revenues from customs duties and the tobacco tax which exceed the total of 130 million [marks]
per annum are to be transferred to the individual federal states on the
same population-related basis that determines the matricular contributions'.[10] The clause actually ensured that the Reich could not
become financially independent; on the contrary, the introduction of
transfers from the Reich and the continuation of the matricular contributions ensured that it was even more irrevocably bound to the states.
The significance of the clause increased because, over the next twenty-

6. J. Conrad, 'Die Tarifreform im Deutschen Reiche nach dem Gesetze vom 15 Juli
1879', in *Jahrbücher für Nationalökonomie und Statistik*, vol. 33 (1879), p. 441.
7. See Gerloff, pp. 157f.
8. On the Prussian constitutional conflict, see Huber, vol. 3, ch. 6.
9. L. Gall, *Bismarck. Der weiße Revolutionär*, Frankfurt, Berlin and Vienna, 1980, p. 583.
10. Quoted from Gerloff, p. 162.

five years, all new sources of tax revenue granted by the Reichstag were subject to it; these included various stamp duties and a tax on spirits. The first moves to solve the problems caused by the linkage of the finances of the Reich and those of the states were not made until 1904. During this slow process, which continued until the outbreak of the First World War, the matricular contributions were in effect changed from fluctuating into fixed payments. In constitutional terms, however, the original subsidiary obligation of the states to provide them remained intact.[11]

As far as financial policy was concerned, the Franckenstein clause clearly reversed the intentions of the customs tariff reform of 1879. Bismarck had recognised this fact; his willingness to accept it in spite of that, thus indicates the priority which he attached to power politics. In addition, he may even have foreseen that the clause would fail to achieve its constitutional and particularistic objectives and would not decisively restrict the financial manoeuvres of the Reich. This conjecture, however, does not invalidate the conclusion that the change in the political climate associated with the genesis of the Franckenstein clause actually presented an almost insurmountable obstacle to the modernisation of the German financial system.

III

The Reichstag hoped to use the issue of matricular contributions as a means of exerting influence over the central government. In making these contributions into a permanent part of the financial system of the Reich, the Franckenstein clause secured for the Reichstag its own continued right of appropriation. *Prima facie*, this seemed to increase its constitutional influence considerably. But as long as the current tariff and tax law remained in force its right to appropriate customs duties and tax revenues was politically ineffective. However, it certainly could exercise its right to appropriate matricular contributions on an annual basis. This was true even when the balance sheet of the Reich budget showed a surplus of revenues over expenditure

11. See P. Laband, 'Die Matrikularbeiträge', *Deutsche Juristen-Zeitung*, vol. 19 (1914), p. 6. For detail on financial policy in the decade before the First World War, see P.-C. Witt, *Die Finanzpolitik des Deutschen Reiches von 1903–1913. Eine Studie zur Innenpolitik des Wilhelminischen Deutschland* (=*Historische Studien*, vol. 415), Lübeck and Hamburg, 1970. Relevant comments also in M. Rauh, *Föderalismus und Parlamentarismus im Wilhelminischen Reich* (=*Beiträge zur Geschichte des Parlamentarismus und der politischen Parteien*, vol. 47), Düsseldorf, 1973, pp. 26ff.

because — in accordance with Article 70 of the Reich Constitution — the matricular contributions had to be included in the preceding budget estimates. The Franckenstein clause thus implanted into the Reich budget an artificial deficit which increased inexorably.

A closer examination also reveals that the annual right of appropriation of the matricular contributions had no real practical significance. Alone, its right to determine expenditure enabled the Reichstag to fix expenditure levels in the budget estimates, to legislate for the collection of revenue and thus to determine the balance. If it was unwilling to introduce new taxes or to raise existing ones in order to cover that difference — although it did not actually possess the right to initiate such legislation — then it had to choose between matricular contributions and bonds. Since bonds were out of the question to cover an ordinary budget, the Reichstag was thus forced to approve matricular contributions to cover the budget deficit. The same factors applied to the supplementary budget if the matricular contributions proved to be insufficient in the actual account. Admittedly, this constraint did not prevent the Reichstag from defining certain items in the budget as extraordinary requirements, from the 1890s on, in order to make bonds available as a source of revenue. Consequently, the indebtedness of the Reich increased rapidly.

In the last analysis, the Reichstag's right of appropriation of matricular contributions, and thus its influence on the financial system of the Reich, only marginally increased the power already provided by its right to appropriate expenditure.[12] However, the paradoxical situation created by the Franckenstein clause emerges fully only when we appreciate the fact that the minor constitutional advantage gained by the retention of the matricular contributions was far outweighed by the particularistic disadvantages associated with it. From the particularist point of view, the matricular contributions proved to be a convenient means of balancing the Reich budget, while bringing the financial systems of the states into continual disarray. Their estimates were dependent on the establishment of the Reich budget and could therefore never be predicted with any degree of reliability. The financial years of the Reich and the states did not coincide, and the Reich budget was usually passed so late that its results could not be included in the

---

12. Laband's excellent analysis of this connection ('Zolltarifgesetz', p. 3) is clearly not universally known. Without it, the most recent survey attributed too much significance to the effect of the Franckenstein clause on the annual right to appropriate revenue; H. Kolms, 'Finanzwirtschaft, öffentliche IV: Geschichte', *Handwörterbuch der Wirtschaftswissenschaften* vol. 9 (1982), pp. 774f.

state budgets of the same year. In addition, the estimates and the actual accounts often diverged wildly. These factors ensured that the states were sometimes confronted with unexpected additional demands which they were unable to meet, forcing them to borrow money.

The states' position was further damaged by the transfers from the Reich prescribed by the Franckenstein clause. The states received almost all the money from the revenues of the Reich which exceeded 130 million marks and, because the expenditure of the Reich always grew faster than its revenues, had to pay correspondingly higher matricular contributions in return. The wording of the clause ruled out any crediting of transfers and matricular contributions only afterwards could it be established whether they had balanced each other or in what measure the states had provided 'uncovered' matricular contributions, that is genuine subsidies. The matricular contributions increased so greatly that they rapidly changed from being an aid to balancing the budget into its most important source of revenue.

The regulation in fact came to endanger the entire financial system of the states, as they were forced to bear the full burden of the economic risks involved. Firstly, the revenues from indirect taxes and duties, which provided the transfers from the Reich, were among those most susceptible to economic fluctuations; secondly, these same economic factors frequently caused the revenues of the Reich and the states to fluctuate, so that the accumulation of these effects could plunge the states abruptly into a financial crisis, while the Reich was relieved of all anxieties over revenue shortfalls or overspending. Gerloff, indeed, has emphasised that the financial system of the Reich developed at the expense of the individual states.[13] Even in the years between 1883 and 1892, when transfers from the Reich exceeded matricular contributions by some 500 million marks and thus provided the states with handsome payments from the Reich, as Franckenstein had intended, this situation did them ultimately more harm than good. It did not ease the burden of taxation as much as had been expected but led to more spendthrift attitudes and tended to obscure the need for fundamental tax reforms. This was particularly damaging to the interests of the municipalities. Above all, however, the sharp fluctuations in their net revenues disturbed the balance of the states' budgets.

The instability produced by the linkage of the finances of the Reich to that of the states, the element of unpredictability in the budget estimates, the sudden surpluses and deficits in the accounts, with

13. Gerloff, pp. 285f.

which the governments always had to cope, with respect to parliamentary pressures, all were factors which hindered the development of financial policies based on reason, continuity and foresight. Such problems persisted for as long as the clause continued to operate. The famous teacher of constitutional law, Paul Laband, recognised at the turn of the century that the Franckenstein clause had not improved the financial position of the states as had been intended; rather, it had 'in reality disrupted the order and stability of the states' finances and, instead of promoting particularistic interests, had made the states completely dependent on the Reich from the financial point of view'.[14]

IV

To consolidate this view of the Franckenstein paradox, I intend to conclude by considering what might have happened if the 1879 Customs Tariff Law had been passed *without* the Franckenstein clause, as Bismarck had intended. This 'counterfactual' method[15] provides an opportunity to discuss the issues of centralism and federalism in the context of the clause more systematically than would have been possible in adhering to the actual course of events. It will be argued that there could have been six positive developments without the clause:

(1) The Reich would have become independent of the states with regard to financial law.

(2) The Reich could have become independent of the states with regard to the financial system.

(3) The financial position of the states could have been improved by the abandonment of the matricular contributions.

(4) The states could at times have had lower net revenues because there would have been no transfers from the Reich.

(5) With the abandonment of the matricular contributions, the distribution of the tax burden among the states could have been improved.

(6) There could have been less pressure on the Reich to borrow money.

14. Laband, 'Zolltarifgesetz', p. 3.
15. On the general use of the 'counterfactual' method in historical research — independent of the *New Economic History* — there is a short but convincing work: A. Demandt, *Ungeschehene Geschichte. Ein Traktat über die Frage: Was wäre geschehen, wenn . . .?* Göttingen, 1984.

Although there would have been other factors involved if the Franckenstein clause had not been adopted, these are not relevant to the following 'contrafactual' discussion.

1. The Reich could have become independent of the states with regard to financial law

This situation could have occurred because the Reich might not have been obliged to make transfers nor have had the right to impose matricular contributions. In constitutional terms, the effects of this self-sufficiency initially appear to be ambivalent. Transfers from the central government to the states always have a unitary tendency, while matricular contributions have a federal effect, or rather, as an analysis of their development reveals, are the *real confederational* element in the federal financial system.[16] Thus far, these two effects could have cancelled each other out. However, our researches have shown that the legal basis for the appropriation of matricular contributions did not *in itself* guarantee the states any increased influence over the fiscal system of the Reich. Without matricular contributions, therefore, the independence of the states would have been increased without damage to the existing fiscal relationship between the Reich and the states. Meanwhile, without transfers, unitary tendencies within Imperial Germany may well have been reduced. Ultimately, the federal powers of the states might have been strengthened.

2. The Reich could have become independent of the states with regard to the financial system

If the Reich had been able to utilise all of its revenues from customs duties and taxes, it could have made relatively light financial demands of the Reichstag. The Reich might have exerted less pressure on sources of taxation, which could then have given the states correspondingly more room for manoeuvre in raising their own taxes. In particular, pressure from the Reich on the states for some share in revenues from direct taxation — conceded in 1906 in the case of death duties — might have been reduced, together with the unitary tendencies involved. Moreover, the Reichstag, being unable to use the matricular contributions as a means of saddling the states with the responsibility for deficits in the budget, might have had more foresight

16. Huber, vol. 3, p. 946.

in setting levels of expenditure. From both points of view, the federal
position of the states might have been strengthened.

3. The financial position of the states would have been improved by the abandonment of the matricular contributions

This aspect has been thoroughly discussed already. The
abandonment of the matricular contributions would have improved the
financial position of the states and simultaneously allowed the development of continuity in their taxation laws, financial policy and budget
provisions. The influence of the Reich on the formal organisation of the
financial systems of the states would also have been reduced[17] and their
overall federal position strengthened.

4. The states could at times have had lower net revenues because there would have been no transfers from the Reich

In the periods from 1883 to 1892 and from 1895 to 1898,
transfers from the Reich exceeded matricular contributions, sometimes
by a considerable margin.[18] This net revenue could have been lost to
the states. The unfavourable financial situation during these years may
well have encouraged their inclination to reform taxation, since the
existing tax structure was clearly no longer able to keep pace with the
demands of economic modernisation. As things stood, tax reforms in
the states could have been based only on the extension of income tax,
which, as the most modern tax, also promised the highest yield. A more
rapid introduction of income taxes could actually have strengthened
the financial position of the states, possibly even to the extent of forcing
the Reich to agree to a system of grants from them, and thus establishing its federal dependence upon them.

5. With the abandonment of the matricular contributions, the distribution of the tax burden among the states could have been improved

As matricular contributions were assessed according to the
population of the various states, the financially weak smaller states
bore the largest burden in comparative terms. They therefore repre-

17. See Gerloff, p. 381.
18. See Gerloff's survey, p. 522.

sented a powerful unitary force in the attempts to open up new sources of revenue for the Reich. The abandonment of the matricular contributions could probably have diminished this tendency and strengthened their particularistic interests in relation to those of the larger states, and especially Prussia.

6. *There could have been less pressure on the Reich to borrow money*

The inadequate tax provisions had forced the Reich into debt at an early stage. This source of revenue had strengthened its independence *vis-à-vis* the states, while simultaneously impeding the access of the states to the money market. If the Reich had not been so indebted,[19] these unitary tendencies might possibly have been less pronounced.

Our 'counterfactual' propositions thus confirm and expose the nature of the Franckenstein paradox. Finally, it should be noted that, during the moves to dismantle the clause after 1904, the states had to make concessions; for example, they were forced to apply for deferment of payment of their matricular contributions, thus making the Reich their creditor. Clearly the Franckenstein clause, totally against the intentions of its author, had actually strengthened the unitary forces in Imperial Germany.

The Franckestein clause led to the creation of an extremely complex fiscal system which resulted in friction and inefficiency. It helped to discredit the federal constitution of the Reich and to make the financial and material — chiefly military — demands of central government appear irrefutable. Moreover, its after-effects ensured that during the First World War the Reich resorted to deficit spending more quickly and comprehensively than other nations; this procedure ultimately ended in disastrous hyperinflation. In addition — and in a form of dialectic response — the Constitution of the Weimar Republic had a distinctly unitarian character which possibly hastened its demise. Only in the Federal Republic of Germany, as far as we can yet judge, has a working balance between unitary and federal interests been achieved.

19. The debts of the Reich on the eve of the First World War surpassed the enormous total of 5,000m. marks (31 March 1914: 5,200m. marks). According to an estimate by Gerloff, this figure was higher than the entire ordinary and extraordinary financial requirement of the Reich at this time (1913: 4,308m. marks). W. Gerloff, 'Der Staatshaushalt und das Finanzsystem Deutschlands', in *Handbuch der Finanzwissenschaft*, vol. 3, Tübingen, 1929, pp. 21, 24.

CARL-LUDWIG HOLTFRERICH

The Modernisation of the Tax System in the First World War and the Great Inflation, 1914–23

'War is the father of all things.' This saying of the Greek philosopher Heraclitus is indeed an exaggeration. Rather, war appears to help fertilise new ideas and developments which have previously germinated in peacetime. Thus came about the establishment of the Bismarck Reich, a federative *Bundesstaat*, as a result of the Franco-Prussian War in 1870–1, and likewise the more strongly centralised Weimar Republic as a consequence of the First World War.

The German Empire was then confronted with heavy financial burdens which it had acquired from the preparation and execution of the First World War and from the settlement of its consequences. This situation was a forcing house for comprehensive financial reforms which occurred within a relatively short period and as the result of which the sturdy foundations of a modern tax system were established, one which exists even today in the *Bundesrepublik*. As a principle for the division of tax revenue between the Reich and the individual states, the solution in the Wilhelmine Empire involved the allocation of 'indirect taxes to the Reich and direct taxes to the individual states'.[1]

In addition to several of its own administrative revenues, the Reich had then at its disposal chiefly the customs duties, and several consumption taxes, particularly on tobacco, beer, brandy, sugar and salt;

1. F. Terhalle, 'Geschichte der deutschen öffentlichen Finanzwirtschaft vom Beginn des 19. Jahrhunderts bis zum Schlusse des Zweiten Weltkrieges', in *Handbuch der Finanzwissenschaft*, 2nd edn, vol. 1, Tübingen, 1952, p. 280.

it also had an early form of turnover tax, in existence since the 1890s, which was dubbed the 'stamp tax'. This dealt primarily with securities and exchanges and with playing cards. Added to these were the surpluses from imperial business concerns such as the postal service and the imperial railways in Alsace-Lorraine.[2] These sources of revenue, however, never generated sufficient funds to cover the expenses of the Empire, which initially, apart from current administrative expenses, consisted entirely of the military budget. Only with the introduction of imperial social security in the 1880s was this situation slightly changed. On the eve of the First World War, the military budget comprised approximately 90 per cent of the total imperial budget, with about 7 per cent reserved for administrative costs and around 3 per cent allotted for subsidies to social security.[3] In 1912, 3.8 per cent of the German National Income was taken up by the imperial military budget, but by 1913 this percentage had risen sharply to 4.9 per cent.[4]

To cover the surplus of imperial expenditures over and above the aforementioned revenues, two financial sources were available to the Reich. The first of these was the so-called 'proportionate levies' (*Matrikularbeiträge*) made by the individual states according to their population. Because of its dependency upon tax revenue from the member states, the Reich was significantly referred to as the 'pensioner [*Kostgänger*] of the states'.[5] The individual states — above all Prussia, which constituted two-thirds of both population and area of the Empire — were jealous of their financial sovereignty. The states and the Reich were never able to work out an equitable method of distributing this burden, nor were they able to create a coherent financial administration. The financial authorities within the individual states raised customs and imperial taxes — to be sure, under the supervision of imperial treasury officials — as well as raising their own taxes, which because of the differing configurations from state to state, led to an inconsistent distribution of tax burdens upon individual taxpayers.[6] An

---

2. For the different types of revenues and their relative importance, see W. Gerloff, 'Der Staatshaushalt und das Finanzsystem Deutschlands', in *Handbuch der Finanzwissenschaft*, 1st edn, vol. 3, Tübingen, 1929, pp. 26–31. Terhalle, pp. 279–82; Peter-Christian Witt, *Die Finanzpolitik des Deutschen Reiches von 1903 bis 1913*, Lübeck, 1970, pp. 18–19, 378–9.

3. Witt, p. 380.

4. Computed from Witt, p. 380 (military expenditures) and from W.G. Hoffmann, *Das Wachstum der deutschen Wirtschaft seit der Mitte des 19. Jahrhunderts*, Berlin, 1965, p. 509 (national income).

5. By Bismarck, the Reich's chancellor.

6. Witt, p. 22.

expert on the matter described the Reich's weak fiscal position as follows:

> Since the Reich possessed in full only one of the three functions of tax sovereignty — the authority to legislate taxation, and this only for customs duties and taxes for the use of the Reich (article 4 of the constitution, paragraph 2), the authority for administration and jurisdiction for this and all other taxes lay with the federal member states.[7]

In times of extreme need, the Reich had at its disposal a further source of finance: imperial loans (or bond subscriptions), which it used to finance up to 28 per cent (in 1909) of the imperial expenses.[8] In 1913 the sum of the imperial debt amounted to 5.2 billion marks, approximately 11 per cent of the national income. In the Federal Republic of Germany in 1982, the highly criticised debts of the federal government amounted to 25 per cent of the national income of the Federal Republic.[9]

Concerning his newly-formed Reich, and consequently its financial constitution, Bismarck did not anticipate a persistent politico-financial flow to the Reich from the individual states; quite the contrary, the indirect tax was for Bismarck and his political soul-mates the tax of the future, and as he declared in 1875; 'I am firmly convinced that where at all possible, the raising of revenue should be through indirect taxation'.[10]

His goal was not the transfer of direct revenue sources from the individual states to the Reich, something which was constitutionally sanctioned. He preferred the repeal of the direct taxes of the federal states and the institution of indirect taxes and customs duties for the benefit of the Reich.[11] Such a position from a conservative politician should not be surprising when one considers that direct taxation either affects the affluent exclusively, as in the case of property taxation, or, when graduated according to social criteria, can be adapted to fit the taxpaying capability of the middle class, as in the case of a progressive income tax. On the other hand, indirect taxation (e.g. excise tax and sales tax) burdens the taxpayer regressively; that is, it falls disproportionately heavily on consumers with lower incomes.

7. H. Leidel, *Die Begründung der Reichsfinanzverwaltung*, Bonn, 1964, p. 35.
8. Witt, p. 379.
9. Computed from *Statistisches Jahrbuch 1983 für die Bundesrepublik Deutschland*. Wiesbaden, 1983, pp. 428, 528.
10. Quoted in Gerloff, p. 25.
11. Ibid.

Long after the Bismarck era, however, the course of events would switch tracks. The financial reform of 1906 procured for the Reich the first, if only quite small, access to sources of direct taxation which the individual states had regarded as their particular preserve, namely in the form of an inheritance tax which went to the Reich. This move generated little revenue for the Reich in actuality, but it did manage to push open slightly a door which had previously been barred. As international tensions increased in 1913 and the German Reich saw itself forced into a state of increased military preparedness, the need to supplement the normal military budget forced the door open further still. In 1913 a one-time property tax, the so-called 'defence subscription' (*Wehrbeitrag*) was implemented, and in three yearly instalments between 1913 and 1915 this tax raised the massive sum of almost 1 billion (i.e. thousand million) marks for the Reich. Simultaneously, a capital-gains tax (*Vermögenszuwachssteuer*) was instituted which raised an annual sum of approximately 185 million marks for the Reich.[12]

Even so, this property tax was no fundamental reform of the Reich's financial constitution. It had been simply intended as a means of subsidising an armaments build-up. Furthermore, the 'defence subscription' was a 'one time only' tax. Its volume was, to be sure, enormous. It flooded the Reich with a new gush of revenue; in fact, its total amount corresponded to approximately one-half of the total imperial revenue of 1912.[13]

It has, however, been claimed that the use of this direct tax, rather than an indirect tax — the Reich's traditional revenue source — to finance the armaments build-up, 'marked the victory of a Social Democratic–Liberal coalition over the Conservatives',[14] after the SPD had won a substantial number of votes in the Reichstag elections of 1912.

During the First World War, the financial weaknesses in the Reich's constitutional system became particularly apparent. The traditional sources of revenue, customs and excise taxes, slowed to a trickle: customs duties sank due to the reduction of foreign trade during wartime conditions, primarily because of the Allied blockade, but also

12. For further details, see Terhalle, p. 286; H. Rohmann, 'Die Entwicklungstendenzen des Finanzsystems im Deutschen Reich und in der Bundesrepublik Deutschland von 1871 bis zur Gegenwart', Diss., Bonn, 1955, pp. 64–72. Witt, pp. 356–76.

13. K. Roesler, *Die Finanzpolitik des Deutschen Reiches im Ersten Weltkrieg*, Berlin, 1967, p. 68; Witt, p. 379.

14. F. Neumark, 'Die Finanzpolitik in der Zeit vor dem Ersten Weltkrieg', in Deutsche Bundesbank (ed.), *Währung und Wirtschaft in Deutschland 1876–1975*, Frankfurt, 1976, p. 91.

because the customs duties on imports — particularly on foodstuffs and raw materials — were cancelled in an effort to attract urgently needed goods to the country, thereby making them cheaper for domestic consumption. But consumption decreased and with it the income from excise taxes, especially on beer, tobacco and brandy.[15] Despite the imperial expenditures which had greatly increased because of the war, the ordinary budget of the Empire could be maintained through sleight of hand: military expenditures, traditionally by far the greatest cost in the imperial budget, were, for the duration of the war, relegated to an extraordinary budget while the debt-servicing allotment for the 'extraordinary wartime expenditures' which were financed with credit, remained in the ordinary budget. Significantly, the share of the debt-servicing allotment in the ordinary or regular budget rose from approximately 26 per cent in 1914 to around 90 per cent by 1916.[16]

In the second half of the war the costs of the war could no longer be financed in this fashion without additional tax increases.[17] In the spring of 1916 the projected ordinary budget showed deficits for the first time. When in the autumn of 1916 the Supreme Command of the Army carried out a further and massive increase in armaments production under the title of the Hindenburg Programme, tax increases became inevitable. Germany then followed the example set by the British government (which already had at its disposal an expanded system of direct taxation before the war, especially income tax): Britain had turned the tax screw, so to speak, immediately after war had broken out. Not until 1916, in light of the budgetary situation, did the German Reich decide to follow suit, and then because in reality the only means left by which it could hope to finance the interest on the war credit was through taxation. While Britain covered between 20–30 per cent of its total war cost by taxes in this fashion, the war was paid for on the German side almost exclusively with war loans and after 1916 was financed increasingly with short-term credit from the Reichsbank to the imperial government.[18] Regardless of the outcome of the war, the potential for serious inflation in the postwar period had been created.

15. On the Reich's revenues and expenditures during the First World War, see Roesler, pp. 196–201.
16. Ibid., p. 197.
17. For details on the tax measures from 1916 to 1918 see Terhalle, pp. 293–4. Roesler, pp. 105–19, 189–94; W. Lotz, *Die deutsche Staatsfinanzwirtschaft im Kriege*, Stuttgart, 1927; H. Jecht, *Kriegsfinanzen*, Jena, 1938.
18. R. Knauss, *Die deutsche, englische und französische Kriegsfinanzierung*, Berlin, 1923, p. 175; R. Will, *Die schwebenden Schulden der europäischen Grossstaaten*, Tübingen, 1921, pp. 28, 109. See also G. Hardach, *The First World War 1914–1918*, London, 1977, pp. 150–69.

The tax increases, which were decided upon by the Reichstag from 1916 onwards, pushed the Reich further towards the institution of direct taxation, which had begun in the period before 1914. In this way the taxes to meet the special war needs of 1916 and 1918 (*Kriegsgewinn-abgaben*) are in the same spirit and show the same rationale as the capital gains tax (*Vermögenszuwachssteuer*) of 1913. It should have gone some way to skim the top off gains in asset values made by private individuals and joint-stock corporations during the war years. The tax rates were strongly graduated and could reach as high as 80 per cent. This brought about a steep rise in imperial tax revenue which in 1916 had raised in total only 2.1 billion marks. The revenue increased by just under 5 billion marks in 1917 and further by approximately 2.4 billion marks in 1918.[19]

In contrast, revenue additions from the increase in indirect tax-ation, the traditional domain of the Reich, decreased in importance: customs on coffee and tea imports, excise taxes especially on tobacco and cigarettes and beer, and several stamp taxes were all raised. In addition to a wine tax, an excise tax on lemonade and mineral water was even instituted. None of the measures was so burdensome, how-ever, as a new excise tax on coal, which was levied in 1917. Of all the measures in the domain of indirect taxation, only one pointed the way towards the creation of the basis upon which our contemporary tax system is built — the introduction of a general turnover tax beginning in 1916 with the so-called 'stamp tax' at the amount of one per thousand on the payments for deliveries of goods. This was expanded in July 1918 into a comprehensive turnover tax at an initial rate of 0.5 per cent. Every transaction involving goods and services was taxed in full and not only that which an enterprise added to the value of semi-finished goods and services. This form of general turnover tax remained in being until the introduction of the present value-added tax in the 1960s. In this way it laid the cornerstone for one of the most productive sources of revenue in the modern state.

Connected with this was another important step towards a modern system of taxation: the establishment of an imperial fiscal court in Munich in 1918. By this measure the Reich delegated to itself the authority of jurisdiction, in any case for the most important taxes which were raised to pay for the war. How much this development was actually connected with the turnover tax law of 1918 is described by one familiar with the matter:

19. Roesler, p. 196.

The success of a tax which was designed to be levied on particular processes along the whole chain of procedures from initial production to the final consumption stage, and in particular on delivery and processing, was in large measure dependent on a systematic penetration of the economic process by a comprehensive administration of the tax laws. Therefore doubts were raised at once over the feasibility of the implementation of the turnover tax through partly deficient tax administrations which would be likely to impede economic life as a result of unequal tax treatment even more than the existing imperial taxes and could endanger the success of the new taxes. . . . How seriously the task of the establishment of the imperial fiscal court was taken by the Reichstag is shown by the fact that the law concerning the fiscal court was bound to the tax reform law of July 1918 as a 'package deal'. . . . If, therefore, the law of the imperial fiscal court was not passed the entire tax proposal would fail. No one could, however, take upon himself such a responsibility in the time of such fiscal urgency — the final year of the war 1918.[20]

Simultaneously, the imperial supervision of tax collection for the Reich was completed. However, an imperially controlled financial administration was not created out of these measures. The later permanent undersecretary (*Staatssekretär*) in the Ministry of Finance, Johannes Popitz, nevertheless saw the imperial fiscal court as a pacesetter along the way towards 'the first visible manifestation of a departure from the system in which imperial tax administration rested solely in the hands of the federal states'.[21]

With the revolution at the end of the war and the proclamation of the republic in 1918, the political order of 1871 was fundamentally altered. Although the administrative structures within the Reich and the individual states in the area of finance remained intact following the revolution, the political situation made far-reaching alterations in the financial constitution seem not only possible but necessary. Already, at the end of the war, the last secretary of state (*Staatssekretär*) of the Imperial Treasury, Graf von Roedern, had recognised the need for a basic redistribution of revenue sources to the Reich's benefit and had begun preparations in this direction.[22] This becomes particularly evident in the justification given in 1919 by the republic's finance minister, Erzberger, for the financial reform towards which he was working:

The Reich has completely changed its structure [since the collapse of the Imperial regime]. It is no longer a federal state, created in response of the

20. Leidel, pp. 54–5.
21. Quoted in ibid., p. 64.
22. J. Popitz, *Die deutschen Finanzen 1918–1928*, in *Zehn Jahre deutsche Geschichte 1918–1928*, ed. H. Müller and G. Stresemann, Berlin, 1928, p. 187.

wishes of a group of monarchs. A great step in a unitarian direction has been made [by a democratic parliament working out a new constitution]. The present structure of the Reich has been created by the will of the German people as a whole [rather than the individual states]. In this fact lies a strong centripetal tendency. The constitutional changes require a comparable change in the authority to tax. The individual states have been until now the practical tax sovereign in Germany. The Reich was, to be sure, theoretically in a position to raise direct taxes, but the hostility of the *Bundesrat* made this a practical impossibility. . . . The Reich will become the primary tax sovereign in the future. The introduction of tax-collecting machinery under its direct control will reflect the changes in the structure of the German constitution.

There are, in addition, compelling practical reasons that require the creation of national tax machinery and the transfer of the most important revenue sources to the Reich. . . . The relationship between the tax needs of the Reich on the one hand and the states and the communities on the other hand has been altered completely. Before the war the Reich required about 40 percent of the total tax yield, the Länder and communities about 60 percent. Today the Reich needs some 75 percent, the Länder and communities only about 25 percent, meaning a complete reversal of the earlier proportions. . . . With such a shift in tax needs it is inevitable that we secure a similar shift in tax authority, namely to give the Reich control over all important revenues while making it responsible for meeting the needs of the Länder and communities.[23]

This was, however, most strongly disputed politically. An expert observed:

Even in the post-revolutionary stage there existed strong forces in the individual states which stood opposed to a basic change in tax sovereignty and the division of tax authority. . . . By far the predominant feeling amongst the public, however, held that both the material considerations of those liable to taxation and the tax authority of the individual states would have to be sacrificed to the necessary reconstruction of the Reich.[24]

The latter tendencies prevailed and formed the financial constitution of the Weimar Republic, which was codified in the Reich Constitution of 1919 and in the consequential legislation enacted by parliament immediately afterwards. It was known as the 'Erzberger Reform' after the then Reich minister of finance. Article 8 of the Reich Constitution transferred to the Reich 'legislation concerning taxes and other revenues insofar as they are claimed in whole or in part for its purposes'; that is, it reaffirmed the tax sovereignty concerning the formal process

23. K. Epstein, *Matthias Erzberger and the Dilemma of German Democracy*, Princeton, 1959, p. 335.
24. Leidel, pp. 66–7.

of tax legislation which, to be sure, had already formally rested with the Reich during the imperial period but whose execution the individual states had hindered. Article 8, however, also provided for the administration of customs and excise taxes by the Reich authorities, something which had not been the case during the Empire. However, the law which rapidly followed concerning the Reich's financial administration — enacted on 10 September 1919 — went far beyond Article 8 and stated that all Reich taxes were to be administered by Reich authorities. The Reich taxation ordinances (*Reichsabgabenordnung*) of 13 December 1919 laid down that all taxes which were raised totally or even partially to the benefit of the Reich were to be administered by Reich authorities. In this way there was set up the basis for a central financial administration encompassing the entire Reich, and this still exists today in the Federal Republic with the Ministry of Finance being its chief administrative body. The former subordinate State Finance Offices (*Landesfinanzämter*) are today the Superior Finance Directories (*Oberfinanzdirektionen*), under which are, finally, the individual tax offices.

The Council of People's Representatives — or Rat der Volksbeauftragten — the government which arose from the revolution, had already in December 1918 proposed a financial programme in which the course was set for the future fundamental principles of taxation. In this proposal was stated by way of introduction:

The World War has laid great burdens upon the German people. These burdens can only be borne if they are justly divided. Therefore property and income in every form are to be taken into account in much sharper form than heretofore. A thorough expansion of a system of direct taxation must form the basis of a new means of revenue and must be tackled immediately.[25]

The finance minister, Erzberger, whose initiative was responsible for the form and parliamentary implementation of the Reich financial administration, also pioneered innovations in tapping sources of revenue.[26] In particular, in 1919 he imposed two strongly graduated one-time property taxes in keeping with the taxes of 1913 and those implemented during the war, namely the extraordinary tax on war

25. *Deutscher Reichsanzeiger vom 31. Dezember 1918, Nr. 307*, as quoted in Leidel, p. 69.
26. On Erzberger's lasting contributions to Germany's fiscal structure see Epstein, pp. 338–48; F. Menges, *Reichsreform und Finanzpolitik. Die Aushöhlung der Eigenstaatlichkeit Bayerns auf finanzpolitischem Wege in der Zeit der Weimarer Republik*, Berlin, 1977, pp. 184–228; Rohmann, pp. 98–118; K. Bräuer, *Die Neuordnung der deutschen Finanzwirtschaft und das neue Reichssteuersystem*, Stuttgart, 1920; E. Respondek, *Die Reichsfinanzen aufgrund der Reform von 1919/20*, Berlin, 1921; Gerloff, pp. 59–64; Terhalle, pp. 297–301.

profits and an extraordinary tax on capital gains. His most far-reaching accomplishment, however, besides the centralisation of railway administration — that is, the transfer of the administration of the German railways from the individual states to the Reich — was the centralisation of income taxation. On 29 March 1920 the Reichstag passed a Reich income-tax law, prepared by Erzberger, as well as a law on corporate tax and a capital-yield tax (*Kapitalertragssteuer*). Personal income was taxed with steeply graduated levies ranging between 10 and 60 per cent, in severe contrast to those of the individual states which had reached, at most, 4 per cent. The tax rates would henceforth be applied to the collective income of a taxpayer; the income from various sources, for example work and capital income, would no longer be determined separately, as had been common in the earlier income taxation of the states. In addition, the system still in operation today, that of revenue deductions for wage and salary earners (PAYE) was instituted along with a social provision, namely tax allowances for every family member — an innovation in German tax law. The capital-yield tax of 10 per cent was also raised at the source. The corporate tax of 10 per cent, in contrast, was assessed after the end of the tax year and consequently did not bring the expected results during the inflation till 1923, as price increases eroded the real value of nominal tax debts.

Income tax became the most significant source of revenue for the Reich. In second place came the turnover tax, whose rate in 1920 was raised to 1.5 per cent, on luxury items even to 15 per cent.[27] An inheritance tax, graduated according to kinship, and a land-acquisition tax were also instituted.

One more pioneering accomplishment of Erzberger's reform work remains to be mentioned: the *Landessteuergesetz*, the intergovernmental tax-distribution law of 30 March 1920. It underlined the prior claims of the Reich to all sources of revenue, it regulated the competencies of the *Länder* and the local authorities, so far as taxation was concerned, and it even obliged them to raise certain taxes — local property taxes, trade taxes and entertainment taxes, for example. Thus a far-reaching re-alignment of the basis of taxation was carried out in the Reich. As compensation for the deprivation of the *Länder*, the Reich apportioned them certain shares of its most important sources of revenue, as for example the present *Länder* in the Federal Republic are given a share of income tax and corporate-tax revenues. As a complete reverse of the

27. Epstein, p. 344.

situation during the Empire, the individual states had become the 'pensioners' of the Reich. Finally, the *Landessteuergesetz* provided for the first time in Germany a system of financial equalisation (*Finanzausgleich*) between the various *Länder*: the poorer ones receiving additional monies from the Reich treasury.[28] Almost more important was the fact that the *Länder* were also forced to carry out a financial equalisation process between the local government districts within their borders.

This monumental accomplishment of Erzberger's reforms did not initially restore the Reich's budgetary situation nor did it prevent the Great Inflation until towards the end of 1923.[29] Its effect revealed itself following the currency stabilisation, however, in that the level of taxes as a proportion of the national income rose dramatically from 9.7 per cent in the year 1913 to 18.1 per cent in 1925.[30] The conditions for the even higher tax proportion of today and the basic structure of the current fiscal constitution were created in the financial crisis during and immediately after the First World War. Specifically:

(1) The turnover, corporate and sharply graduated income taxes to benefit the Reich.
(2) The process of revenue deductions in wage-payments (PAYE).
(3) The Reich financial jurisdiction.
(4) The Reich financial administration.
(5) The financial equity between *Länder*.

While the 'Reich' has in the meantime become the 'Bund', these essential fiscal innovations have stayed with us in Germany until today.

---

28. Terhalle, p. 301; in more detail, H.E. Hornschu, *Die Entwicklung des Finanzausgleichs im Deutschen Reich und in Preussen von 1919 bis 1944*, Kiel 1950; H. Thierauf, 'Der Finanzausgleich in der Weimarer Republik', Diss., Würzburg, 1961; H. Stumpp, 'Die Entwicklung des Finanzausgleichs in Deutschland von 1871 bis zur Gegenwart', Diss. Würzburg, 1964, pp. 49–62.
29. See C.-L. Holtfrerich, *The German Inflation 1914–1923: Causes and Effects in International Perspective*, Berlin and New York, 1986.
30. Computed from Hoffmann. pp. 509, 801. For a detailed comparison of the pre-war and post-war fiscal system in Germany, see Statistisches Reichsamt (ed.), *Die Deutsche Finanzwirtschaft vor und nach dem Kriege* (= *Einzelschriften zur Statistik des Deutschen Reichs*, vol. 14), Berlin, 1930.

PETER-CHRISTIAN WITT

Tax Policies, Tax Assessment and Inflation: Towards a Sociology of Public Finances in the German Inflation, 1914–23

I

It was no accident that during the First World War the work on public finance of Rudolf Goldscheid and Joseph A. Schumpeter was stimulated in a new direction. Until this time the uncontested view was that the study of finance was the 'theory of the state budget'.[1] In light of the finance policies practised by the central powers of Germany and Austria-Hungary, and in light of the methods chosen by these two states for defraying the enormous costs of war and for solving simultaneously the problem of distributive policy, this appeared to be too formal an approach, which was unsuitable not only for identifying the problems but also for the development of solutions to the problems. In any case, science of public finance, so Rudolf Goldscheid believed, must eventually make its central research interest the 'conditioning by society of the state budget and its reciprocal function as a conditioner of social development'.[2] In this way it would become capable — that is, both economically and politically — of developing strategies for the

1. See. W. Gerloff, 'Grundlegung der Finanzwissenschaft', in *Handbuch der Finanzwissenschaft*, vol. 1, Tübingen, 1926, pp. 1ff.
2. R. Goldscheid, 'Staat, öffentlicher Haushalt und Gesellschaft. Wesen und Bedeutung der Finanzsoziologie', in ibid., p. 147; idem, *Staatssozialismus oder Staatskapitalismus*, Jena, 1917.

shaping of public finances during and, still more important, after the war. Joseph A. Schumpeter took up and generalised this idea with his own intellectual sharpness and precision of language. According to his own apodictically formulated view:

> Finances are one of the best points of attack for researching the social mechanism, and especially, but not exclusively, the political mechanism. Namely, at each point of application — or better, periods of application — in which the existing [methods of functioning] are dying out and beginning to give way to the new, and while there are continual financial crises under the old methods, the great fruitfulness of this view is demonstrated. This is the case as much with respect to causal factors, in so far as developments in the realm of state finances are an important element at every change, as it is also, with respect to symptomatic factors, in so far as everything that occurs impinges upon the realm of finances.[3]

The point of Schumpeter and Goldscheid is that with the formulation of a new, future-orientated and, in contrast to the traditional existing scale, decidedly expanded set of problems for the study of finance, a much more promising beginning for the investigation of the past was also definitely being offered. In particular, a means was being presented to investigate the most recent past from the beginning of the industrial age in which an ever larger portion of the social product in whatever form was involved in state-regulated taxation and distribution policy. However, in the study of finance there were some research problems which, despite some very promising beginnings,[4] were not pursued in sufficient measure — namely, analysing the state budget from the point of view of its 'conditioning by society . . . and its reciprocal function as a conditioner of social development' and using this as a scale of measurement for the 'political and social condition of the state,' and how this reciprocal conditionality functioned as a means of inducing as well as hindering the process of social and political

---

3. J.A. Schumpeter, 'Die Krise des Steuerstaates', in *Aufsätze zur Soziologie*, Tübingen, 1953, pp. 5ff (1st edn, 1918).
4. The most important works on this are by F.K. Mann: 'Finanzsoziologie, Grundsätzliche Bemerkungen', in *Kölner Vierteljahreshefte zur Soziologie*, vol. 12 (1933), pp. 1–20; 'Beiträge zur Steuersoziologie', in *Finanzarchiv NF*, vol. 2 (1934), pp. 281–314; 'Zur Soziologie der finanzpolitischen Entscheidungen', in *Schmollers Jahrbuch*, vol. 57 (1933), pp. 705–30; 'The sociology of taxation', in *Review of Politics*, vol. 5 (1943), pp. 225–35; 'The fiscal component of revolution', in ibid., vol. 9 (1947), pp. 331-49; 'Die Finanzkomponente der politischen Revolutionen', in *Kölner Zeitschrift fur Soziologie*, vol. 4 (1951/2), pp. 1–18; *Steuerpolitische Ideale. Vergleichende Studien zur Geschichte der politischen und ökonomischen Ideen und ihres Wirkens in der öffentlichen Meinung 1600–1935*, Jena, 1935; in the new textbooks as, for example, in G. Schmölders, *Finanzpolitik*, 3rd rev. edn, Berlin, Heidelberg and New York, 1970, the concepts of finance sociology, tax sociology, and so on, are not even mentioned.

change.[5] In the discipline of history, on the whole the analysis of state finances has been almost entirely neglected.[6]

The investigation of public finances is a decidedly very promising point of departure for the analysis of the sources and consequences of hyperinflation (therefore explicitly not for the study of previously 'normal' inflationary development, ranging up to the 30 per cent annual price increases experienced by some industrial states today) and particularly as all hyperinflation in the twentieth century is causally connected with the state's tax-raising and distributive policies during war and in the confusion of revolution. Certainly, the analysis of the state budget cannot be satisfied with the formerly held naïve assumptions as they were recently again expressed by Heinz Haller in his study on 'The Role of State Finances for the Inflationary Process'.[7] In this paper he says that Germany was pulled into inflation through the war and that the postwar inflation was 'finally the unavoidable result of the lost war'. In addition, Germany did not find itself, as Great Britain did, in the 'fortunate situation of having disposal over a system of taxation which could be immediately harnessed for war financing'. And in the postwar period, had Germany had 'a government which would have immediately put rigorous tax measures into effect . . . [it would have had] as good as no chance of survival'. More emphatically, it was precisely the renunciation of rigorous taxation and the conscious acceptance of inflation which 'secured the parliamentary system for the period of the Weimar Republic'. The last assertion could be easily made ironic — the parliamentary system of the Weimar Republic to whose security the 'Great Inflation' apparently contributed so decisively, did not last all that long as a functioning entity but was already finished as such by 1930. And, although it could be pertinently argued following Haller's reasoning that if the avoidance of a higher tax burden in the postwar period was a goal of the administration at all, which according to this argument first gave it a chance of survival, then attention should be given at this point to an important fact in Haller's presentation of evidence: he concedes without reservation — completely in agreement with the results already produced at the time by

5. P.-C. Witt, 'Finanzpolitik und sozialer Wandel', in H.-U. Wehler (ed.), *Sozial-geschichte Heute. Festschrift fur Hans Rosenberg zum 70. Geburtstag*, Göttingen, 1974, pp. 565ff.
6. For the most recent work on German finance history which includes finance sociological considerations, only my own work can be referred to, *Die Finanzpolitik des Deutschen Reiches 1903–1913. Eine Studie zur Innenpolitik des Wilhelminischen Deutschland*, Lübeck and Hamburg, 1970, as well as a series of essays in periodicals and collections.
7. In Deutsche Bundesbank (ed.) *Währung und Wirtschaft in Deutschland 1876–1975*, Frankfurt, 1976, pp. 115–55, esp. p. 150.

contemporaries — that the public finance economy of Germany in and after the First World War was a decisive causal factor in the German inflation between 1914 and 1923. But with the merest assertion of this phenomenon his interest ends, while in reality it must be the point of departure for further inquiry — because finance policy or public financial systems are definitely not abstract creations, and because efficient and inefficient tax systems are not the result of some kind of 'happy' coincidence. The ability to react or not to react to altered situations with altered methods as, for example, with 'rigorous taxation', is also in no way determined by fate but is the result of social and political power constellations; it is the analysis of the latter which presents the real task.

If it is therefore correct to say that the public-finance economy of Germany represents the essential source of inflation, so with reference to Rudolf Goldscheid's dictum for the analysis of the conditioning by society of inflation and the reciprocal function of its conditioning of social development, a structural investigation of the public finances in war and the postwar period becomes theoretically a particularly promising point of departure. However, within the limits of this essay this objective is naturally not realisable. Thus, following a short analysis of wartime financial policy as an expression of the distribution of power in the German Empire, and following a similarly brief sketch of the conceptions of financial and tax policy held by postwar governments, which above all stresses the novel quality of the financial policies developed by them, we will turn to the social conditioning of inflation and its reciprocal function as a conditioner of social development with the assistance of an analysis of the causal relationship between tax assessment and inflation. The shift of the question to be investigated from the connection between tax *policy* and inflation to the connection between tax *assessment* and inflation can be easily justified theoretically and is significant in that only this kind of formulation can lead to satisfactory answers.[8] In practical application this procedure necessitates climbing into the quagmire of 'low' politics and of the even 'lower' administrative procedure — certainly a reason why the insights and practical investigation in this area have split so far away from each other.

8. Compare, for example, recent studies such as J. Daviter, J. Könke, O. Graf Schwerin, *Steuernorm und Steuerwirklichkeit*, vol. 1: *Steuertechnik und Steuerpraxis in Frankreich, Grossbritannien, Italien und Deutschland*, Cologne and Opladen, 1969; B. Beichelt, B. Biervert, J. Daviter, G. Schmölders, B. Strümpel, *Steuernorm und Steuerwirklichkeit*, vol. 2: *Steuermentalität und Steuermoral in Grossbritannien, Frankreich, Italien und Spanien*, Cologne and

II

There are few differences of opinion among researchers on the actual results of German wartime financial policies; namely, the inability to finance a significant portion of the additional expenditure for the war from current or additional tax income[9] resulted, up to the end of 1916, in a rapidly rising long-term indebtedness. And since the end of 1916, as the consolidation of intermediary financing through treasury-bond credits was no longer successful, the result was a rapidly accelerating increase in the short-term debt and the money supply.[10] The policies of distribution were of particular significance because the interest and amortisation of the national debt required the entire tax income of the central government. The situation in the federal states in general looked somewhat better owing principally to the fact that much of their mandatory expenditure was transferred to the central government.[11] For the communal finances, on the other hand, which were particularly affected by social expenditure, there are only a few reliable accountings and absolutely no general balance. Certainly, one can assume with a high degree of probability an increased imbalance between income and expenditure, since the local authorities too were allowed to practise large-scale financing of their expenditure through

---

Opladen, 1969; among the older studies are the excellent works by F. Meisel, 'Wahrheit und Fiskalismus bei der Veranlagung der modernen Einkommensteuer', in *Finanzarchiv*, vol. 31, no. 2 (1914), pp. 144–68 and *Britische und deutsche Einkommensteuer, ihre Moral und Technik*, Jena, 1925. Particularly stimulating for the main questions is the collection of essays by F.K. Mann, *Finanztheorie und Finanzsoziologie*, Göttingen, 1959.

9. The estimates in the literature vary between 0 and 13 per cent for the proportion of war expenditure financed by taxes. See R. Knauss, *Die deutsche, englische und französische Kriegsfinanzierung*, Leipzig, 1923; R. Will, *Die schwebenden Schulden der europäischen Grossstaaten*, Tübingen, 1921, p. 28; W. Lotz, *Die deutsche Staatsfinanzwirtschaft im Kriege*, Stuttgart, Berlin and Leipzig, 1927, pp. 105ff. My own calculations — based on published statistics, with the addition of unpublished material from the federal treasury which after the end of the war assign to the total war-costs the final army and navy costs — come to the conclusion that the expenses authorised through the war, including servicing the debt, to the extent of about 156 billion (i.e. thousand million) marks was covered up to 97.7 per cent through loans (see P.-C. Witt, 'Die Finanz- und Wirtschaftspolitik des Deutschen Reiches 1918–1924', unpub. ms, Table 4a, 4b, pp. 14f.). Of the 211.6 billion marks total expenditure of the Reich and the federal states in the budget years 1914–18, 11.1 per cent was covered about through taxes, about 7.1 per cent through surpluses/profit from public enterprises and about 81.8 per cent through loans.

10. See C.-L. Holtfrerich, 'Political Factors of the German Inflation', in N. Schmukler and E. Marcus (eds.), *Inflation through the Ages: Economic, Social, Psychological and Historical Aspects*, New York, 1983, pp. 400–3.

11. In the budget years 1914–18, the Reich received in total 17.4 billion marks in tax yields, while debt-servicing required about 17.6 billion marks. In the federal states 6.1 billion marks were received from taxes, 3.5 billion of which went to servicing their debts. (Cf. footnote 9).

new indebtedness.[12] All three administrative bodies of the state refused
to finance by taxes either the increased direct or indirect burdens of the
public sector which developed as a result of the war. At the same time,
they did not even succeed in raising sufficient long-term loans; on the
contrary, they financed about half through the establishment of short-
term loans.

This very comparison of the financial policy of all three types of
territorial bodies in the Reich during the First World War shows that
an interpretation of Germany's wartime financing that primarily em-
phasises the weak constitutional position of the Reich in financial
matters falls short of the mark. It can, to be sure, explain why the Reich
was capable or wanted to employ direct taxes on income and property
only towards the end of the war, and then very hesitatingly, but it
would help little in explaining the failure of the federal states and the
local authorities to increase drastically these taxes, which fell within
their provenance under the dominant constitutional interpretation.[13]
Of equally slight explanatory value is reference to the fact that the
responsible statesmen and public opinion were seduced for a long time
by the idea of being able to place the 'lead weight' of the war costs on
the enemy.[14] Also, the interpretation which argues that the political
truce introduced at the beginning of the war drastically reduced the
freedom of action of responsible leaders and made impossible practically any alteration in the financial jurisdiction between the central
government and the federal states as well as any redistribution of the
relative burdens among the various social strata, is too bound by
superficial phenomena. This interpretation can, however, be the point
of departure for an analysis of the causes. This has to apply first to the
distribution of expenditures and income among the federal government, the states, and the local authorities. Without going into the fine
details, the distribution of expenditure was as follows: the central
government had to bear, besides the financially almost insignificant
functions such as the establishment of legal uniformity and representing the nation abroad, only the defence or war burdens as really
cost-intensive functions. In contrast, the states and local authorities
divided among themselves all the remaining expenditures; in particu-

12. See, in addition, the petitions of the lord mayor of Essen of 17 October 1918 and of
the *Deutscher Städtetag* of 24 April 1919 to the Prussian finance minister, ZStA Merseburg,
Rep. 151 II, no. 823.
    13. See on this complex question Witt, *Die Finanzpolitik des Deutschen Reiches 1903–1913*,
pp. 17ff.
    14. K. Helfferich (at that time secretary of the Treasury) on 20 August 1915 in the
Reichstag, *Stenogr. Berichte über die Verhandlungen des Reichstags*, vol. 306, p. 225.

lar, they took care of almost all the welfare functions. To meet these expenditures the indirect (consumption) taxes and excises stood at the central government's disposal; at the states and local authorities' disposal, next to their extensive productive property in agriculture, transport and industrial enterprises, stood in the first place the taxes on personal income and property as well as inheritance. Such a system of division of expenditures and finance sources between superior and subordinate territorial bodies was and is not unusual in federal states. The actual problem developed in Germany because the political representation — the chance for individual social groups and political parties to achieve their goals, or even the possibility of participating in the political decision-making process at the different levels of nation, states and local authorities — were sundered from each other in the extreme. At the national level, at least in principle if not in fact, a democratic suffrage was in effect. In contrast, at the states' and local authorities' level an unequal, chiefly plutocratic suffrage was in effect.[15]

This constellation was the cause of the inflexibility in the scheme for distributing the sources of finance between the federal government on the one side and that of the states and local authorities on the other, and was already evident before the world war. It also blocked all attempts to create a new organisation during the war, although the expenditures of the central government had increased drastically while those of the states and local authorities were relatively reduced. The slogan which the Conservatives expressed before the war with remarkable frankness was that direct taxation could not be allowed to rest 'in the hands of a parliamentary body elected on equal suffrage'.[16] This opinion, to be sure, was no longer articulated with the same kind of brutal openness. Rather, it was referred to in terms of its legitimisation by the historical nature of the system.[17] However, in practice and with little foresight the ruling Conservatives in the Prussian parliament clung tightly to this goal and, through the Prussian State Ministry, which was dependent upon them, managed to block any attempts by the federal government at further exploiting direct taxation for its own

15. See on this section P.-C. Witt, 'Finanzpolitik und sozialer Wandel in Krieg und Inflation', in H. Mommsen et al. (eds.), *Industrielles System und politische Entwicklung in der Weimarer Republik*, Düsseldorf, 1979, pp. 404ff, and 'Reichsfinanzminister und Reichsfinanzverwaltung', *VJZG*, vol. 23 (1975), pp. 4ff.

16. The leader of the Conservatives, Ernst v. Heydebrand und der, Lasa on 10 July 1909 in the Reichstag, *Stenogr. Berichte über die Verhandlungen des Reichstags*, vol. 237, p. 9322.

17. O. Frhr. v. Zedlitz-Neukirch, *Neuaufbau der Finanzen nach dem Krieg und qualitative Sparsamkeit*, Stuttgart, 1917, p. 7.

purposes.[18] However, the blocking of this transfer of direct taxation to the Reich did not hinder the federal states from at least tapping these sources of revenue themselves. But, with the exception of smaller and financially weaker states, which saw themselves compelled to make a considerable increase in the tax rate, the states declared themselves satisfied with minimal corrections[19] and beyond that undermined at the very outset the efforts, undertaken too late in any case, to unify or at least strive for similar tax schedules among the federal states.[20]

Perhaps still more politically and financially significant — in any case, more burdensome to future tax policies than the unsuccessful extension of the direct taxes — was the fact that the dominating Conservatives in Prussia successfully opposed the creation of a special-ised technical tax administration, maintaining, as a kind of old-estate privilege, the system whereby all direct-tax assessment was subject only to the vote of the *Landräte*, officials chosen from their own social class.[21] Therefore it was made certain, as one of those involved put it, that 'the Prussian Junker had and held so much that his ancestral estate was maintained and that he was able to send his sons into the service of the king as soldiers and officials'.[22] In other words, the 'ruling class' used their position of strong political privilege, through the Prussian voting system, and strong social privilege, through the selec-tion of officials during the war,[23] and additionally by their tax power, 'to heighten their own prosperity and to strengthen their economic position'.[24] It is the social and political division of power and not constitutional abstractions which determined the war-financing of the German Reich and which laid extensive foundations for the inflation of the postwar years.

18. See on these manoeuvers the documents ZStA in Merseburg, Rep. 151 HB no. 1444, and ZStA Potsdam, Rkz no. 219; the statements by Roesler, pp. 103ff, limited themselves to a very superficial reference to the tax programmes.
19. For particulars, see the article 'Einkommensteuer' by Johannes Popitz, in *Handwörterbuch der Staatswissenschaften*, 4th edn, vol. 3, Jena, 1926, pp. 400–91, here pp. 439–45.
20. See the protocol on the results of the meeting with the federal states' finance minister on 23/24.9.1918, in GLA Karlsruhe, 237/31922, Aufz. Wagner 26,9.1918; St A. Hamburg, Senatskommission für die Reichs- und Auswärtigen Angelegenheiten II, II A 1 fasc. 3 Bd. 1, Aufz. Schaefer, 25.9.1918.
21. See P.-C. Witt, 'The Prussian Landrat as tax official, 1891–1918', in G. Iggers (ed.), *The Social History of Politics*, Leamington Spa, 1985, pp. 137–54.
22. ZStA Potsdam, Rkz no. 951, v. Klitzing to Bethmann Hollweg, 3 May 1912.
23. See, in addition, the report of the general director of the direct taxes in the Prussian Finance Ministry of 5 November 1918, ZStA Merseburg, Rep. 151 II no. 117.
24. F.K. Mann, *Finanztheorie und Finanzsoziologie*, Göttingen, 1959, p. 117.

III

The political revolution of November 1918 swept away the barriers which had stood until then against rational disposal of finances, against severe taxation of income, property and inheritance and against an effective tax administration. That was also understood by the representatives of the previously privileged strata,[25] and in the first months of the revolution the later so-called Erzberger finance programme, which laid the basis of reform, was conceived.[26] However, there was a fact of more importance: the popularly mandated cabinet (Rat der Volksbeauftragten) put together a series of resolutions affecting expenditure which, with the rest of the projected budget year 1918 and the budget year 1919, added a debt of approximately 20.6 billion marks.[27] The financial means of covering this debt (besides the issuing of treasury notes) existed neither theoretically nor practically, because the building up of the new system of German taxation necessarily required more time due to the legal diversity inherited from the Empire.[28] Apparently, the practice which had originated in the Empire simply repeated itself. The ruling social class — and this was the workers during the relevant time period, between November 1918 and spring 1919 — essentially used their control over government expenditures 'to increase their own prosperity'. Naturally, it is incontestable that almost all of these additional expenditures served the broad mass of the population in some form of social security and were explicitly directed towards winning greater distributive justice. To emphasise this point of view alone, however, would not satisfactorily characterise the goals which were pursued at that time. For in reality the finance policy was imbedded in a well-thought-out concept of an integrated economic, social and financial policy which should overcome the evident economic difficulties after the war's end. This would be achieved through a cyclical policy financed with deficit spending which

25. See, in addition, the memoranda of the Conservative Otto Hoetzsch of 5 November 1918, published with an introduction by the author in *VJZG*, vol. 21 (1973), pp. 337ff.

26. See particularly the protocol of the Finance Ministers Conference of 29/30 January 1919, ZStA Merseburg, Rep. 151 HB no. 1444, maschinenschriftliches Protokoll, 146 pp.

27. Witt, 'Die Finanz- und Wirtschaftspolitik des Deutschen Reiches', Table 12, p. 94.

28. In anticipation of a federal regulation of the tax rate, the federal states raised the income tax strongly (from 1913 on the average 4.6 per cent, on 1919 on the average 13.1 per cent of taxable income including the communal surcharges on the state income tax) without — in so far as this judgement is possible given the desolate condition of the finance statistics — there being any increase in income. See 'Die deutsche Einkommenbesteuerung vor und nach dem Kriege', *Statistik des Deutschen Reiches*, vol. 312, Berlin, 1925, p. 24ff. (Tax rates), pp. 46ff. (Assessment results), *Vierteljahreshefte zur Statistik des Deutschen Reiches*, vol. 4 (1922), pp. 71–113 (for the actual results of the tax assessment).

would simultaneously guarantee economic growth, social security and political democracy.[29] Such a policy at first appeared to improve the lot of everyone without hurting anybody; the financing of the additional expenditures was authorised through short-term loans and their inflation-stimulating tendencies were consciously taken into account by both the government and all socially relevant interest groups. Certainly, the government had only foreseen deficit financing for the period of the 'transition economy' (*Übergangswirtschaft*''). Thereafter it promised, on the basis of the comprehensive finance programme developed at the same time, not only to be able to cover the current expenditures but also to create a surplus for loan amortisation.[30] The particulars of this finance programme cannot be gone into here; however, its essential legal characteristics were as follows: (1) exclusive competence of the Reich — legal jurisdiction and administrative sovereignty were assumed by the central government over all taxes and levies; (2) the central government was required to establish a legal framework for the entire tax law and for the management of public income and expenditures; (3) the central government claimed all taxes falling on income, property and inheritance, all consumption taxes and excises, and permitted the states and local authorities a certain amount of freedom in negotiating taxes on real property. That meant that the subordinate administrative units would be very much dependent for their income from subsidies out of the national taxes. Materially, the finance programme contained, on the one hand, the increase of the existing excises and consumption taxes as well as an essential increase in the general sales tax which had already been introduced during the war. On the other hand, the programme received a bundle of completely newly-conceived direct taxes, of which the most important were the inheritance tax (legacy duty, estate duty and gift tax), property tax (capital levy, tax on wartime property value increases) and finally the income tax (income tax on earned and unearned income, capital-gains tax as a base tax, corporation tax). The yield relationship between indirect and direct taxes in their final state should have contributed 35

29. See here P.-C. Witt, 'Bemerkungen zur Wirtschaftspolitik in der "Übergangswirtschaft" 1918/19,' in D. Stegmann et al. (eds.), *Industrielle Gesellschaft und politisches System*, Bonn, 1978, pp. 79–96; P.-C. Witt, 'Staatliche Wirtschaftspolitik in Deutschland 1918–1923: Entwicklung und Zerstörung einer modernen wirtschaftspolitischen Strategie', in G.D. Feldman et al. (eds.), *Die Deutsche Inflation*, Berlin, 1982, pp. 151–79.

30. The future financial requirements of the Reich and its coverage: Memoranda of the Reich finance minister, 5 August 1919, *Stenogr. Berichte über die Verhandlungen des Reichstags*, vol. 337, pp. 601–14, For the origins of the programme see K. Epstein, *Matthias Erzberger und das Dilemma der deutschen Demokratie*, Berlin, 1962, pp. 369ff, as well as my own study, 'Die Finanz- und Wirtschaftspolitik des Deutschen Reiches'.

per cent against 65 per cent, respectively. This programme was pressed
through the law-making machinery of the Reich between August 1919
and March 1920 with relatively few changes in the government's
proposals. Measured by the prewar finance programme, which spent
much less, this was a very short period of time for passage. Therefore
the leading politicians and particularly Erzberger were repeatedly
reproached for their haste, which prevented the Reichstag from explor-
ing all the legal ramifications and made it constantly necessary to pass
amendments to improve the new tax laws. However, measured against
the financial necessities of the government, this already constituted a
fatal delay in the attempt to cut short the budget deficit as one
important source of the inflation. Central government had to raise its
floating debt by around 53 billion marks to approximately 130 billion
marks once again between August 1919 and August 1920, when finally
the revenue from the new tax programme started to flow in. To be sure,
one can assume that the successful passage of parts of the programme
at the end of 1919 and the mere existence of the reform programme
exercised a positive influence in support of the value of the mark, and
the final passage of all of the laws at the end of March 1920 essentially
contributed to a relatively stable mark throughout the following year
and beyond.[31]

IV

In the end, Matthias Erzbergers' tax reform never fulfilled
the expectations. In the budget year 1920 the taxes brought exactly 36 per
cent, in 1921 barely 45 per cent, in 1922 around 35 per cent and in the
rump budget 1923 (March to December) only 11 per cent of the
necessary income to cover expenditures.[32] Exceptional increases in
expenditures did not play a decisive role; on the contrary, in the budget
years 1920 to 1922 the public expenditures of all territorial entities
continuously diminished. Only in 1923 did they increase, again as a

31. C. Bresciani-Turroni, *The Economics of Inflation*, London, 1931, pp. 54ff.; with
respect to this, see my essay, 'Finanzpolitik und sozialer Wandel', in Mommsen et al.,
pp. 395–426, here p. 418. I would also not want to exclude the effects of the proclam-
atory nature of the tax programme. It is possible in the unexplained tax incidence
problem that the announced tax increase shifted the problem onto the consumer by
raising the prices in advance of the tax increase; that is, the announcement of the tax
increase caused a price increase some months before the passing of the bill.
32. See Table 8.2, and *Deutschlands Wirtschaft, Währung und Finanzen*, Berlin, 1924, p. 30.

result of the Ruhr occupation.[33] This failure was only to a limited
extent caused by later amendments to the tax laws, which had the effect
of somewhat reducing direct taxes.[34] Certainly, these later laws reflected the agitation against the alleged 'unbearable tax burdens'
carried out by interest groups from industry, commerce, the middle
class and agriculture, but the alterations in the tax laws which actually
came into effect were too insignificant to explain the meager net
result.[35] In this context other factors were much more important. To
begin with, the German tax system operated with respect to indirect
(consumption) taxes and tariffs, mainly using taxation schedules based
on quantity; that is, a tax levy of a set amount in marks on a legally
established quantity of a product. In this system the price of the
product was of no importance to the taxing authorities. Only in a few
cases was it foreseen in the tax or customs regulations that the tax
contribution by quantity did not always remain the same, but that with
increased quality and price the tax also increased. However, in these
cases too, no attempt was made to make some link between the price of
the product and the level of the tax in the form of a proportional tax
payment which varied with price. In this system, with increasing
currency depreciation the real proportional tax per quantity of a product
continuously went down — in other words, this system of tax rates
exhibited little responsiveness to inflation. If the originally intended tax
burden was to be restored, legal measures would be required, which
would entail tedious political conflicts. Only in three cases did the
German system deviate from their general principles of organisation;
namely, in the general sales tax and in the coal tax, established during
the First World War, which taxed a fixed percentage of sales (i.e. the
sales price determined the tax burden) and in a series of tariffs which in
1919 managed to encompass the actual import price beyond the
so-called gold excise premium. The higher responsiveness to inflation
of the latter taxes and excises ensured, however, that the relative
significance of the indirect taxes and excises for the entire tax intake,
with the exception of the year 1920, lay continuously above Erzberger's
intended 35 per cent quota in the finance programme.[36]

33. See P.-C. Witt, 'Finanzpolitik und sozialer Wandel', in Mommsen et al., p. 424,
Table 1.
34. Ibid., pp. 417ff.
35. See in addition the documents in ZStA Potsdam, RFM nos. 915–31 and 941; the
flood of their own publications of the interest-group organisations, the petitions to the
Reichstag and the other publicity sources cannot be named here separately.
36. 1920, about 35 per cent; 1921, about 38 per cent; 1922, about 53 per cent; 1923
(until November), about 48 per cent: *Deutschlands Wirtschaft, Währung und Finanzen*, p. 34;
see Table 8.2.

The same problem was exhibited in the tax rates of the so-called direct taxes; that is, the income, capital-gains, corporation taxes, estate and legacy duties and gift tax as well as of the property tax, which was conceived as an one-time tax in the form of a capital levy. The applied graduated rate made necessary relatively high rates of assessment in the higher brackets of income and property or inheritances in order to reach the wished-for intake. To be sure, all the politicians and officials who were responsible for the setting of the tax rates, but also those who were really affected by the high progressive assessment at the top rate levels, were aware that the average tax burden was very much less oppressive than it appeared.[37] It was, however, maintained — and not only for sensible practical reasons or because this system was the traditional one, but because in two respects it permitted the exercise of first-rate demagoguery. In the face of the enemy's demands for reparations, one could maintain that despite the imposition of maximally oppressive taxes, the country was still unable to pay reparations.[38] And in internal political conflicts one could maintain the same to all groups demanding that a heavier burden should fall upon the 'economy' or the 'rich'. It is to be noted that this system, which became a vehicle of tax demagoguery for political purposes, was not originally created by opponents of an effective progressive taxation of large incomes and wealth, but by social-democratic makers of tax policy, who in the individual federal states after the revolution had set, for example, the income-tax schedules for 1919 for especially high incomes in the last tax bracket at over 100 per cent of the income liable to taxation, at the same time carefully making sure that in their tax districts there were no taxpayers with earnings above that level.[39]

While the existing *tax-rate system* negatively influenced the tax yield only through most of the indirect taxes and excises (though the door was opened wide to political demagoguery through the direct taxes), the system of *tax assessment* revealed itself to be a financial catastrophe.

37. See, in addition, as an explanation, the discussion on income tax, Berichte über die 1.–5. Sitzung der Finanzkommission, 15 May 1919 to 27 June 1919, GLA Karlsruhe, 237/13318; Bericht der Unterkommission für die Einkommensteuer, 18 June 1919, ZStA Potsdam, RFM no. 915.
38. The Reich's Finance Ministry's ongoing calculations were produced on the alleged tax distribution for the purposes of propaganda which — as all those involved knew perfectly well — had nothing to do with reality. See, for example, ZStA Potsdam, RFM no. 775.
39. See *Die deutsche Einkommenbesteuerung vor und nach dem Kriege, Statistik des Deutschen Reiches*, vol. 312, pp. 36ff. In Mecklenburg-Strelitz, to give an example, the tax rate for the 5-million-mark excessive incomes was set at over 100 per cent; this cost nothing since, according to the statistics on income tax, in this state there had never even been a taxpayer whose income exceeded 1 million marks.

Before the fragmented bureaucratic authorities of the separate states could introduce the new taxes, they had at the same time to laboriously create a unified finance administration.[40] This fact played an important but not a decisive role. More important were the factors immanent in every assessment system: after the legally stipulated period the tax-payer declared the relevant tax particulars to the tax office. The tax office was only then in a position to assess the amount of tax due and demand payment. This tedious process — which, depending on the kind of tax being assessed, could require between the determination and the payment of the tax debt a period of from a few months up to two or three years — was often dependent on very complicated material. After the first legally correct assessment, the point at which the system began to be effective, under stable monetary conditions this time lapse posed only a minor problem because advance payments could be required for the current tax period. The critical point was the first assessment, since no income flowed for a certain time. The situation became even more critical where nothing resembling stable monetary conditions obtained, but rather open inflation. Then the deficit in the state budget would grow as a consequence of the missing tax yields, thereby heating inflation and serving as an incentive to the taxpayer to delay in each of the separate steps of tax assessment and payment: making a tax declaration, getting the tax amount and paying it. This delay was accomplished by using all the legal devices in all the tax laws which necessarily provide for the protection of the taxpayer.

In Germany, generally speaking, even for most indirect taxes, an *ex post facto* assessment system was in effect in the case where the person owing the tax and the actual taxpayer were not the same person. For example, for the turnover tax a quarter-year was foreseen as the tax period after which the taxpayer had to send in a record of his sales. A month after expiry of this tax period a tax declaration had to be submitted, and after the subsequent determination of the tax indebtedness by the tax office, payment had to be made within fourteen days.[41] In practice this meant that, even during periods of stable money values, the person owing the tax had an interest-free operating credit for several months. Under inflationary conditions this meant that in real terms the treasury only received a portion of the outstanding amount owed while the taxpayer profited from the interest, and also — as he quickly recog-

---

40. See Witt, 'Reichsfinanzminister', *VJZG*, vol. 23 (1975), pp. 1–61.
41. See sections 35ff of the sales-tax law of 26 December 1919, as well as the implementation regulations and decrees of the Reich Finance Ministry, ZStA Potsdam, RFM no. 1630.

nised — from the difference between the real value of the taxes when they fell due (e.g. at a sale) and when they were paid. The consumer in principle bore the full intended tax burden.[42] As the consumption taxes through the assessment system revealed themselves under inflationary conditions as a system of redistribution among private persons, so did the assessment system of the direct taxes lead (with the exception of the capital-gains tax, which was deducted at the source and only *ex post facto* included in the assessment to the income tax) not only to a radical reduction of the intended tax debt, but also the planned distribution of the tax burden among the taxpayers was radically reversed. This will be illustrated here by the central focus of the Erzberger tax reform, income tax.[43]

In the planning of finances in 1919 it was projected that the income tax should bring in approximately one-third of the national tax income and that by the same token it should realise from the estimated 25 million taxpayers on small and medium incomes of up to 14,000 marks per year (at the time the law became effective this corresponded to approximately 2,600 marks in 1913 prices) about 30 per cent of receipts, while the approximately 5 million taxpayers with higher incomes would provide about 70 per cent. The tax rate schedule and the progression of tax brackets were arranged with this objective in mind.[44] But actually, with the exception of the year 1922, the portion of the receipts from income tax never reached what had been planned, and the distribution of the tax burden on small and medium incomes on the one hand and on larger incomes on the other turned out dramatically differently from that which the creators of the income-tax law had anticipated. If one searches for the causes of this development, one is compelled to consider the problem of assessment. Because of the very different legal arrangements among the old state income taxes, and as a result of the fact that the utilisation of their assessments for purposes of convenience by the Reich for the first year of the national income tax would have produced differing tax burdens for persons with the same income, the tax law had foreseen a complete renovation of the assessment system. After the expiry of the tax or fiscal year 1920, the

42. This statement turns to paper all the lovely calculations about the distribution of the tax burden among the population which the Reich Finance Ministry put together on the basis of the tax intake into the Treasury in so-called goldmarks (adjusted against the cost-of-living index).
43. Owing to the shortage of space I omit discussion of the corporation tax as an income tax on juridical persons, the capital levy or the inheritance taxes. It must be emphasised, however, that the assessment system had quite similar effects for them also.
44. See J. Popitz, 'Einkommensteuer', in *Handwörterbuch der Staatswissenschaften*, vol. 3, 4th edn, Jena, 1926, pp. 446ff.

first assessment according to the new law should be made in order to create the same conditions for all taxpayers.[45] On the other side, the officials creating the law saw clearly that the initial assessment, involving more than 30 million taxpayers, would inevitably lead to a complete breakdown of the tax administration; furthermore, that for the many millions of taxpayers, who only received income from wages or salaries, an *ex post facto* application of taxes would be accompanied by considerable practical difficulties — this was in any case the experience with older federal states' income taxes. Therefore they had an ingenious idea: to burden all wage and salary earners with a straight tax rate of 10 per cent and obligate the respective employer to deduct this tax from the wage or salary payments at the source. With this method two birds would be killed by one stone: first the tax offices would be freed of an immense work-load, and at the same time they would be assured that the tax on wage and salary earners would actually be applied. Certainly, an *ex post facto* assessment was also projected for them, but because the tax rate was chosen in such a way that a great majority of the wage and salary earners actually had paid their taxes by a wage deduction, this *ex post facto* assessment was not relevant financially and also could be omitted if need be. Through these technical tax regulations developed, in principle, three classes of income tax payers: (1) those who only paid wage taxes; (2) those whose wage or salary income was not sufficiently burdened through the 10 per cent base deduction and/or had other sources of income; (3) those who gained income from property-owning, industry or capital investment, or self-employment and lay exclusively under *ex post facto* assessment.

In Tables 8.1 to 8.3 the financial results of the income tax for the years from 1920 to 1922 are shown.[46] An important fact becomes quite clear from Table 8.2, namely the relative significance of the income tax under the total tax income, even if the projections were never fulfilled. The other important fact is that in fiscal year 1920 only wage tax was paid in, and with the exception of just a few months in the first half-year 1922, the wage tax continuously paid in a far higher portion of the tax yields than the assessed income tax; only in a single month, in February 1922, did the relationship between the wage tax and the assessed income tax stand at 30 per cent to 70 per cent, respectively, somewhat as the drafters of the law had conceived (cf. Table 8.1). The

45. See in this context especially the report of the Undercommission for Income Tax, 18 June 1919, ZStA Potsdam, RFM no. 915.
46. The following exposition is based on a series of documents, RFM nos. 915–31, 1100–22 and 1197–9, ZStA Potsdam; reference to single documents will be omitted.

relatively high ability of wage tax to respond to inflation as a base tax made this result just about impossible to avoid, although attention must be drawn to the fact that the real tax income out of the wage tax could have been very much higher had the employers not increasingly delayed in paying the deducted wage tax and had they not created for themselves at the cost of the employee and the state treasury an interest-free operating credit whose real repayment value declined with the increasing acceleration of the inflation.[47] In Table 8.3 an attempt is made to compare the theoretical assessment results and the real yields of the wage and income tax. Here it is shown that the assessment results (which were, by the way, continuously used in political propaganda both internally and externally)[48] were as good as worthless. Then, according to the assessment, those taxpayers who only paid on their wages (57–67 per cent of all taxpayers) should contribute only approximately 28 per cent in 1920, approximately 18 per cent in 1921 and approximately 14 per cent in 1922. However, they actually paid for 1920 approximately 52 per cent, for 1921 approximately 53 per cent and for 1922 approximately 37 per cent of the assessed tax balance. That was related to the fact that they continuously paid 100 per cent of their tax in real terms, while the other assessed taxpayers brought in in real terms only about 36 per cent for 1920, about 19 per cent for 1921 and about 27 per cent for 1922.

The question why this evident disproportionality was tolerated cannot be explained without knowledge of the actual process of assessment. Although severe political conflicts had taken place at the actual introduction of the wage tax and the payers of the wage tax had opposed deductions with strikes,[49] in the end all the political and social groups were of one opinion that the utilisation of the 'pay as you earn' system for the wage tax was unavoidable for administrative and financial reasons. And they all recognised, at least verbally, that the

47. See as example the report of the president of the State Finance Office, Hannover, of 4 September 1922 (ZStA Potsdam RFM no. 1107), in which is indicated that, along with the reluctance to pay over the wage tax deductions by the employer, in an increasing number of cases the deducted wage taxes never, or only in part, reached the Reich Treasury.

48. It is, by the way, a special perfidy that Popitz in his article on the income tax in the *Handwörterbuch der Staatswissenschaften* reproduced the distribution of the income tax according to tax levels for the year 1920, through which it would be suggested to the unbiased reader that the approximately 27.3 million income taxpayers with incomes up to 14,000 marks had paid only around 27 per cent of the tax while the remaining 3.2 million with higher incomes had paid 73 per cent. As director of the tax department of the Reich Finance Ministry, Popitz naturally knew well that the assessed and actually paid taxes were divergent in the extreme.

49. See the documents in BA Koblenz, R 43 I no. 2414; for the strike in Württemberg *Vorwärts* nos. 429, 435 and 444 of 28 August, 1 and 7 September 1920.

Table 8.1.   Yield of income tax

(1)	Total (mill. mks) (2)	PAYE (3)	% of col. 2 (4)	Assessed income tax (5)	% of col. 2 (6)
1920 Apr.	—	—	—	—	—
May	—	—	—	—	—
June	44.3	44.3	100	—	—
July	394.3	394.3	100	—	—
Aug.	553.9	553.9	100	—	—
Sept.	769.6	769.6	100	—	—
Oct.	1080.7	1080.7	100	—	—
Nov.	1403.4	1403.4	100	—	—
Dec.	1458.1	1458.1	100	—	—
1921 Jan.	1321.6	1321.6	100	—	—
Feb.	1239.7	1239.7	100	—	—
Mar.	1975.4	1975.4	100	—	—
Budget 1920/1	10241.0	10241.0	100	—	—
1921 Apr.	1040	968	93	72	7
May	1103	957	87	146	13
June	1163	963	83	200	17
July	1367	879	64	488	36
Aug.	1409	764	54	645	46
Sept.	1276	653	51	623	49
Oct.	1791	980	55	811	45
Nov.	2064	1026	50	1038	50
Dec.	2763	1584	57	1179	43
1922 Jan.	3489	2264	65	1225	35
Feb.	4431	1349	30	3082	70
Mar.	7816	3390	43	4426	57
Budget 1921/2	29712	15777	53	13935	47

continued on page 155

wage-tax regulation demanded as a necessary compensation a speedy assessment of those taxpayers subject only to an assessed income tax and a similarly speedy collection of the tax burden established for these persons for 1920, as well as the resulting prepayments for 1921 and correspondingly for 1922 thereby established. The sharply worded instructions which were issued particularly by the finance minister, Wirth, to the tax authorities emphasised this point constantly: that it

Table 8.1. *continued*

1922	Apr.	4299	2192	51	2107	49
	May	5746	2871	50	2875	50
	June	5812	3397	58	2415	42
	July	7687	4773	62	2914	38
	Aug.	9933	5675	57	4258	43
	Sept.	13851	8079	58	5772	42
	Oct.	21895	15757	72	6138	28
	Nov.	29119	22071	75	7048	25
	Dec.	48053	39506	82	8547	18
1923	Jan.–					
	Mar.	387046	336580	87	50466	13
Budget						
1922/3		533441	440901	83	92540	17

The total yield of the income tax as well as the yield of PAYE and assessed income tax for the budgets 1920 to 1922 are fairly meaningless; only the monthly figures show the relative importance of PAYE and assessed income tax, respectively. Nevertheless, the figures for the budgets are important in one respect: they were used in the political manoeuvres of political parties and economic interest-groups.

Sources: ZSTA Potsdam, RFM nos. 1100–20 (files on the assessment and date of payment of the income tax — 'pay as you earn' — system and assessed income tax).

was absolutely necessary to get on with the work of assessment with the greatest of speed so that 'the complaints of the wage and salary earners about their priority in being burdened in contrast to the other tax-payers would finally lose its basis'.[50] At first these warnings continued without result; only in the last quarter of 1921 were the tax offices able to send out the tax bills for 1920 and thereby also demand realistic prepayments for 1921, and finally in the months between May and July 1922 the tax bills for those with particularly large incomes were sent out in substantial numbers.[51] For the first time in the taxation of incomes the assessed taxpayers appeared to be required to make realistic payments. However, this progress was destroyed through an

50. On 16 September 1921 to all presidents of the State Finance Offices, ZStA Potsdam, RFM Nr. 1100, there were further similar decrees which came out every two or three months regularly demanding a speeding up of the assessment process.

51. ZStA Potsdam, RFM nos. 1100–20, Compilations on the State of Assessment, the sent out tax instructions and the resultant tax debts for the tax years 1920/1921/1922. These compilations show significant regional differences which cannot be expanded on due to lack of space.

Table 8.2. Income of the central government

(1)	Total income (mill. mks) (2)	Treas. bills (%) (3)	Total taxes (%) (4)	Income tax, PAYE (%) (5)	Income tax, assess (%) (6)	Capital levy (%) (7)	Estate (etc.) duties (%) (8)	Sales tax (%) (9)	Alcohol, tobacco (%) (10)	Import duties (%) (11)	Export duties (%) (12)	Coal tax (%) (13)	Misc. taxes (%) (14)
1920 Apr.	419.6	80.48	16.87	—	—	0.02	3.47	2.54	3.64	2.92	—	3.16	1.12
May	700.7	83.77	14.64	—	—	0.51	3.25	1.09	2.99	1.90	—	3.95	0.95
June	1244.3	85.73	13.37	0.33	—	1.33	2.23	0.67	2.08	1.53	—	3.32	1.88
July	1133.1	79.08	19.95	3.28	—	1.12	2.42	0.59	2.48	1.29	—	3.67	5.10
Aug.	880.8	73.95	23.98	6.11	—	0.69	3.23	0.97	2.62	0.93	—	4.22	5.21
Sept.	1111.6	77.37	21.64	6.85	—	0.99	2.54	0.98	0.95	1.04	1.95	3.67	2.67
Oct.	527.4	41.05	56.84	19.15	—	5.14	6.62	2.16	4.99	3.15	3.05	6.22	6.36
Nov.	1032.5	60.39	38.32	12.12	—	4.96	3.68	1.48	2.87	1.81	2.71	3.65	5.04
Dec.	1083.8	42.01	56.97	11.60	—	20.23	7.48	1.34	2.81	1.73	1.17	3.91	6.70
1921 Jan.	805.0	27.78	70.84	13.89	—	23.41	4.53	7.99	3.63	2.41	2.75	3.66	8.57
Feb.	1145.5	47.89	51.14	9.41	—	11.81	4.61	9.86	2.98	1.95	1.66	3.06	5.80
Mar.	1181.6	48.15	50.91	10.04	—	12.36	3.91	8.50	4.13	1.62	1.07	3.87	5.41
Budget 1920/1	11265.6	62.51	36.31	7.65	—	7.26	3.90	3.30	2.86	1.72	1.18	3.77	4.67
1921 Apr.	1040.7	53.76	45.43	8.23	0.61	13.38	4.42	8.26	2.58	2.18	1.05	1.35	5.95
May	911.6	39.26	59.82	9.37	1.43	14.67	9.30	10.21	3.29	2.33	0.58	3.51	5.13
June	1223.0	58.78	40.53	6.73	1.40	8.74	5.22	5.54	2.93	2.06	4.60	2.80	0.51
July	905.2	49.88	49.19	7.77	4.31	7.88	7.21	6.25	3.41	3.68	0.62	3.42	4.64
Aug.	1302.3	69.72	29.64	4.41	3.72	3.39	4.04	3.72	2.29	2.06	0.47	2.57	2.97
Sept.	921.1	60.31	38.78	5.18	4.95	3.16	4.99	3.94	4.78	3.35	0.74	4.33	3.36
Oct.	913.1	54.04	45.04	7.15	5.92	3.43	7.39	5.17	3.15	5.33	1.02	4.03	2.45
Nov.	892.4	54.59	44.46	6.50	6.57	4.52	6.22	5.49	3.27	3.93	1.52	3.42	3.02
Dec.	1484.5	71.43	28.00	5.53	4.12	1.64	4.42	3.19	2.25	1.60	1.57	2.03	3.29

	Total income (col. 2)	Borrowing (col. 3)	Total taxes (col. 4)	(5)	(6)	(7)	(8)	(9)	(10)	(11)	(12)	(13)	(14)
1922 Jan.	868.7	49.38	49.65	12.78	6.91	1.80	7.25	6.07	2.68	2.99	2.76	4.58	1.83
Feb.	692.7	42.08	56.71	7.95	18.16	1.33	6.89	6.16	3.64	3.44	2.74	4.76	1.64
Mar.	808.6	38.92	60.04	11.46	15.19	1.06	6.85	8.21	3.69	4.34	3.38	4.63	1.23
Budget 1921/2	11963.6	55.40	44.52	7.47	5.44	5.46	5.96	5.80	3.07	2.95	1.73	3.28	3.36
1922 Apr.	650.2	40.28	59.06	9.80	9.42	1.11	7.66	11.32	7.81	3.23	3.97	4.06	0.68
May	686.4	31.83	67.54	11.01	11.02	2.13	8.99	16.74	3.89	3.28	3.74	6.09	0.65
June	573.2	24.48	74.77	14.28	10.15	1.26	10.22	10.15	6.23	5.72	3.95	12.30	0.51
July	640.3	36.92	62.41	13.83	8.44	0.77	6.15	11.48	3.31	5.22	4.58	7.93	0.70
Aug.	712.4	42.55	56.88	10.27	7.70	1.19	4.79	16.66	3.86	3.40	3.79	5.67	0.29
Sept.	1139.9	78.75	20.87	5.32	3.80	0.21	2.03	1.99	1.54	1.72	2.67	1.51	0.08
Oct.	923.9	74.92	24.61	7.73	3.01	0.23	2.01	3.60	1.16	2.13	3.19	1.47	0.08
Nov.	892.4	69.03	30.41	6.47	2.07	0.18	2.07	5.08	2.29	1.90	8.07	2.21	0.07
Dec.	1155.5	82.87	16.75	4.99	1.08	0.06	1.42	1.25	1.05	1.17	3.20	2.51	0.02
1923 Jan.	779.7	67.18	32.27	9.42	1.40	0.09	2.20	4.95	1.50	2.20	2.80	7.70	0.01
Feb.	702.1	81.19	18.20	4.87	0.73	0.01	1.61	4.47	1.37	1.13	3.10	1.45	0.83
Mar.	1237.4	85.32	14.34	4.65	0.69	0.01	2.09	1.18	0.82	0.71	1.33	2.82	0.04
Budget 1922/3	9965.0	64.07	35.41	7.90	4.29	0.50	3.73	6.35	2.52	2.36	3.46	4.13	0.17

Sources: Übersicht der Einnahmen des Reiches, *Reichsministerialblatt* 1920–3; *Übersicht über die Bewgungen der Reichshauptkasse 1920–1923*, BA Koblenz, R 43 I nos. 2356ff.; ZSTA Potsdam, RFM no. 859; ZSTA Potsdam, RFM nos. 1100–20. The figures are adjusted according to the original accounts of the Reichshauptkasse. Total income (col. 2) has been adjusted against the cost-of-living index; government borrowing (col. 3) and total taxes (col. 4) are shown as a percentage of total income. Total taxes equals the sum of columns 5 to 14.

Table 8.3   Income tax: Number of taxpayers, yield of tax assessment, real
value of income tax paid

	Budget 1920/1 (Apr.–Mar.)	Tax year 1921 (Apr.–Dec.)	Tax year 1922 (Jan.–Dec.)
(1) Number of taxpayers (mill.)	30.5	29.8	29.7
(2) Taxpayers only subject to PAYE (mill.)	17.4	16.8	20.1
(3) % of total	57.1	56.4	67.7
(4) Taxpayers subject to PAYE and assess. income tax (mill.)	7.9	7.9	4.7
(5) % of total	25.9	26.5	15.8
(6) Taxpayers only subject to assess. income tax (mill.)	5.2	5.1	5.0
(7) % of total	17.0	17.1	16.5
(8) Total yield of income tax (mill. mks)	28297.0	42316.0	490000.0
(9) Yield of income tax by taxpayers only subject to PAYE (mill. mks)	7900.0	7545.0	68000.0
(10) Yield of income tax of taxpayers subject to PAYE and assess. income tax (mill. mks)	20397.0	34771.0	422000.0
(11) Real value of yield of income tax adjusted against cost of living index (mill. mks)	2586.0	3030.0	3258.0
(12) Real value of PAYE cf. row 9 (mill. mks)	722.0	540.0	452.0
(13) Real value of PAYE and assess. income tax, cf. row 10 (mill. mks)	1864.0	2490.0	2806.0
(14) Real value of PAYE paid by taxpayers only subject to PAYE (mill. mks)	722.0	540.0	452.0

Table 8.3 *continued*

(15) Real value of PAYE by taxpayers subject to PAYE and assess. income tax (mill. mks)	140.0	94.0	426.0
(16) Real value of assess. income tax paid by taxpayers (mill. mks)	528.0	388.0	331.0
(17) Rows 15 and 16 as % of row 13	35.8	19.4	27.0
(18) Yield of income tax actually received by the Reichshauptrasse (mill. mks)	862.0	977.0	1592.0

Notes and sources:

Rows 1–7A: *Schlußnachweisungen über die Zahl der Lohnd Einkommensteuerpflichtigen im Deutschen Reich*, ZSTA Potsdam, RFM nos. 1100–20. For 1922 the figures are estimates of the Reichsfinanzministerium as the income tax assessment had never been settled in some of the revenue offices of the occupied territory.

Rows 8–10: *Zusammenstellung des Steuersolls 1920–1922*, ZSTA Potsdam, RFM nos. 1106, 1120. The figures for the yield of income tax by taxpayers subject to PAYE are merely the receipts of the Reichshauptkasse; no attempts have been made to adjust the figures according to subsequent assessment.

It isn't possible to split the yield of income tax in row 10 into tax on earned income (subject to PAYE) and on unearned income (only subject to assessed income tax).

Rows 11–13: The real value of the income tax had been calculated on the base of monthly figures, but it should be understood that these estimates are only a very rough calculation.

Rows 14–16: *Anschreibungen der Reichshauptkasse und des Reichsfinanzministeriums über den Eingang von Einkommensteuer*, ZSTA Potsdam RFM nos. 1100–20. The Reichsfinanzministerium and the Reichshauptkasse did not only put down the amount of income tax paid in during a given time period (1920 and 1921 monthly; 1922 and 1923 weekly), but the amount was split down into income tax deducted from wages (PAYE), income tax for 1920, 1921 and 1922 and prepayments on income tax for the corresponding year. By this it is possible to calculate the real value of the payments of income tax for the corresponding year.

Row 18: *Deutschlands Wirtschaft, Währung und Finanzen*, Berlin 1924, p. 34.

explosive increase in the price indices and the real income from the assessed income tax began once again to sink until its monthly contribution in early 1923, at the end of the budget year 1922, was still only a few million gold marks (deflated against the cost-of-living index). The multiplier which was finally introduced in March 1923, for the prepayments and the income-tax debt of 1921, in principle changed nothing as it was introduced too late and with much too small a factor.[52] The temporal sequence of events, which becomes evident from the assessment documents, suggests the interpretation that, outside of other factors such as the preparedness of the Reichsbank to discount commercial bills, the murder of Walther Rathenau in June 1922 and the growing doubts about the political stability and in the economic promise of Germany, the system of tax assessment, particularly but not exclusively that for income tax, contributed to the fact that in June–July 1922 German inflation finally became hyperinflation. At this time the first assessed income tax and also corporation tax[53] became perceptible burdens, and this led to greater opposition to the taxes by high-income earners as well as by judicial persons (i.e. joint stock companies, limited liability companies, limited partnerships),[54] and also certainly encouraged willingness to avoid the tax burden, with the help of inflation.

52. See Witt, 'Reichsfinanzminister *VJZG*, vol. 23 (1975), pp. 58ff.
53. See ZStA Potsdam, RFM no. 1625, Zusammenstellungen über die Veranlagung und das Ergebnis der Körperschaftssteuer.
54. See the rapidly increasing number of claims against the tax instructions (from the compilation in ZStA Potsdam, RFM nos. 1100–20) as well as the complaints before the finance courts (see the unpublished decisions of the Reich finance court in ZStA Potsdam, RFM nos. 1256–9, and the collection of decisions and recommendations of the Reich finance court, vols. 1–17, Munich 1920–5).

About the Contributors

Harm-Hinrich Brandt Born 1935. Professor of History, University of Würzburg. His published works include *Wirtschaftspolitik und gewerbliche Mitbeteiligung im nordhessischen Raum 1710–1960* (1960); *Wirtschaft und Wirtschaftspolitik im Raum Hanau 1597–1962* (1963); *Die Industrie- und Handelskammer Kassel* (1963); *Der österreichische Neoabsolutismus: Staatsfinanzen und Politik 1848–1860*, 2 vols (1978).

Carl-Ludwig Holtfrerich Born 1942. Professor of Economic History, Free University of Berlin. His publications include *Quantitative Wirtschaftsgeschichte des Ruhrkohlenbergbaus im 19. Jahrhundert* (1973); *Die deutsche Inflation 1914–1923. Ursachen und Folgen in internationaler Perspektive* (1980) (trans. as *The German Inflation 1914–1923: Causes and Effects in International Perspective*, (1986); co-editor of *Beiträge zu Inflation und Wiederaufbau in Deutschland und Europa 1914–1924*, 9 vols (1982–6).

Jürgen Baron von Kruedener Born 1938. Professor of History, President of the University of the *Bundeswehr* Munich. His published works include *Die Rolle des Hofes im Absolutismus* (1973); co-editor of *Technikfolgen und sozialer Wandel* (1981).

Kersten Krüger Born 1939. Professor of History, University of Hamburg. His published works include *Die Einnahmen und Ausgaben der dänischen Rentmeister 1588–1628* (1970); *Finanzstaat Hessen* (1980); co-author of *Sozialstruktur der Stadt Oldenburg 1630 und 1678* (1986); editor of *Der Ökonomische Staat Landgraf Wilhelm IV.*, vol. 3 (1977).

Hans-Peter Ullmann Born 1949. Professor of History, University of Giessen. His writings include *Der Bund der Industriellen* (1976); *Bibliographie zur Geschichte der deutschen Parteien und Interessenverbände* (1978); *Staatsschulden und Reformpolitik 1780–1820*, 2 vols (1986); co-editor of *Deutschland zwischen Revolution und Restauration* (1981).

161

Peter-Christian Witt   Born 1943. Professor of History, University of Kassel. His publications include *Die Finanzpolitik des Deutschen Reiches* (1970); *Friedrich Ebert. Parteiführer-Reichskanzler-Volksbeauftragter-Reichspräsident* (1971; 4th enl. and rev. edn, 1987); co-author of *Die Republik von Weimar*, 2 vols (1979; 2nd edn, 1984) and *Arbeiterfamilien im Kaiserreich* (1983); co-editor of *Industrielle Gesellschaft und politisches System* (1978) and *Deutscher Konservatismus im 19. und 20. Jahrhundert* (1983); co-editor of *Beiträge zu Inflation und Wiederaufbau in Deutschland und Europa*, 9 vols (1982–6).

Heide Wunder   Born 1939. Professor of History, University of Kassel. Her published works include *Siedlungs- und Bevölkerungsgeschichte der Komturei Christburg* (1968); co-author of *Einführung in die Geschichtswissenschaft* (1975) and *Gesellschaft und Geschichte* (1976); *Die bäuerliche Gemeinde in Deutschland* (1986); editor of *Das Pfennigschuldbuch der Komturei Christburg* (1969) and *Feudalismus* (1974).